To Tuni and Pat

Gītagovinda of Jayadeva

LOVE SONG OF THE DARK LORD

Krishna's incarnation as the cosmic Dwarf is painted in Gujarati style of the fifteenth century. The leaf includes a fragment of Mānānka's commentary on the *Gītagovinda*. Reproduced from the *Journal of the University of Bombay*, 6 (1937) plate IX.

GĪTAGOVINDA OF JAYADEVA

Love Song of the Dark Lord

Edited and Translated by
BARBARA STOLER MILLER

MOTILAL BANARSIDASS PUBLISHERS
PRIVATE LIMITED • DELHI

Reprint: Delhi, 2007
First Indian Edition: Delhi, 1984

ISBN : 81-208-0366-3 (Cloth)
ISBN : 81-208-0367-1 (Paper)

MOTILAL BANARSIDASS
41 U.A. Bungalow Road, Jawahar Nagar, Delhi 110 007
8 Mahalaxmi Chamber, Warden Road, Mumbai 400 026
203 Royapettah High Road, Mylapore, Chennai 600 004
236, 9th Main III Block, Jayanagar, Bangalore 560 011
Sanas Plaza, 1302 Baji Rao Road, Pune 411 002
8 Camac Street, Kolkata 700 017
Ashok Rajpath, Patna 800 004
Chowk, Varanasi 221 001

UNESCO COLLECTION OF REPRESENTATIVE WORKS
INDIAN SERIES

This book has been accepted in the Indian Series of the Translations Collection of the United Nations Educational, Scientific and Cultural Organization (UNESCO)

PRINTED IN INDIA
BY JAINENDRA PRAKASH JAIN AT SHRI JAINENDRA PRESS,
A-45 NARAINA, PHASE-I, NEW DELHI 110 028
AND PUBLISHED BY NARENDRA PRAKASH JAIN FOR
MOTILAL BANARSIDASS PUBLISHERS PRIVATE LIMITED,
BUNGALOW ROAD, DELHI 110 007

Translations From The Oriental Classics

PREFACE

Deliverance is not for me in renunciation.
I feel the embrace of freedom in a
thousand bonds of delight.

Rabindranath Tagore
Gitanjali 73

Jayadeva's dramatic lyrical poem *Gītagovinda* is a unique work in Indian literature and a source of religious inspiration in both medieval and contemporary Vaishnavism. The poem is dedicated in devotion to the god Krishna. It concentrates on Krishna's love with the cowherdess Rādhā in a rite of spring. Intense earthly passion is the example Jayadeva uses to express the complexities of divine and human love.

Although the poem originated in eastern India in the twelfth century and remains most popular there, it spread throughout the subcontinent in the centuries following its composition. As early as the thirteenth century it was quoted in a temple inscription in Gujarat, in western India. Established traditions of commentary and manuscripts exist in every part of India. Its songs are an important part of the devotional music and literature of Orissa, Bengal, and South India. The songs were introduced into Kerala in the sixteenth century and are still sung in temples there. Portions of the poem represent one of the major subjects in medieval Rājput painting.

Critical acclaim of the poem has been high, but its frank eroticism has led many Indian commentators to interpret the love between Rādhā and Krishna as an allegory of the human soul's love for God. The condemnation of Jayadeva's eroticism made by the seventeenth-century esthetician Jagannātha in his *Rasagaṅgādhara* (Kāvyamālā 12, Bombay, 1888, p. 52) is exceptional. Learned and popular audiences in India and elsewhere have continued to appreciate the emotional lyricism the poem expresses in its variations on the theme of separated lovers' passion.

Commenting on F. H. van Dalberg's German rendering of the *Gītagovinda,* Goethe wrote, "What struck me as remarkable are the extremely varied motives by which an extremely simple subject is made endless" (note to Schiller dated Jan. 22, 1802, quoted from *Correspondence between Goethe and Schiller,* translated by L. D. Schmitz, London, 1909, vol. 2, p. 395). Dalberg's version was based on the first English translation of the *Gītagovinda* by William Jones, published in the *Transactions of the Asiatic Society, Calcutta,* in 1792 and reprinted in London in *Asiatik Researches,* 3 (1799), 185–207. A verse translation by the German poet Friedrich Rückert, begun in 1829 and revised according to the edited Sanskrit text and Latin translation of C. Lassen (Bonn, 1836), appeared in *Zeitschrift für die Kunde des Morgenlandes,* 1 (Gottingen, 1837), 128 ff.

The poem has also been translated into most modern Indian languages and many other modern European languages. Notable English versions include Edwin Arnold's *The Indian Song of Songs* (London, 1875); George Keyt's *Sri Jayadeva's Gita Govinda: The Loves of Kṛṣṇa and Rādhā* (Bombay, 1940); S. Lakshminarasimha Sastri's *The Gīta Govinda of Jayadeva* (Madras, 1956); Duncan Greenlees' Theosophical rendering, *The Song of Divine Love* (Madras, 1962), and Monica Varma's "transcreation," *The Gita Govinda of Jayadeva,* published by Writers Workshop (Calcutta, 1968).

My own interest in the *Gītagovinda* began when I heard it sung in Orissi style in the home of Sulakshana and Debi Prasanna Pattanayak in Poona in 1966 and attempted to translate some of the songs. None of the available translations seemed to convey the literary richness or the religious significance of the original. My early work toward a verse translation of the poem convinced me that my English version should be based on a critical edition of the text and an extensive study of the traditions associated with the poem at various levels of Indian culture.

While I have concentrated my effort on textual aspects of the *Gītagovinda,* I have also gathered and studied substantial material relevant to its cultural contexts. I have heard and recorded the songs of the poem in different musical versions in Orissa, Bengal, Bihar, Madras, Mysore, and Kerala, as well as Nepal. Because of the role of the songs in the nightly worship of the deity in Jagannātha Temple at Puri, they are venerated and sung throughout Orissa. Their performance is an essential aspect of Orissi dance, which has developed through the religious art of temple dancers called Maharis who still dance *Gītagovinda* songs before Jagannātha. The significance of the legendary life of Jayadeva that identifies the poet's muse as a temple dancer of Puri is discussed in the first section of my introduction. I have learned much about the emotional content of the poem from watching Sanjukta Panigrahi and Ritha Devi perform *Gītagovinda* songs in Orissi style. I spent many pleasant hours in Cuttack in consultation with Kalicharaṇ Patnaik and Akshaya Mohanty discussing and listening to the music of *Gītagovinda*. A seventeenth-century palm-leaf manuscript of the text, with the commentary *Sarvāṅgasundarī* and superb illustrations, was examined in the collection of Kalicharan.

In Bengal, the singing of *Gītagovinda* is especially prominent at an annual spring fair in the village of Kenduli in Birbhum district, which is identified as the birthplace of Jayadeva in Bengali tradition. The influence of the poem on the devotional music of Bengal is analyzed in an article by Swami Prajnananada entitled "The *Gītagovinda-padagāna* in the Background of the *Padāvalī-kīrtan* of Bengal," published in the *Journal of the Music Academy, Madras,* 36 (1965), 176–82.

In Nepal, the *Gītagovinda* is sung during the spring celebration in honor of the goddess Sarasvatī, in which worship is offered to the god of love, Kāmadeva, and his consort. I did not hear an actual performance, but learned about it in a talk with the father of my friend Dr. Prasanna Chandra Gautam, who read the description and chanted a portion of the poem from his brahman family's old manual of annual ceremonies, entitled *Vārṣikavratapaddhati*. In the Bir Library collection in the National Archives in Kathmandu, I found the earliest known manuscripts of the *Gītagovinda,* dated 567 and 616 in the Nepali era (ca. A.D. 1447 and 1496). Norvin Hein discusses the theatrical rendering of the *Gītagovinda* in regions where Śākta influence prevails, with special reference to its performance in Nepal and Bihar (*The Miracle Plays of Mathurā,* New Haven, 1972, pp. 267–71). He quotes the account of Sylvain Lévi of an evening performance by popular players in Kathmandu on March 7, 1898, in which the plot and songs were based on the *Gītagovinda*.

In much of South India the poem is sung according to the classical Karnatic system of music. An edition of the text with musical notation according to this system by Semmangudi R. Sreenivasa Iyer was published by the Sanskrit College Committee, Tripunithura, Kerala, in 1963. The text is prefaced by this note: "*Ashtapadi,* as the poem is popularly known, is sung daily in many of the temples of Kerala, as the pious Hindus consider it a devotional song of the highest order. It is also sung invariably during Kathakali performances, but the way of singing in

Kerala is different from that of Bhajanapaddhati which has been adopted by Mr. Sreenivasa Iyer." With the help of the music scholar K. P. S. Menon of Calicut, I was able to hear *Gītagovinda* songs as they are sung by members of a drummer caste in the courtyard of Guruvayur and other temples of Kerala while certain rituals are being performed by brahman priests within the sanctuary. Mr. Menon also provided me with an English text of Rama Varma's nineteenth-century version of the *Gītagovinda,* based on Kathakali technique. The Malayalam text, entitled *Ashtapadi Attaprakaram,* was edited by K. Raghavan Pillai and published in the Kerala University Malayalam Series (Trivandrum, 1964). The text came to my attention through a review of it by L. S. Rajagopalan in the *Journal of the Music Academy, Madras,* 37 (1966), 221–22. Mr. Rajagopalan's correspondence with me on the performance of the *Gītagovinda* in Kerala temples has provided many suggestions for further work on this subject.

In order to better understand the lyrical structure of the *Gītagovinda,* I have studied the theory and practice of both classical Hindusthani and classical Karnatic music. I studied the North Indian flute with Vasant Rai, a disciple of Allaudin Khan and the director of Alam School of North Indian Music in New York, and I took lessons on South Indian flute with V. Deshikachar at the Mysore College of Fine Arts. I have consulted a text of the *Gītagovinda* with annotations of the gestures (*abhinaya*) for every word in the first seventeen songs of the poem; this was edited by K. Vasudeva Sastri and published in the Tanjore Sarawati Mahal Series (Tanjore, 1950). Certain songs belong to the current repertoire of Bharata Natyam, and I relished the opportunity to watch and analyze some of these in the classes of Veṅkaṭalakshmyammā, also at the Mysore College of Fine Arts. These studies have informed my translation and analysis of the poem, but I have not attempted a technical discussion of its music and dance performances in deference to the excellent work by scholars in this area. In March 1967 Sangeet Natak Akademi and Lalit Kala Akademi sponsored a conference in New Delhi entitled "Geet Govind Celebrations." Published conference papers by C. S. Pant, Premlata Sharma, N. S. Ramachandran, Dilip Kumar Mukherjee, Rukmini Devi, and E. Nilakanta Singh analyze aspects of music and dance associated with the poem. Kapila Vatsyayan, author of the excellent book *Classical Indian Dance in Literature and the Arts* (New Delhi, 1968), is currently preparing an extensive study of the poem's expression in Indian music, dance, and the plastic arts. She presented a general paper on the subject at the International Sanskrit Conference in Delhi in 1972 that is scheduled for publication in the proceedings of that conference. Her analysis of the *Gītagovinda* in Manipuri dance, presented at the Manipur Sahitya Sangeet Natak Akademi in 1973, is being prepared for publication.

My appreciation for the visual imagery of the *Gītagovinda* has been enhanced by published volumes of paintings from various schools. These include R. P. N. Sinha's *Geeta Govind in Basholi School of Indian Painting* (New Delhi, 1958); M.S. Randhawa's *Kangra Paintings of the Gītagovinda* (New Delhi, 1963); and Moti Chandra's two portfolios in the Lalit Kalā Series, both entitled *Gītagovinda* (New Delhi, 1965).

In my introduction, I have tried to analyze and trace the sources of formal and thematic elements that have been relevant to my understanding of Jayadeva's poetic creation. I have not tried to survey the wide influence of the poem on later Indian religious literature, poetry, and the arts. This material belongs to the study of Dr. Vatsyayan, whose published work promises to complement the present volume. The importance of the *Gītagovinda* in later Bengali Vaishnavism is well documented in the studies of Dasgupta, De, Dimock, and Harekrishna Mukhopādhyāya cited in the notes to sections two and three of the introduction. Its place in the broader development of Indian religious eroticism is central to a recent Oxford University doctoral thesis by Lee Siegel, entitled "Sacred and Profane Dimensions of Love in Indian Traditions as Exemplified in the *Gītagovinda* of Jayadeva" (Oxford, 1975). Several scholars have compiled descriptive lists of the literary imitations of the *Gītagovinda:* V. W. Karambelkar, "Three More Imitations of the *Gītagovinda,*" *Indian Historical Quarterly,* 25, no. 2 (1949), 95–101; K. N. Mahapatra, "Some Imitations of the Gītagovindam," *The Orissa Historical Research Journal,* 15, nos. 3 and 4 (1971), 95–130; V. Raghavan, "In the Footsteps of Jayadeva: Nanjaraja's *Saṅgīta Gaṅgādhara,*" unpublished typescript of 1972, revised from an article published in *The Hindu,* Madras, in 1936.

Documentation of my critical study of the *Gītagovinda* is presented, with the edited Sanskrit text, only in the hardcover edition of this book. It seemed unreasonable to increase the size of the paperback edition with material that would be of interest only to scholars. The hardcover edition also includes a glossary of Sanskrit words: this too is intended mainly for scholarly readers. Because the vocabulary of the poem is highly concentrated, the glossary serves as an alternative to repetitive textual notes. The translation is not directly annotated. I hope that the detailed discussions of the poem in various sections of the introduction will provide all that necessary for the general reader to enjoy and understand my

English version of Jayadeva's poetry. The discussions are supplemented by extensive bibliographic and textual notes. Because the bibliography differs so much from section to section, no general list of references is given. In preparing both the glossary and the introduction, as well as the translation itself, I have depended heavily on the interpretations and analyses of various commentators. The contents of selected commentaries are described as part of the evidence for the critical edition. References to variant interpretations of ambiguous phrases and technical terms are found in the glossary and the notes to the introduction.

The research for this book has taken me to India three times. My search for manuscripts in the summer of 1971 was supported by grants from the National Endowment for the Humanities and the American Philosophical Society. A grant from the American Council of Learned Societies enabled me to spend time in Madras and Orissa in January 1973 to consult manuscripts in the Adyar Library, the Orissa State Museum, and the Raghunandan Library, and to experience performances of the *Gītagovinda*. My residence at Mysore University during the winter of 1974–75 was supported by the American Institute of Indian Studies. A Guggenheim Fellowship for "A Textual and Contextual Study of Medieval Sanskrit Poetry and its Modern Interpretations" gave me time to consider the *Gītagovinda* in the broader context of medieval literature and to explore theories of the relationship between religion and art in Indian civilization. It also enabled me to work in Nepal in the autumn of 1974.

In the five years I have spent gathering and preparing the *Gītagovinda* material for publication, many people have given me invaluable help. My special thanks are to the Pattanayaks, who have often shared with me and my family the warmth and cultural life of their home. My formal affiliation at Mysore University was with the Central Institute of Indian Languages, of which Dr. Pattanayak is the director; the resources of the institute greatly facilitated my work. In Mysore, I was also helped by research scholars at the Oriental Institute and the Office of the Chief Epigraphist. I enjoyed many hours at the Oriental Institute discussing Sanskrit *kāvya* and analyzing aspects of the *Gītagovinda* with H. V. Nagaraja Rao. It was under his supervision that the Devanagari text of my critical edition was typeset at Sree Kantha Power Press, publishers of the Sanskrit newspaper *Sudharmā*. Without his gracious help, this book would not be in its present form. Thanks are due to Theodore Riccardi, Lynn Bennett, and Gabriel Campbell for their help in locating and identifying the Nepali materials that have been so central to my critical text;

and also to Neil Gross, who patiently collated the references for the glossary.

I am indebted to Daniel H. H. Ingalls for the example of his own work and for his encouragement of this translation through the endless revisions I submitted to his attention. For their generous and detailed criticism at various stages of the translation, I thank Susan Bergholz, Edwin Gerow, Jeffrey Masson, Agueda Pizarro, David Rubin, Burton Watson, and my husband James. William Bernhardt, Karen Mitchell, and Andrée Mounier of Columbia University Press have all contributed to the conception and form of the book; I appreciate their skills and standards.

James and Gwenn have shared my travels in the Indian subcontinent and much of my adventure in studying the *Gītagovinda*. Their appreciation for the music of Jayadeva's poem and for my involvement with it have made this work pleasurable.

Barbara Stoler Miller

NEW YORK, 1976

CONTENTS

A NOTE ON SANSKRIT PRONUNCIATION

In reading Sanskrit words, the accent is usually placed on the penultimate syllable when this is long; otherwise it is placed on the antepenultimate. A syllable is long if it contains a long vowel (*ā, ī, ū*), a diphthong (*e, o, ai, au*), or a vowel followed by more than one consonant. It should be noted that the aspirated consonants *kh, gh, ch, jh, th, dh, ph, bh,* and so on are considered single consonants in the Sanskrit alphabet.

Vowels are given their full value, as in Italian or German:

a	as *u* in c*u*t
ā	as *a* in f*a*ther
i	as *i* in p*i*t
ī	as *i* in mach*i*ne
u	as *u* in p*u*t
ū	as *u* in r*u*le
ṛ	a short vowel; as *ri* in *ri*ver
e	as *ay* in s*ay*
ai	as *ai* in *ai*sle
o	as *o* in g*o*
au	as *ow* in c*ow*
ṁ	nasalizes and lengthens the preceding vowel
ḥ	a rough breathing, replacing an original *s* or *r*; lengthens the preceding vowel and occurs only at the end of a syllable or word

Most consonants are analogous to the English, if the distinction between aspirated and nonaspirated consonants is observed; for example, the aspirated consonants *th* and *ph* must never be pronounced as in English *th*in and *ph*ial, but as in ho*th*ouse and she*ph*erd. (Similarly, *kh, gh, ch, jh, dh, bh.*) The differences between the Sanskrit "cerebral" *ṭ, ṭh, ḍ, ḍh, ṇ,* and "dental" *t, th, d, dh, n* are another distinctive feature of the language. The dentals are formed with the tongue against the teeth, the cerebrals with the tongue turned back along the palate. Note also:

g	as *g* in *g*oat
ṅ	as *n* in i*n*k, or si*ng*
c	as *ch* in *ch*urch

ñ as *ñ* in se*ñ*or (Spanish)
ś, *ṣ* as *sh* in *sh*ape or *s* in *s*ugar.

Kṛṣṇa and Viṣṇu are spelled Krishna and Vishnu for the convenience of the reader.

Introduction

1 Jayadeva: The Wandering Poet

Jayadeva, wandering king of bards
Who sing at Padmāvatī's lotus feet,
Was obsessed in his heart
By rhythms of the goddess of speech,
And he made this lyrical poem
From tales of the passionate play
When Krishna loved Śrī.

Jayadeva, the poet's signature in the *Gītagovinda,* is the name by which he is known as a poet-saint in Indian tradition.[1] It is a name he shares with Krishna, the divine hero of his poem; he invokes Krishna in the second song with the refrain *jaya jayadeva hare,* "Triumph, God of Triumph, Hari!" In the context where the poet's name becomes an epithet of Krishna, the name in turn gains a dimension of sacred meaning. The listener is reminded of Jayadeva's special relation to Krishna as his name is repeated in the signature verse that ends each song.

The lyrical, religious eroticism of the *Gītagovinda* earned sainthood for Jayadeva and a wide audience for his poem. All versions of the legend that sanctifies Jayadeva's life say that he was born in a brahman family and that he became an accomplished student of Sanskrit and a skilled poet.[2] However, he abandoned scholarship at a young age and adopted an ascetic life, devoting himself to God. As a wandering mendicant, he would not rest under one tree for more than a night for fear that attachment to the place would violate his vow. His ascetic life ended when a brahman of Puri insisted that Jagannātha, "Lord of the World," himself had ordained the marriage of Jayadeva with the brahman's daughter Padmāvatī, who was dedicated as a dancing girl in the temple. Padmāvatī served her husband and he shared her devotion to Jagannātha. As Jayadeva composed, she danced—thus the *Gītagovinda.* In the process of writing the poem, Jayadeva conceived the climax of Krishna's supplication to Rādhā as a command for Rādhā to place her foot on Krishna's head in a symbolic gesture of victory (X.8). But the poet hesitated to complete the couplet, in deference to Krishna. He went to bathe and in his absence

Krishna appeared in his guise to write the couplet; then Krishna ate the food Padmāvatī had prepared for Jayadeva and left. When Jayadeva returned, he realized that he had received divine grace in exalting Krishna's loving relation to Rādhā.

Various local versions of this legend have grown into conflicting traditions about Jayadeva's place of birth and region of poetic activity. Modern scholars of Bengal, Orissa, and Mithila have put forth claims locating the village of his birth in their respective regions. Two strong traditions say that the "Kindubilva" cited in the *Gītagovinda* (III.10) is either a village near Puri in Orissa or a village in the modern Birbhum district of Bengal. A third tradition identifies the village of Kenduli near Jenjharpur in Mithila as Jayadeva's birthplace. The argument is well known and has been summarized in favor of Jayadeva's Bengali origins in a recent monograph by Suniti Kumar Chatterji.[3] Although the Bengali position remains tenuous, both legends and historical documents suggest that Jayadeva lived and composed in eastern India during the latter half of the twelfth century.

The dating of Jayadeva's literary activity is established by the composite evidence of various literary and historical documents. Most prominent is the presence of verses attributed to Jayadeva in Śrīdharadāsa's *Saduktikarṇāmṛta,* an anthology compiled in Bengal in A.D. 1205 (Śāka era 1127), at the end of the reign of Lakṣmaṇasena, who ruled about A.D. 1179–1205.[4] Among the thirty verses attributed to Jayadeva in S. C. Banerji's edition of the anthology, two are in the critical text of the *Gītagovinda.*[5] In the *Gītagovinda* (I.3), Jayadeva compares himself with poets named Umāpatidhara, Śaraṇa, Govardhana, and Dhoyī,[6] all of whom are quoted in the *Saduktikarṇāmṛta*. Dhoyī composed a court epic entitled *Pavanadūta,* "Wind-messenger," to glorify a campaign by Lakṣmaṇasena into the south.[7] The other poets are less directly associated with Lakṣmaṇasena, but their works relate them to the period and region of his reign.[8]

It seems clear from the contents of the *Saduktikarṇāmṛta* and from the inscriptions of Lakṣmaṇasena that the king was a patron of Sanskrit learning and of Vaishnavism. The Senas were Karnatic kings who employed Sanskrit for their official documents, the standard practice in North India at this time.[9] The inscriptions of Lakṣmaṇasena open with an invocation to Vishnu (*aum aum namo nārāyaṇāya*) instead of to Śiva, as had been the practice of his predecessors. The king is described by the epithet "Highest Vaishnava" (*paramavaiṣṇava*).[10] A court that promoted Sanskrit learning and the highly syncretic Vaishnava worship of this time would have provided an appreciative audience for the *Gītagovinda*. It is impossible to know whether Jayadeva composed the work at Lakṣmaṇasena's court; perhaps he composed it elsewhere and performed it there.

The South Indian Vaishnava devotional cults that were influential in Bengal in the twelfth century were equally active in Orissa. Traditional accounts record that Rāmānuja, the great Vedānta philosopher and apostle of the Śrīvaishnava cult, visited Puri in the early part of the twelfth century and established a school there. It is claimed that he met and influenced the King of Puri and worked to introduce the ritual of Śrīvaishnavism into the Jagannātha temple, against the strong opposition of resident Śaiva priests.[11] The king whom he met was probably Anantavarman Choḍagaṅgadeva, the Gaṅga king who ruled in Orissa about A.D. 1078–1147. Later Gaṅga records suggest that Choḍagaṅgadeva initiated major construction of the Jagannātha temple, which was completed during the reign of his grandson Anaṅgabhīmadeva in the late twelfth century. From the evidence of his inscriptions, Choḍagaṅgadeva, like Lakṣmaṇasena of Bengal, came under Vaishnava influence. Two sets of copperplate inscriptions illustrate the shift in his sectarian allegiance. In A.D. 1081 (Śāka era 1003), Choḍagaṅgadeva expressed traditional Gaṅga devotion to Śiva by granting land to support worship of *Rājarājeśvara,* a name of Śiva. In A.D. 1118 (Śāka era 1040), in a grant of land to a brahman named Mādhava, his inscription begins with an invocation to Lakṣmī, and the king is described as "Highest Vaishnava" (*paramavaiṣṇava*). Temple records show that since the time of Choḍagaṅgadeva, Jagannātha has been continuously worshipped as the supreme form of Vishnu, whose power is expressed through the energy of his consort, Lakṣmī or Śrī.[12]

Although the legend of Jayadeva's life has no historical value, it does tell us that in the course of his wanderings Jayadeva visited Puri, where he came under the influence of the Jagannātha cult and formed a special relationship with Padmāvatī. The identification of Padmāvatī as Jayadeva's wife is not supported by either of the early commentators on the *Gītagovinda*. Both Mānāṅka and Kumbhakarṇa identify *Padmāvatī* (I.2; X.9; XI.21), or *Padmā* (I.25), as names of Krishna's divine consort *Śrī* (I.2; I.23), or *Lakṣmī* (XI.22), who is also called *Kamalā* (I.17) in the poem. The "marriage" of Jayadeva and Padmāvatī in the legend may be a veiled allusion to his initiation in the Śrīvaishnava cult that was established in Puri under Rāmānuja's influence. The role of Krishna's cowherdess consort Rādhā in the *Gītagovinda* takes its cosmic significance from the context of recurrent references to Śrī. Jayadeva's use of the epithet *Jagadīśa,* "Lord of the World," for Krishna in the first song is too similar to *Jagannātha* to be accidental—the *Gītagovinda* may well have taken shape in the richly syncretic environment in Puri in the twelfth century.[13]

By the fifteenth century, the *Gītagovinda* was sufficiently popular in Puri to be incorporated into the ritual of the Jagannātha temple. An inscription located on the left side of the Jayavijaya doorway, written in Oriya language and script and dated A.D. 1499, prescribes the performance of the *Gītagovinda* in the temple.[14] An English translation of the inscription reads:

> On Wednesday the tenth lunar year of Kakaḍā, bright half in the ninth mark of the warrior, the elephant-lord, the mighty Pratāparudradeva Mahārāja, king over Gauḍa and the ninety millions of Karṇāta and Kalabaraga, orders as follows: "Dancing will be performed thus at the time of food-offerings (*bhoga*) to the Elder Lord (Balarāma) and the Lord of the *Gītagovinda* (Jagannātha). This dancing will continue from the end of the deities' evening meal to their bedtime meal. The dancing group of the Elder Lord, the female dancers of Lord Kapileśvara, and the ancient dancing group of Telangana will all learn no song other than the *Gītagovinda* from the Elder Lord. *Aum.* They will sing no other song. No other dance should be performed before the great God. In addition to the dancing, there will be four singers who will sing only the *Gītagovinda.* Those who are not versed in singing the *Gītagovinda* will follow in chorus—they should learn no other song. Any temple official who knowingly allows any other song or dance to be performed is hostile to Jagannātha."

In the early sixteenth century, the great Vaishnava mystic Caitanya made a pilgrimage to Puri and settled there. It is recorded in the spiritual biography of Caitanya by Kṛṣṇadāsa Kavirāja, entitled *Caitanyacaritāmṛta,* that Caitanya derived great joy from hearing the *Gītagovinda,* as well as the songs of the Bengali poet Caṇḍīdāsa and the Maithili poet Vidyāpati.[15] There is no reference to the origin of Caitanya's devotion to the songs of the *Gītagovinda,* but it is likely that he heard them in the temple of Jagannātha. His love for Jayadeva's songs led to the canonization of the *Gītagovinda* within the Vaishnava Sahajiyā cult and its interpretation according to the doctrines of Bengali Vaishnavism.[16] Sahajiyā tradition claims Jayadeva as a practicer of its unorthodox ritual and the "original preceptor" (*ādiguru*) of the cult.[17] Jayadeva's ritual practice is not revealed by his poem, but the place of his songs in the Caitanya cult complements the Oriya tradition that nightly performance of the songs in worship of Jagannātha at Puri has been continuous for more than seven hundred years.[18]

By the end of the thirteenth century, the *Gītagovinda* was known in western India. A stone inscription of Mahārāja Sāraṅgadeva Vāghelā of Aṇahillapattan, dated A.D. 1291 (Vikrama era 1348), opens with Jayadeva's invocation to Krishna in his ten incarnate forms (I.16).[19] The inscription records the levying of a revised tax on the inhabitants of Pālhanapura (modern Palanpur) to defray the expenses of temple offerings to Krishna. The *Gītagovinda* was probably brought to Gujarat by Vaishnava pilgrims who heard it at Puri or some other eastern center of the Krishna cult.

Further evidence of the poem's wide dissemination in the centuries following its composition includes the existence of one palm-leaf manuscript in Newari hooked characters dated ca. A.D. 1447 (Nepali era 567) and another in Newari script dated ca. A.D. 1496 (Nepali era 616).[20] The text of this version accords well with the text on which Mānāṅka based his simple commentary. The fifteenth-century date given to an early paper manuscript of the *Gītagovinda,* accompanied by Mānāṅka's commentary and illustrated with paintings of the ten incarnations of Krishna in the Gujarati style of the mid-fifteenth century, is corroborated by the date, ca. A.D. 1512 (*saṁvat* 1569), on another manuscript of Mānāṅka's commentary.[21] The literary critical commentary of Kumbhakarṇa, called *Rasikapriyā,* is dated the mid-fifteenth century according to the dates of the ruler of Mewar named Kumbhakarṇa (A.D. 1433–68), with whom the commentator is identified.[22] By the sixteenth century Jayadeva's poem was recognized throughout northern India for the intensity of its poetic and its religious expression.

2 *The Lyrical Structure of Jayadeva's Poem*

The *Gītagovinda,* deceptively simple in its surface beauty, has a wealth of meaning embedded in structurally intricate forms and concepts drawn from various levels of Indian literary tradition. In the process of preparing this textual analysis and translation, I have come to appreciate how masterfully Jayadeva interwove formal and thematic elements to create a work of high art and religious intensity that remains appealing to popular audiences throughout the Indian subcontinent. In order to translate the lyric drama into an English form that conveys its sense and characteristic texture, I have found it essential to unravel these elements, trace their sources, and understand how Jayadeva used them in his own innovative ways.

I have tried to find a diction within current English that would be receptive to the letters, words, meanings, and textures of Jayadeva's Sanskrit—a medium in which the translation could become a representation of the original. The choice has not been between translation of words (*śabdānuvāda*) and translation of feeling (*bhāvānuvāda*). Words derive meaning from the contexts in which they occur. Words in their various levels of denotative, connotative, and suggested meanings, as well as in their grammatical forms and structural relations, are the stuff out of which feeling is made in poetry. To paraphrase I. A. Richards, word and feeling are interlinked so closely that to dissect one from the other is a perilous operation.[1] Word and feeling have functioned inseparably in the translation process. Critical analysis of Jayadeva's language, style, and concepts has helped to integrate these throughout.[2]

In Sanskrit literature creative expression was circumscribed by strict conventions, which served to expand the significance of words and images beyond their given meaning. Sanskrit poets sought to awaken response by manipulating complex language, figures of speech, and imagery in skillful improvisation. Classical poets like Kālidāsa and Bhartṛhari appealed exclusively to an educated audience of men who were familiar with poetic techniques and were capable of understanding the linguistic subtleties of Sanskrit grammar.[3] Jayadeva seems to have been consciously appealing to a more diverse audience, characterized by broader literary taste and religious devotion. Verses in the *Gītagovinda* (e.g., I.2, 4; XII.22) express the poet's intent to reach an audience sympathetic to the creative purpose of enjoying Krishna's divine love through esthetic experience.

Jayadeva seems to have searched the literary expressions of his poetic heritage and contemporary experience to distill a genre appropriate to his vision of Krishna's springtime rite of love. The form of the *Gītagovinda* defies categorization in any classical genre of Sanskrit literature. The lyricism and dramatic movement of the poem may be based on some nonclassical form, but the complex structures Jayadeva uses to integrate religious, erotic, and esthetic meaning suggest that his inspiration for the *Gītagovinda* also came from works like Kālidāsa's classical epic, the *Kumārasambhava*, "The Birth of the Prince," and the same author's unique lyric poem, the *Meghadūta*, "The Cloud-messenger."[4] Jayadeva's application to Sanskrit of elaborate sound patterns of rhyme, alliteration, and measured rhythm offers concrete evidence of how he used techniques of "popular" songs to exploit the lyric potential of the classical language.[5]

The *Gītagovinda* is best characterized as a dramatic lyrical poem. It is expressed as a cycle of songs[6] interspersed with recitative portions in the metrical forms of classical *kāvya* verses. These *kāvya* verses function as independent grammatical and esthetic entities. Most of them are narrative verses identifying the singer of a song or elaborating its context. Others, like verse I.47, are relatively independent of the story and serve primarily to reinforce the esthetic atmosphere of the poem. Such verses may be recalled and enjoyed like miniature paintings from an album.

Winds from sandalwood mountains
Blow now toward Himalayan peaks,
Longing to plunge in the snows
After weeks of writhing
In the hot bellies of ground snakes.
Melodious voices of cuckoos
Raise their joyful sound
When they spy the buds
On tips of smooth mango branches.

The brief *kāvya* verses in the *Gītagovinda* may contain dense descriptions and complex ideas. Classical ornamentation (*alaṁkāra*) is used to expand meaning. Alliterations and sensuous vocabulary, which are general characteristics of the songs, occur in some verses. Subtle forms of metaphor (*upamā*) employed in the verses are recognized by the commentators.[7]

Since contrasting metrical patterns are basic to the structure of the *Gītagovinda,* the distinction between syllabic meter (*akṣaravṛtta*) and two types of moric meter (*tālavṛtta*) must be recognized.[8] The basic patterns of both syllabic and moric meters depend on the quantity of individual syllables in a unit of verse. Syllabic meters are generally characterized by fixed sequences of short, or "light," and long, or "heavy," syllables repeated in each quarter of a verse. The musical moric meters are defined by the number of beats (*mātra*) in a line, with each light syllable counting as one beat and each heavy syllable as two beats. Most moric meters are further patterned into measures (*gaṇa*), the most common type being a measure of four beats (*caturgaṇa*).

Within the seventy-two *kāvya* verses included in the critical edition of the *Gītagovinda,* twelve different syllabic meters occur.[9] There are also three verses in the moric meter Āryā (VI.1; VII.2; IX.1). Āryā is the most extensively used moric meter in Sanskrit poetry. It is the characteristic meter of poetry in Prākrit dialects of the classical period, exemplified by the contents of Hāla's anthology, the *Sattasaī,*[10] and by Prākrit verses in Sanskrit dramas. Although the classical Āryā meter is organized in terms of beat and measure, like the songs of the *Gītagovinda,* its formal articulation makes it distinct from the types of measured meters that order the songs.[11]

In comparison with the compact form and contained grammar of the classical *kāvya* verses, the structure of the songs is broader and more complex. A composite pattern of three interdependent formal units is repeated in each of the twenty-four songs.[12] The fixed unit in each song is the *dhruvapada,* a "refrain" that is repeated after each couplet; it is the stable unit of sound and meaning in the song. Its content provides a context for the descriptive details of the couplets and intensifies their meaning. Where the *dhruvapada* contains the grammatical subject to which descriptive compounds and phrases refer, it resolves the "dangling" syntax of the couplets. The refrains are characterized by syntactic simplicity and a core vocabulary of recurring words that suggest correspondences between Rādhā and Krishna at different stages of their separation. Just as a refrain unifies a song, the network of refrains unifies the poem.

The varying unit in each song is the *pada,* a stanza that is one of a series of rhymed couplets occuring in a particular moric metrical pattern. From this comes the designation of the songs as *padāvalī,* "stanza-series," a term that Jayadeva introduces in the *Gītagovinda* (I.4). Since the stanzas usually number eight, the songs are also referred to as *aṣṭapadī,* "eight-stanza song."

The final formal unit is the *bhaṇita,* the last *pada* in each song. Each *bhaṇita* repeats the poet's signature, Jayadeva, and usually some form of the root $\sqrt{}$*bhaṇ,* which means "saying" or "singing." This stanza reaffirms the affinities of the poet's creative activity and the audience's esthetic experience to the developing erotic relationship between Rādhā and Krishna. It functions in each song to give the perspective of esthetic and religious perception to the emotional intensity of the preceding stanzas and the refrain.

The system of moric meters in the *Gītagovinda* songs gives the poem its rhythmical structure. A particular meter relates couplets within a song, and the metrical system relates the songs to one another. Jayadeva's skillful variation of a few selected metrical patterns sustains the aural appeal of his long poem.

As I have already suggested, the moric meters of the songs contrast with the traditional moric meters like Āryā in several ways. The severely restricted occurrence of heavy syllables is most striking. Heavy syllables are relatively rare in the songs; they are limited mainly to initial position within the *gaṇa* units and to the ends of lines. This gives the songs their lilting quality and definite rhythmical beat. The rhythmical element is further emphasized by repetitious sound patterns of alliteration, assonance, consonance, and end rhyme. These devices are all used in earlier Sanskrit literature, but nowhere else with the persistence that characterizes the *Gītagovinda*.

The meters of the songs and the mode of their articulation clearly resemble the meters of medieval poetry in the vernacular languages known as Apabhraṁśa. Although few of Jayadeva's meters are specifically identifiable with those known from either Jain Apabhraṁśa poetry of western India or Buddhist Caryāpada poetry of eastern India, the predominant metrical pattern of the songs corresponds with the basic rhythmic design of such non-Sanskrit medieval poetry. The correspondence had led scholars like Pischel, Renou, and Chatterji to suggest that the songs, or even the entire poem, were originally composed in Apabhraṁśa and then translated into Sanskrit.[13] A close reading of the songs and a comparison of the songs with the *kāvya* verses in the poem suggest instead that Jayadeva adapted the musical moric meters of vernacular poetry in order to create a medium of song within conventional poetic Sanskrit. If one analyzes Jayadeva's style in terms of meter, ornamentation, and structure, the classical elements drawn from Sanskrit and Prākrit sources are as significant to the songs as the Apabhraṁśa meters. Jayadeva's adaptation of Apabhraṁśa meters to Sanskrit is not an isolated phenomenon. It is the most sustained and successful of several such experiments that are known from the tenth century and after, when the bonds of classical Sanskrit literature were loosened by attempts to broaden its appeal.[14]

The most prominent meter in the *Gītagovinda* songs repeats a pattern of couplets structured into lines of seven four-beat measures, exemplified by the opening couplet of the third song (I.27):[15]

lalitala|vaṅgala|tāpari|śīlana|komala|malayasa|mīre|
madhukara|nikaraka|rambita|kokila|kūjita|kuñjaku|tīre ||

⏑ ⏑ ⏑ ⏑ | - ⏑ ⏑ | - ⏑ ⏑ | - ⏑ ⏑ | - ⏑ ⏑ | ⏑ ⏑ ⏑ ⏑ | - - |
⏑ ⏑ ⏑ ⏑ | ⏑ ⏑ ⏑ ⏑ | - ⏑ ⏑ | - ⏑ ⏑ | - ⏑ ⏑ | - ⏑ ⏑ | - - ||

This meter and its variants, which maintain the four-beat measure, govern nineteen of the twenty-four songs in the *Gītagovinda*.[16] The dominant metrical unit of the songs reflects the four-beat subdivision of the most common rhythmical pattern (*tāla*) of both Hindusthani and Karnatic classical music. The meter of a song can provide the rhythmical component of the song's music. It seems significant that no *tāla* designations are given in two of the oldest manuscripts of the *Gītagovinda,* though each song in these manuscripts is defined by the name of a melodic pattern (*rāga*). Where *tāla* names do accompany *rāga* names in other manuscripts, there is enormous variability with regard to the *tāla* names.[17]

Most of the refrains are in moric metrical patterns that maintain the same measured beat as that of the associated couplets.[18] They generally contrast with the couplets in length only. Refrains usually consist of one line or two rhyming lines of unequal length. The rhythmic cadences of the refrains tend to be heavier than those of the couplets, thus giving their words greater emphasis.[19]

Rhyme, in its several varieties, highlights the rhythmic patterns of the songs. Alliteration (*anuprāsa*) in Sanskrit poetry involves the echo of repeated sounds in a line; it is not limited to the initial sounds of words. Alliteration is the rhyming device most commonly used to produce emphasis and euphony in classical *ḳāvya*.[20] In the *Gītagovinda* alliterative combinations of consonants and vowels reinforce the meters and the sensuous imagery of the songs. They often contribute to the rhythmical complexity of a line by forcing syllables into a syncopation of the metrical accent.[21]

End-rhyme (*antānuprāsa*) is a universal feature of the couplets. It serves to mark the close of each metrical cycle. This consistent use of end-rhyme is rare in classical Sanskrit poetry, though internal rhyme is common, as it is in the *ḳāvya* verses of the *Gītagovinda*.[22]

The eminent critic Ānandavardhana warns that a poet's preoccupation with repetitions of sound, like word-play, alliteration, and assonance, is an obstacle to the production of erotic mood.[23] But most Sanskrit critics consider these devices essential to the sweetness of poetry (*madhura, mādhurya*).[24] These critics seem to agree with the practicing poets that sense and sound must complement each other to create intensity in the expression of erotic mood.

The entire *Gītagovinda* abounds in various forms of word-play as well as rhyme. The repetition and shifting meaning of key words like *rasa* (taste), *madhu* (honey), and *vilāsa* (seduction), relate levels of content within the poem and often expand the context of a verse or song. Jayadeva puns on the names of certain meters he uses in the *kāvya* verses.[25] He plays on the names of heavenly nymphs to describe Rādhā (X.14). He plays on the epithets of Krishna, especially *Mādhava, Madhusūdana,* and *Hari.* The poet's own name, Jayadeva, which is also used as an epithet of Krishna, is repeated as the poet's signature at the end of each song.[26]

The grammar of the songs is simplified. Certain forms are repeated frequently. Prominent are the locative, which is often used in its absolute function, the instrumental, and various participles. In the tenth song, unvarying grammatical parallelism governs each of the couplets.

In the *Gītagovinda* repetitive patterns of sounds, syllables, words, and phrases serve to reinforce and supplement the metrical structures of the songs. All Sanskrit poetry contains generous amounts of sound elaboration (*śabdālaṁkāra*); [27] in the songs of the *Gītagovinda* the redundancies are incessant, complex, and multileveled. They create a sensuous surface of verbal ornamentation that suggests comparison with the sculptured surfaces of the medieval Hindu temples of Bhubaneswar and Khajuraho. In the rhythmic disposition of a basic ground plan and the superimposition of repetitive shapes along a vertical axis, each temple moves to a point of intense concentration, where it simultaneously plunges into the womb-house of the deity and transcends itself.[28] The intricate vertical and horizontal design that emerges in the *Gītagovinda* from the repetitions of metrical units, refrains, rhymes, alliterations, technical words, puns, and syntactic devices unifies the entire poem and concentrates its movement.

All known manuscripts of the *Gītagovinda* indicate the names of various *rāgas,* or melodic patterns, for individual songs. The Indian *rāga* is a melodic formula that includes particular embellishments and tone colors. The technique of improvisation, which is essential to the formal presentation of a *rāga,* uses dense combinations of grace notes and microtonal ornaments. The *rāga,* in the form of either a song or an instrumental piece, is identifiable in performance by its characteristic turns of phrase and dominant tones. In theory, every *rāga* is associated with a particular mood, time, and seasonal setting.[29]

The songs of the *Gītagovinda* are sung in regions of eastern and southern India in a variety of different *rāgas.*[30] Although the oldest manuscripts show striking agreement in designating a group of eleven different *rāgas* for the twenty-four songs, there has been no traditional transmission or notation to assure that these names designate the same melodic patterns they do in later times. The fact that many commentators are preoccupied with defining the *rāgas* in terms of Indian music theory suggests that the songs were variously interpreted throughout their history.

3 *Jayadeva's Language for Love*

Poetry is distinguished from ordinary modes of speech by the controlled and stylized ways it strives to transcend the limits of ordinary language. The lyrical techniques of Jayadeva's songs combine with the conventional language of Sanskrit erotic poetry to express the intimate power of divine love.[1] As Jayadeva's elaborates the passion of Rādhā and Krishna, he creates an esthetic atmosphere of erotic mood (*śṛṅgārarasa*) that is bliss for devotees of Krishna. The poet's aim is implied in an opening verse of the *Gītagovinda* (I.4):

> If remembering Hari enriches your heart,
> If his arts of seduction arouse you,
> Listen to Jayadeva's speech
> In these sweet soft lyrical songs.

The relation between esthetic and spiritual experience is made explicit in the signature verse of the final song of the poem (XII.19):

> Make your heart sympathetic to Jayadeva's splendid speech!
> Recalling Hari's feet is elixir against fevers of this dark time.
> She told the joyful Yadu hero, playing to delight her heart.

The concept of mood, *rasa,* is at the heart of all Indian artistic expression. *Rasa* is literally the taste or flavor of something. The *rasa* of a verse, song, dramatic scene, or musical performance is the flavor of a pervading emotion (*sthāyibhāva*). Sanskrit poets and critics came to realize the unique power and the esthetic potential of sexual passion (*ratibhāva*) in its aspects of pain and pleasure.[2] The erotic mood that emerges from passion was expressed in the antithetical modes of "separation" (*vipralambhaśṛṅgāra*) and "consummation" (*saṁbhogaśṛṅgāra*). To experience this mood in the interplay of its two modes was considered the height of esthetic joy.[3] Jayadeva created the religiously potent atmosphere of the *Gītagovinda* by exploring the poignant mood of separation within the broader play of divine passion in consummation.

Passion is transformed into erotic mood when a poet distills essential qualities from the confusion of spontaneous emotion and then patterns them according to universalizing rules of composition. Passion is made palpable through sensuous descriptions of movements and physical forms. Seasonal changes in nature and bodily signs of inner feeling are colored richly to create a dense atmosphere of passion.[4] The theorists dictated that the gestures exposing a character's mental states must be subtle, expressive enough to arouse a sensitive audience but never so crudely detailed that they stimulate wanton desire.[5] In the *Gītagovinda*, this restraint functions to make potentially pornographic subject matter the material of esthetic and religious experience.

In Jayadeva's environment of springtime (*sarasavasanta*, I.27 *), Rādhā and Krishna are vehicles (*vibhāva*) for the universalization of erotic emotion. These youthful figures with gleaming flesh and lotus-petal eyes manifest signs of emotion (*vyabhicāribhāva, sāttvikabhāva*) to communicate the passion of their separation. For Jayadeva, their longing and reunion is the concrete example of religious experience in which the disquieting distinction between "I" and "mine" versus "you" and "yours" is calmed.[6] The esthetic experience of their love is the means for breaking the imaginary barrier dividing human from divine.

The poet's direct presence throughout the poem dramatizes his view that the discipline of esthetic perception is a way to enjoy Krishna's graceful love. Each signature verse is a variation on the idea that the emotional states of Rādhā and Krishna have religious power through the medium of the poet's lyric presentation.

Insight into Jayadeva's conception is found by following the way he presents his characters through the movement of the poem's twelve parts. After evoking Rādhā and Krishna in their secret erotic relationship and stating his own aim, Jayadeva invokes the ten cosmic incarnations of Krishna. He proceeds to present increasingly intimate aspects of Krishna's relation to existence, focusing on the suffering he shares with Rādhā in the frustration of their love. Krishna's ecstatic reunion with Rādhā within the forest thicket in springtime allows the poet's audience to witness the center of existence. The vision (*darśana*) of Krishna revealed through Rādhā at the end of the poem is a vision of the soul of his erotic mood (*ekarasa*, XI.24–31, song 22). Its effect is comparable with Krishna's manifestation to Arjuna in the eleventh chapter of the *Bhagavadgītā*. Rādhā's heart, strengthened by the long trial of their separation and by the force of Krishna's suffering, is filled with erotic mood (*sarasamanas*, XII.1) that is the consummation (*sambhogaśṛṅgāra*) of the erotic, esthetic, religious experience Jayadeva creates for himself and his audience. This vision is contained within the structure of the poem, like the vision that climaxes a worshipper's controlled approach to the deity in the womb of a Hindu temple. On another level, the poetic perspective follows the movement of Rādhā's friend (*sakhī*), who goes between the parted lovers to describe the condition of each to the other. This perspective begins on Rādhā's side, but it subtly shifts to mediate between Rādhā and Krishna and bring them into union. The friend, the poet, and the audience share the experience of secretly participating in the play of divine love.[7]

The *Gītagovinda* begins with a classical verse indicating the subject of the poem.[8]

"Clouds thicken the sky.
Tamāla trees darken the forest.
The night frightens him.
Rādhā, you take him home!"
They leave at Nanda's order,
Passing trees in thickets on the way,
Until secret passions of Rādhā and Mādhava
Triumph on the Jumna riverbank.

The place, the time, the characters, and their relationship in the poem are superficially clear in this verse. But details of the episode are rich in symbolism and have encouraged complicated interpretations of Jayadeva's meaning.[9] Most interpretations turn on the identification of the speaker of the first half of the verse and on the reference to Krishna's "fear" and Rādhā's role as his guide through the dark forest. The opening speech is variously attributed to Krishna,[10] Rādhā,[11] Nanda,[12] or even the friend of Rādhā.[13] Jayadeva is characteristically ambiguous here—the many voices that are possible in the verse all direct the sexual energies of Krishna toward Rādhā, but each voice slightly shifts the quality of the darkness and of Krishna's fear. When we hear Krishna's foster-father, the cowherd-chief Nanda, address Rādhā, Krishna's youthful fear of the dark is suggested. When we hear Rādhā speaking to herself, the words suggest a woman sensing the sexual fear of her adolescent lover. When we hear Krishna himself speaking he is courting Rādhā in the veiled language of love, where feigned fear is a device of seduction. The composite voice further suggests that fear may relate to the cosmic age of darkness, the Kali Yuga, for which the union of Rādhā and Krishna is the cure.[14]

The darkness of the night in the forest is described in voluptuous sounds and imagery that echo through the entire poem.[15] It is in this secret, sexually stimulating environment that Krishna and Rādhā enact the initial triumph of their divine love and then suffer the long night of separation that ends in their reunion. They follow the path through the forest as a pair, which Jayadeva calls Rādhā-Mādhava.[16] The triumph of their passions occurs in this dual state, which is the defining structure of their relationship in the *Gītagovinda.* The "home" to which Rādhā brings Krishna is a forest thicket (*kuñja*), the secret place of their divine love, in which they meet again at the end of their journey.

The erotic mysticism of the *Gītagovinda,* which inspired the Vaishnava saint Caitanya, was interpreted allegorically by Caitanya's followers in terms of the Sahajiyā doctrine of devotional esthetics (*bhaktirasa*);[17] they used love as a metaphor whose primary reference was a metaphysical conception. Although many elements in the *Gītagovinda* are codified in the Sahajiyā doctrine of love, this reading seems artificial. Jayadeva's verses nowhere praise unbodied joy; they are explicitly sensual, and celebrate the sensual joy of divine love. Through imagery, tone color, and rhythm, Jayadeva interweaves levels of physical and metaphysical associations, and the cosmic energy of Krishna's love with Rādhā is condensed into a religious ecstasy.

4 Krishna: Cosmic Cowherd Lover

Krishna's mythology is ancient and complicated, emerging in the earliest levels of the epic *Mahābhārata* and developing through the various phases of Purāṇic literature. The history and significance of the Krishna legend has been analyzed in numerous scholarly studies; the summary that follows borrows freely from them.[1]

The process of Krishna's deification is discernible in epic literature. In the accounts of him in the *Mahābhārata* and the *Harivaṁśa,* his character is a transparent composite of a cowherd hero and a tribal chief who is also a form, or an incarnation (*avatāra*), of the god Vishnu. The mundane and cosmic levels of his activity are interwoven in the narratives to encompass elements from various sources in a complex mythic structure.[2] The basic account includes Krishna's miraculous birth, his concealment among cowherds to protect him from his demonic uncle Kaṁsa, his childhood pranks and miraculous deeds in the cowherds' village, his youthful sexual play in the forest with the cowherdesses of Vraja, his destruction of demons, his defeat and killing of Kaṁsa, his role in the Bhārata war as the cunning and unscrupulous counsellor-cousin of the five Pāṇḍava brothers, and his violent death. In the *Bhagavadgītā,* he teaches a syncretic religion of devotion to his Pāṇḍava companion Arjuna and reveals himself to be the all-God, who is called Vishnu.[3] The fusion of Krishna with Vishnu involved a transfer of many of Vishnu's epithets, as well as his functions, to Krishna.[4] The divine-cowherd episodes of Krishna's legend became the focus of the medieval devotional cults that emphasized erotic mysticism, and in the process his divinity became distinct from the other incarnations of Vishnu. Krishna emerged as the supreme god of the Kali Yuga, the cosmic age of darkness.[5]

From ancient times, Indian culture has attributed extraordinary power to names and the act of name-giving, especially the naming of gods. The traditional practice in Hindu ritual of chanting a series of a god's thousand names (*sahasranāmastuti*) is evidence of this. Epithets are characterizing names, frequently taking the form of descriptive compound words (*bahuvrīhisamāsa*) in Sanskrit. Although some epithets are petrified into obscure ornamental formulas, most of them function to delineate the subject's character by evoking his deeds, relations, physical forms, and qualities.[6] The particular names and epithets a sophisticated poet like Jayadeva chose from among the myriad names of Krishna must have been meant to set the figure in a pattern of specific associations.

Most of Krishna's epithets in the *Gītagovinda* are traceable to older sources. The epithet *Bhagavat,* Lord, which is prominent in the *Mahābhārata,* the *Harivaṁśa,* and various Purāṇas and which is referred to in the title of the *Bhagavadgītā,* is notably absent in the *Gītagovinda.* Its absence, along with the absence of terms like *dharma, karma,* and *bhakti,* encourages the speculation that Jayadeva was consciously distinguishing the Krishna he worshipped from the object of the orthodox Bhāgavata cult.[7] This is consonant with the poet's concentration on Krishna's special relation to Rādhā, the isolated figure who contrasts with the cowherdess group and who is ignored in early Bhāgavata texts.[8] The epithets *Jagadīśa,* Lord of the World, and *Jayadeva,* God of Triumph, are textually associated with Krishna for the first time in the *Gītagovinda.* Their use in the opening songs is crucial to appreciating the conceptual framework and movement of the poem. The epithets *Daśavidharūpa* and *Daśākṛtikṛt,* referring to Krishna in his ten incarnations, are similarly significant.

The various epithets are defined below, in order of their appearance in the text of the poem, with references to other sources. Chapters and verses in the text of the *Gītagovinda* are referred to by Roman and Arabic numerals; an asterisk placed after a verse number indicates a refrain.

MĀDHAVA (I.1; III.2; IV.1, 2*, 7; V.7; VII.12, 39; VIII.2*; IX.2*; XI.14*) literally means "related to *madhu.*" *Madhu* may mean "springtime," or "honey," or "the progenitor of Krishna's own Yadu clan." The relation of the progenitor Madhu to the demon Madhu whom Krishna destroys is unclear. Daniel H. H. Ingalls suggests that the whole myth of the demon rests on a misunderstanding of the name Mādhava, "springtime."[9] It may be that the "misunderstanding" was intended by storytellers to amplify the meaning of the epithet as it applies to Krishna. In the *Gītagovinda, madhu* is used to mean "honey" (I.36; VI.2; VII.6; X.2*; XI.18), "springtime" (I.46), and "the demon Madhu" (I.20). The epithets *Madhusūdana,* "killer of Madhu" (I.25, 40; II.17; VII.9), *Madhuripu,* "enemy of Madhu" (II.9, 18; V.1, 14; VI.5; VII.13, 29; XII.9), and *Madhumathana,* "tormentor of Madhu" (XI.2*) indicate that Krishna conquered *madhu,* but it remains uncertain how *madhu* is to be understood. If these epithets and *Mādhava* are understood as a complex of related meanings, they seem to suggest that Krishna conquered and absorbed into himself the power of what he conquered, whether it was "springtime" or "honey" or Krishna's own progenitor, all of which are potentially dangerous and so "demonical." Springtime, personified in Indian literature as the companion of the god of love, is erotically powerful and painful for parted lovers. Honey, the prized raw food of the forest, is cited as an aphrodisiac of power and danger in early brahmanical literature.[10] Lévi-Strauss offers an analysis of honey in South American myths as a paradisaical seducer and disrupter of marital ties,[11] and one can see a parallel relation between Krishna's seductive, antinomian sexual behavior and his metaphoric association with honey. The conventional Indian sexual image of the bee acting like a lover in producing and drinking honey further widens the meaning of Krishna's association with honey. Bees are referred to in the poem by the common Sanskrit epithets *madhukara,* "honey-maker" (I.27; VII.25), *madhupa,* "honey-drinker" (I.36; V.4; XI.4, 18), and *madhuvrata,* "busy with honey" (II.1). The dominant meanings of *madhu* thus provide a strongly erotic context for the verbal play of *Mādhava* and related epithets in the *Gītagovinda*.[12]

VĀSUDEVA (I.2) refers to Krishna's royal birth in the Yadu clan as the son of Vasudeva and Devakī. It is a common epithet of Krishna throughout epic literature.[13]

HARI (I.4, 5*, 17*, 27*, 34, 38*, 39, 43, 46; II.1, 2*; IV.9, 17; V.14, 15; VI.2*, 6, 7; VII.3, 7, 10, 14, 29, 38; IX.1, 2, 4, 6, 8, 9; XI.6, 8, 9, 13, 24*, 31; XII.1, 19) literally means "the tawny one," but Vaishnava commentators interpret it to mean "the destroyer of pain," derived from the Sanskrit root √ *hṛ*. Hari is a common name of Vishnu in his cosmic form and his various incarnations in the epics and Purāṇas. It is probably borrowed from the Vedic name of Indra, whose characteristics Vishnu and Krishna absorb.[14] The ambiguity of reference in the name *Hari* reflects the identification of Krishna, as *Jagadīśa,* with the cosmic form and function of Vishnu.[15] The similarity between *Hari* and Śiva's name *Hara,* "the destroyer" (III.11), is exploited by Jayadeva for ironical effect.

KEŚAVA (I.5*, 45; IV.11*; VIII.2*; XI.1) means "long-haired." It is traditionally related to Krishna's killing of the horse-demon Keśin.[16] Like *Hari,* it refers ambiguously to Vishnu and Krishna in epic and Purāṇic literature.

JAGADĪŚA (I.5*) means "Lord of the World." In the refrain of the song of invocation, it indicates Krishna's cosmic supremacy. In the Jagannātha cult of Orissa, which probably provided the context for the composition of the *Gītagovinda,* Krishna is identified with the composite Buddhist-Śaivite-Vaishnavite form of Jagannātha.[17]

DAŚAVIDHARŪPA (I.15) means "having a tenfold form." It indicates that Krishna is at once all of the ten forms of cosmic power he assumes in his awesome aspect (*aiśvarya*) in order to save the world. The same is meant by *Daśākṛtikṛt* (I.16). The ten forms of *Jagadīśa* are a variant of the ten incarnations of Vishnu; in Purāṇic literature Krishna instead of Balarāma is usually the eighth incarnation. The incarnations were originally independent legends that came to center on Vishnu as the preserver of order when it is imperiled. Various aspects of the legends are emphasized in different texts. The content of the *Gītagovinda* song is not traceable to any single source.[18]

The awesome aspect of Krishna, which the ten forms vividly portray, recedes as Krishna's lover-hero role (*nāyaka*) is elaborated in the poem to dramatize his honey aspect (*mādhurya*) in relation to Rādhā. But the cosmic power remains a background for the intimacy of the lovers throughout the poem; the intimacy offers a dimension of cosmic power on which human perception can focus. The complex and powerful manifestations of cosmic reality are concentrated in emotions that are carefully patterned for esthetic experience.[19] In the terminology of Indian esthetics, the song of invocation to Krishna's tenfold form expresses the mood of wonder (*adbhutarasa*), whose presence is essential to Jayadeva's religious transformation of the mood of erotic love (*śṛṅgārarasa*).[20]

Jayadeva presents the ten forms of *Jagadīśa* as follows:

1. MĪNAŚARĪRA (I.5), the Fish-form, more commonly called *Matsyāvatāra*. The ancient myth of the deluge and man's rescue by a giant fish, which is told in the *Śatapatha Brāhmaṇa* (I.8.1–6), is the basis of later versions. The *Gītagovinda* refers to the theft of the Vedas from Brahmā by a sea demon as the former is entering the sleep of cosmic dissolution. Hari takes on the form of a fish and, by means of the deluge, destroys the demon and recovers the Vedas.[21]
2. KACCHAPARŪPA (I.6), the Tortoise-form. The *Gītagovinda* refers to the creative power of the giant tortoise in relation to earth, an association that is made in the *Śatapatha Brāhmaṇa* (VII.5.1.5). This form is better known, as *Kūrmāvatāra,* for supporting Mt. Mandara when the gods and demons churn the sea to obtain the elixir of immortality.[22]
3. ŚŪKARARŪPA (I.7), the Boar-form, another name for *Varāhāvatāra.* The giant boar rescues the earth by raising it out of the ocean depths on one of his tusks.[23]
4. NARAHARIRŪPA (I.8), the Man-lion form, another name for *Narasiṁhāvatāra.* It is the form in which Hari destroys the infidel King Hiraṇyakaśipu, who threatened his own son Prahlāda with death because of the son's devotion to Hari. Hiraṇyakaśipu had been given a boon of invulnerability by day or night, by god, man, or beast, inside or outside his palace, and to overcome it the god appears at twilight as a man-lion inside a pillar and reaches out to dismember the king.[24]
5. VĀMANARŪPA (I.9), the Dwarf-form. The three cosmic strides of Vishnu form the basis of the dwarf myth.[25] The demon Bali, usurper of Indra's power, grants three paces of land to Hari when he comes to him in the guise of a dwarf. Then Hari assumes his cosmic shape

and traverses earth, atmosphere, and heaven. The *Gītagovinda* refers to Hari's wet feet, which the demon, in his hospitality, has washed to welcome his guest.[26]

6. BHṚGUPATIRŪPA (I.10), the form of the Bhṛgu chief better known as *Paraśurāma,* "axe-wielding Rāma," who reestablishes order in the world by putting an end to the tyranny of the warrior class.[27]
7. RĀMAŚARĪRA (I.11), the form of the "charming" Rāmacandra, Prince of Ayodhyā, who is alternately called *Raghupatirūpa.* He is the hero of Vālmīki's epic *Rāmāyaṇa* and of the *Rāmopākhyāna* of the *Mahābhārata* (III.258–76). His purpose as an incarnation of Hari is the killing of the ten-headed demon king Rāvaṇa, whose evil power threatens the world. The abduction of his wife Sītā by Rāvaṇa and his defeat of Rāvaṇa and Rāvaṇa's general Duṣāṇa, "the corrupting one," are referred to in the second song of the *Gītagovinda* (I.16, 22).[28]
8. HALADHARARŪPA (I.12), the form of the plowman Balarāma, elder brother of Krishna. *Haladharasodara,* "brother of Haladhara," refers directly to Krishna (VII.28). Balarāma and Krishna are alternative incarnations of Vishnu in some texts; in other texts they are both partial incarnations, each representing a hair of Vishnu, one white and one black.[29] Balarāma is known for his addiction to wine, paralleling Krishna's addiction to women. The *Gītagovinda* refers to the episode where he drunkenly orders the Jumna river to move close so he can sport there. When the river fails to obey, he throws his weapon, the plowshare, into her and makes the river bend to him.[30]
9. BUDDHAŚARĪRA (I.13), the form of "the enlightened one," Gautama Buddha. Buddha is not an incarnation in the *Mahābhārata* or the *Harivaṁśa,* but he appears as such in the texts of early Purāṇic literature.[31] The orthodox Hindu view stresses that Buddha's emphasis on moral values, as opposed to Vedic ritual, is valuable only in confusing men and fostering the social chaos that marks the decline of the Kali Yuga. Jayadeva's linking of Buddha's condemnation of Vedic ritual with his compassion for animal victims is a more positive view, consonant with the syncretism characterizing the worship of Krishna as *Jagadīśa* in the *Gītagovinda.*[32]
10. KALKIŚARĪRA (I.14), the form of the avenger, Kalki, who appears with a blazing sword on a white horse at the end of the Kali Yuga to punish barbarians and sinners.[33]

KṚṢṆA is anglicized as *Krishna* in this volume to render recurring reference to the hero of the *Gītagovinda* less artificial for English readers (I.16, 26; II.10; VIII.3, 7; X.5; XII.21); it literally means "black," or "dark." It is a prominent name of the epic hero who is identified with Vishnu in the *Mahābhārata* and who is counted as one of the standard incarnations of Vishnu. Kṛṣṇa Devakīputra is mentioned in the *Chāndogya Upaniṣad* (III.17.6) as a pupil of the mythical teacher Ghora Aṅgiras; scholars have made much of the reference, but it is too isolated to be significant. In the *Gītagovinda,* Krishna is *Jagadīśa,* the cosmic power of the Dark Age. His relationship with Rādhā is set in the context of his youthful adventures among the cowherds and his adolescent erotic play with the cowherdesses in Brindaban forest.[34]

JAYADEVA (I.17*) is interpreted as a dependent compound (*tatpuruṣasamāsa*) meaning "God of Triumph." This is derived by reading the refrain of the second song as *jaya jayadeva hare,* "Triumph, God of Triumph, Hari!" to parallel the refrain of the first song, which is *jaya jagadīśa hare,* "Triumph, Lord of the World, Hari!"[35] The commentator Śaṅkaramiśra, referring to the opening verse of the poem, points out that Krishna's triumph as the hero (*nāyaka*) of the *Gītagovinda* is in sexual play (*keli*). Rādhā is called "Love's living goddess of triumph," *anaṅgajayajaṅgamadevatā* (III.15). The epithet of Krishna is identical with the name of the author of the *Gītagovinda.* In this function, *Jayadeva* occurs in the signature stanza (*bhaṇita*) of each song, as well as in some verses (I.2, 4, 15, 24, 34, 45; II.9, 18; III.10; IV.9, 18; V.6, 15; VI.9; VII.10, 20, 29, 38; VIII.9; IX.9; X.9; XI.9, 21, 31; XII.9, 19, 21, 22).[36]

HAṀSA, (I.18), the Indian wild goose, which migrates to the Himalayas every spring to mate on Lake Mānasa, according to legend. It is symbolic of the Universal Spirit (*parabrahman*). *Mānasa* also means "mental" and the poet's reference is to Krishna as the Universal Spirit in the minds of sages.

MURĀRI (I.37; V.12; VII.21, 22*; XI.21), or *Muravairin* (X.9), means "enemy of Mura." Mura is a demon who is associated with another demon named Naraka in the *Mahābhārata* (I.59, etc.), as in the *Gītagovinda* (I.20).[37]

PĪTAVASANA (I.38; II.7), or *Pītāmbara* (XII.20), means "wearing a yellow cloth." It is an ancient epithet of Krishna, referring to the light garment that contrasts with his dark skin.[38]

VANAMĀLIN (I.38; V.2*, 8*; VII.31*) means "wearing a garland of forest flowers" and symbolizes Krishna's sensual presence in the forest.[39]

GOVINDA (II.19; V.17; VI.1; XI.23; XII.21) is probably a Prākritic form of *gopendra* (*gov' inda*), which means "chief of the cowherds." It can also be derived from *go* $\sqrt{}$*vid* to mean "protector of cows."[40] In either case, the epithet refers to Krishna's adolescence in the forest among the pastoral people of Vraja, the period of his awesome feats of strength, seductive flute playing, and sexual rites. The title *Gītagovinda* has these associations; the young dark lord of the forest is the subject of the poet's singing.

KEŚIMATHANA (II.11*) means "tormentor of the demon Keśin." In the *Harivaṁśa* (62.69), Keśin is called "the meanest of horses," *turagādhama*.[41]

KAṀSĀRI (III.1) means "enemy of Kaṁsa." It refers to the rivalry between Krishna and his uncle, the demonic King Kaṁsa.[42]

UPENDRA (IV.20) means "Indra's younger brother."[43] In the *Gītagovinda* verse it is used to form a pun on the name of the meter *upendravajrā*.

JANĀRDANA (VII.12) means "exciting to men." It is a common epithet of Krishna in the *Mahābhārata*, the *Harivaṁśa*, and the *Bhāgavata Purāṇa*.

NĀRĀYAṆA (XII.2*) literally means "related to *nara*, man." In the *Śatapatha Brāhmaṇa* (XIII.3.4.1) it is an epithet of Puruṣa, the primordial man. Throughout the *Mahābhārata* it is the name of Vishnu or Krishna in the role of cosmic creator.[44]

YADUNANDANA (XII.12, 12*) means "joy of the Yadu clan." Like the epithet *Vāsudeva*, it refers to Krishna's royal birth.

In addition to the epithets that Jayadeva chose to characterize Krishna, references to characters, places, and events from various Vaishnava myths are used to expand the context of the poem. The role of Krishna's foster-father, the cowherd-chief Nanda, in the opening verse is barely indicated by the adverbial compound *nandanideśataḥ*, "at Nanda's order." But the presence of the name emphasizes that Krishna is young as his sexual play begins.[45] References to Krishna's defeat of the serpent-king Kāliya (I.19)[46] and the bird-demoness Pūtanikā (VIII.8)[47] evoke heroic events of his legend. Kāliya was punished for befouling the Jumna waters and Pūtanikā was killed when the baby Krishna sucked her life from her by taking the poisoned breast she offered him. Garuḍa (I.20) is the anthropomorphized eagle who usually serves as Vishnu's vehicle.[48]

The sexual freedom enjoyed by the adolescent cowherd is symbolized by Krishna's simple bamboo flute, which is called *vaṁśa* (I.43; II.2, 19) or *veṇu* (V.9).[49] Like the flower arrows shot by the god of love, Krishna's magical flute is an adolescent instrument for arousing and sustaining sexual desire. Both the arrow and the flute, with their obvious phallic significance, function in this way in the myths of many societies.[50] The culminating effect of Krishna's flute-playing is the ritual circular dance, called *rāsa* (I.43; II.2*), which he performs under the full moon of autumn with the cowherdesses. The common version of the story recounts Krishna's seduction of the cowherdesses by the melodious call of his flute in the woods of Brindaban (*Vṛndāvana*) on the banks of the river Jumna (*Yamunā*).[51] Krishna remains elusive, but promises to dance with the girls in autumn, when the heat and rains are finished. On a night of the full moon, Krishna goes toward the forest playing his flute. The cowherdesses follow and form a circle around him, like stars around the moon. By his magic power, he multiplies himself to dance with all the cowherdesses at once.[52] This rite of autumn acts as a foil for his springtime play with his cowherdess consort Rādhā.

In Indian myth, spring is the ally of Kāma, the god of love. The sexual aggression of Love is portrayed in the myth of his body's destruction by Śiva when he interrupted Śiva's meditation with flower arrows to arouse the divine ascetic's desire for Pārvatī, the daughter of Himālaya. In his relation to Rādhā, Krishna is both the object of Love's attack and the embodiment of Love's creative sensuality.[53]

By representing his divine hero with a complex of characteristics known from older religious sources, Jayadeva thus sets Krishna's relation with Rādhā in a sacred framework. Krishna's relation to all living beings is expressed through his ten incarnate forms. His personal spiritual relation to human beings is expressed through the form of the flute-playing adolescent cowherd. His intense spiritual intimacy with an individual human being is expressed through the divine sensuality of his love with Rādhā.

As the divine lover and object of the poet's worship, Krishna is the embodiment of erotic mood (*śṛṅgāramūrtiman,* I.46) and the essence of esthetic experience (*ekarasa,* XI.24*). His relation with Rādhā epitomizes the classical pattern of erotic love in Sanskrit drama and poetry. Krishna is referred to by standard forms of address given for the dramatic hero (*nāyaka*) in Bharata's *Nāṭyaśāstra,* such as "beloved" or "lover" (*kānta,* VII.11, XII.10, 11; *dayita,* I.41, VII.17, 30; *priya,* IV.21, V.16, VII.30, VIII.1, X.12, XI.32, 33, XII.5, 13; *vallabha,* VII.30),[54] "cheat" (*kitava,* VI.10),[55] and "rogue" (*śaṭha,* VII.30).[56] These familiar forms of address complement the sensuous surface that emerges from descriptions of Krishna's ornamented physical presence and his manifestations of emotion. By such means the poet encourages his audience to approach the divine lover through esthetic experience. The ingenious integration of religious, erotic, and esthetic meaning that Jayadeva achieves in the structure of the *Gītagovinda* is basic in the character of Krishna too.

5 *Rādhā: Consort of Krishna's Springtime Passion*

Rādhā is one of the most obscure figures in early Indian literature. Until Jayadeva made her the heroine of his poem, she appeared only in stray verses scattered through various Purāṇas, anthologies of Prākrit and Sanskrit poetry, works of literary esthetics, grammar, poetry, drama, and a few inscriptions. In the *Gītagovinda,* Rādhā is neither a wife nor a worshipping rustic playmate. She is an intense, solitary, proud female who complements and reflects the mood of Krishna's passion. She is Krishna's partner in a secret and exclusive love, contrasted in the poem with the circular *rāsa* dance Krishna performs with the entire group of cowherdesses. Krishna disappears after this dance, deserting the cowherdesses; but he stays with Rādhā to admire and ornament her. Her relationship with Krishna culminates in their union and mutual "victory" (*jaya*) over each other. In Jayadeva's view, the profound intimacy of Krishna's concentration on Rādhā, in contrast with the diffusion of erotic energy in his play with the cowherdesses, is the perfection of Krishna's nature.[1]

Jayadeva's reference to his heroine focuses on one name, *Rādhā* (I.1, 26; II.1; III.1; IV.20; V.1; VI.2*; XI.1, 13, 14*, 24, 32; XII.1, XII.11) and its diminuitive, *Rādhikā* (I.37; III.2; IV.1, 11*; X.9, XI.2*; XII.2*). Names of Krishna's divine consort, such as *Śrī* (I.2; I.23), *Padmāvatī* (I.2; X.9; XI.21), *Kamalā* (I.17), *Padmā* (I.25), and *Lakṣmī* (XI.22), occur to place Rādhā in the appropriate cosmic context. Rādha's role as the female counterpart of her lover is consonant with the meaning of her name, which is related to the word *rādhas*. In Vedic and Purāṇic literature, *rādhas* and other forms of the root √*rādh* have meaning of "perfection" and "success," even "wealth."[2] The Vedic god most closely associated with *rādhas* is Indra, who bears the epithet "Lord of Success" (*rādhaspati*).[3] In the *Mahābhārata* and various Purāṇas, the rivalry between Indra and Vishnu/Krishna results in the transference of elements of Indra's great power to Vishnu/Krishna. Among these elements are female powers associated with Indra, such as Śrī in the episode of the churning of the ocean.[4] Indra lost Śrī through a curse by the sage Durvāsa and Vishnu reclaimed her as his spouse. A similar pattern may well account for Krishna's role as "Lord of Success" (*rādhaspati*) in relation to *Rādhā,* the feminine personification of *rādhas.* This explanation helps to clarify the parallelism between the pair Śrī/Lakṣmī-Vishnu/Krishna and the pair Rādhā-Krishna that is suggested in many stray verses antedating the *Gītagovinda.* There is no need to construct fanciful etymologies for the word *rādhā,* but this has been the approach of the Sanskrit commentators on the *Gītagovinda* and more recently of the linguist Sukumar Sen.[5] Such accounts offer no clue to why the association between Rādhā and Krishna was made.

In the absence of direct textual evidence it remains impossible to know when and in what circumstances the Rādhā-Krishna pair originated. What we find in the available Prākrit and Sanskrit sources suggests that the poets and critics are dealing with a familiar subject. The name Rādhā seems to carry overtones of meaning from astral mythology. Although there is no reference to the pair in Vedic literature, the word *rādhā* occurs in the *Atharva Veda* (XIX.7.3) in relation to the two stars called *viśākhā.*[6] Later references to *rādhā* as the name of a feminine constellation or star-cluster (*nakṣatrā*) associate her with Indra. Indra is called a "cowherd" (*gopā*) and is paired with a *viśākhā* in several Vedic contexts. In the *Taittirīya Brāhmaṇa* (3.1.1.11) [7] two *viśākhās* are described as the chief female consorts (*adhipatnī*) of the male constellations (*nakṣatra*) and are paired with Indra and Agni, who are called the two best cowherds. In the *Taittirīya Saṁhitā* (4.4.11),[8] in the section where the building of the fire altar (*agnicayana*) is described, the layers of bricks are pairs of feminine constellations and masculine deities. The feminine *viśākhās* are paired with the masculine deities Indra and Agni. These associations are especially significant when it is recalled that Indra is the "Lord of Success" (*rādhaspati*).

In the same *Taittirīya Saṁhitā* passage the pairs of months of the various seasons are named; the months of spring (*vāsantikāv ṛtū*) are named *madhu* and *mādhava.* In the *Mahābhārata,* Vishnu is related to the constellations by his epithet *Nakṣatrin,* "Lord of Constellations," and to spring by the epithets *Mādhu* and *Mādhava* that he shares with Krishna.[9] *Mādhava* is a major epithet of Krishna in epic and later literature. Krishna is also associated in several contexts with various feminine constellations.[10] Whether or not the equation of *rādhā* with *viśākhā* in commentaries on the *Atharva Veda* passage is based on a "misunderstanding" of the word *anurādhā,* as Whitney suggests, it is clear that by the fifth century, *rādhā* was held to be another name for the constellation *viśākhā.*[11] With the equating of month names and constellation names, *viśākhā* became one of the months of spring, creating another link between *rādhā* and *mādhava.* The somewhat esoteric character of these associations may have increased the appeal of Rādhā as a consort for Krishna in a secret relationship. In these two aspects, she represents, like Lakṣmī, the power of "success" and she incarnates, like Śiva's Pārvatī, a phenomenon of nature. Both aspects illuminate her association with Krishna.[12]

Because of the fluidity of Purāṇic texts, it is impossible to date or locate the relationship of Rādhā and Krishna from them. However, the pattern of Rādhā's presence and absence in some major Purāṇas is relevant to the problem. As disciples of the sixteenth-century Vaishnava saint Caitanya, who was considered an incarnation of the divine lovers Rādhā and Krishna, the Gosvāmins searched Purāṇic literature to find references that would establish Rādhā's old and high status within orthodox Vaishnavism.[13] References to Rādhā by name in early Purāṇas such as the *Matsya,* the *Linga,* and the *Varāha* are significant, but few. Rādhā's elaborate treatment in the *Brahmavaivarta* and *Padma* Purāṇas seems to postdate the Caitanya movement.[14] There is no direct reference to Rādhā in the *Harivaṁśa,* the *Viṣṇu Purāṇa* or the *Bhāgavata Purāṇa.* But the mention of a favored cowherdess who is "worshipped" or "desired" (*ārādhitā*) by Krishna in the tenth book of the *Bhāgavata Purāṇa*[15] led the Gosvāmins to derive the name Rādhā from *ārādhitā* and to claim Rādhā's place in the text.[16]

The heroine of the *Gītagovinda* is so complex that it seems absurd to seek Jayadeva's model for her in the allusions to the arrogant girl (*dṛptā*) of the *Bhāgavata* episode. Krishna's special mistress is presented there to criticize the exclusivism that Krishna's relationship with her represents. If the *Bhāgavata* authors are referring to Krishna's consort Rādhā, they seem to be rejecting her relationship with Krishna as an inappropriate model for the devotee. The possessive attitude manifested in her secret encounter with Krishna is antithetical to the values presented in the *Bhāgavata* and the attitude is criticized for its perversity (*daurātmya,* X.30.42). It is not unlikely that the authors of the *Bhāgavata* knew a rival cult centering on Krishna and his cowherdess-consort and were critical of it.

Charlotte Vaudeville, in her article entitled "Evolution of Love-

Symbolism in Bhagavatism," [17] has stated her supposition that the author of the *Bhāgavata* was specifically rejecting the figure of Nappiṇṇai, as she appears in the Tamil Āḷvār poetry of Āṇḍāl and Nāmmāḷvār. Here Nappiṇṇai is the daughter, or daughter-in-law, of Nandagopāl and the wife of Krishna; she is an incarnation of Vishnu's consort Nīladevī.[18] It is possible that Nappiṇṇai is the source of the Rādhā conception in Prākrit and Sanskrit literature, but the two figures more likely represent independent variants; their characteristic relations with Krishna are different. In the ritual dance called *kuravai,* Krishna dances with his wife Nappiṇṇai, while Krishna's relationship with Rādhā is a secret, erotic rite.[19]

The character of Rādhā and her unique association with Krishna that Jayadeva brought to his *Gītagovinda* from earlier literature is not apparent from any single source, but details emerge from the collection of stray verses that refer to her. A chronological catalogue of these references suggests an old tradition surrounding the secret love of Rādhā and Krishna.[20]

From the *Sattasaī* of Hāla (dated first to seventh centuries by various scholars): [21]

> Krishna, removing cow-dust from Rādhikā
> With the breath of your mouth,
> You sweep away the high esteem
> These other cowherdesses have for you. (86)

From the *Gaüḍavaho* of Vākpati (late seventh or early eighth century): [22]

> Let nailmarks Rādhā makes remove your pain—
> They are rich with mood.
> They are shining on Krishna's chest
> Like his magical kaustubha gem. (22)

From the *Veṇīsaṁhāra* of Bhaṭṭa Nārāyaṇa (antedates A.D. 800): [23]

> Angered in sensual play, she lost her mood for love
> In the rāsa dance on sandbanks of the Jumna river.
> When Kaṁsa's foe followed Rādhikā
> As she left in a choking veil of tears,
> His body hairs seemed to bristle
> From his steps touching her footprints
> And from her calmed, loving looks—
> May you prosper from Krishna's innocent plea! (2)

From the *Dhvanyāloka* of Ānandavardhana (mid-ninth century):[24]

> Say, friend, if all is well still with the bowers
> that grow upon the Jumna bank,
> companions to the dalliance of cowherd girls
> and witnesses to Rādhā's love.
> Now that there is no use to cut their fronds
> to make them into beds for love,
> I fear their greenness will have faded
> and they grown old and hard. (2.6)
>
> Gracious love, Rādhā is difficult indeed to please—
> Her tears fall even as you wipe them away
> With the cloth that covered some true love's loins.
> "Women's hearts are hard, so enough flattery! Leave me alone!"
> He was told this whenever Hari tried to placate her—
> May he grant you his blessing! (3.41)

From the *Dhvanyālokalocana* of Abhinavagupta (early tenth century):[25]

> Then when demon Madhu's foe had gone to Dvāravatī,
> Rādhā embraced a sweet vine growing on the Jumna bank,
> A little bent from the way he made it quiver—
> Rādhā's lamenting
> In a faltering voice choked by heavy tears
> Made even the waterbirds wail regretfully.

From the *Kāvyamimāṁsa* of Rājaśekhara (late ninth or early tenth century), as an illustration of the poetic figure *tulyadehitulya,* an imitation that resembles the similarity between two similar persons:[26]

> Then we are going to give the different types of the imitation *tulyadehitulya.* . . . the change of subjects gives a different shape to the same theme: this is the change of subject.
>
> May the winds of Śiva's sighs protect you
> As they arise from the hollow of his right nostril,
> Making lines in the ash-dust on his body,
> Disrupting his yogic breathing exercise,
> Licked by the serpent sheltered in his ear,
> Stealing coolness the moon gives,
> Witnessing the agony his mind suffers
> When his body is parted from angry Pārvatī.
>
> May Hari's sighs protect you
> As they burn from the fire deep within,

Boiling the lotus-honey from his navel,
Wilting the garland on his breast,
Drunk in and spit out because of their heat
By the trembling serpent who forms his couch,
Witnessing his memory of Rādhā's love,
And heard jealously by goddess Śrī.

The occurrence of Rādhā's name in the two oldest-known Sanskrit compositions in mixed prose and verse (*campū-kāvya*) is significant. But the name occurs only once in the *Damayantīkathā* (early tenth century), and once in the *Yaśastilakacampūkāvya* (A.D. 959) and the passages are spare in detail relating to Rādhā.[27] In the *Damayantīkathā* passage the name Rādhā is part of an elaborate pun. The *Yaśastilaka* reference simply says, "Thus indeed—formerly, did Gaṅgā not sport with Maheśvara, Rādhā with Nārāyaṇa, Bṛhaspati's wife with the Moon, Tārā with Valin?"

From inscriptions (dated A.D. 974, 982, and 986) of Vākpati-Muñja, a Paramāra ruler of Malwa, in which the same two verses open each inscription, one in praise in Śiva as the lord of Pārvatī and this one in praise of Krishna as the deserted lover (*virahin*) of Rādhā:[28]

May the active body of demon Mura's enemy protect you!
Lakṣmī's face could not please it, the ocean's waters could not cool it,
The lotus in the lake of his own navel was powerless to pacify it,
Fragrant breath from serpent Śeṣa's thousand mouths could not soothe it—
It was so sick with the pain of Rādhā's desertion.

From the *Sarasvatīkaṇṭhābharaṇa* of Bhoja (ca. A.D. 1000–55)[29] is a verse (2.294) that is an exercise in word play known as *kavināmāṅkāṣṭapattrabandha.* Here the poet's name, Rājaśekhara, is hidden in a poem in palindromes and puns; the name emerges through a diagram of an eight-petaled lotus. The diagram was executed by H. S. Phātak of the Mysore Oriental Research Institute. The verse can be paraphrased roughly as follows: "She who bestowed a kingdom of defects, a knower of *rasa* that gives expansion ($\sqrt{ra}$), who speaks pretentious speech, who does wrong to the world, the full-moon maiden, whose eyelashes are like serpent Śeṣa, whose eye leads to *nītiśāstra,* she who travels in the sky, whose love is praiseworthy, who is charming, whose penance is several, carrier of the moon, Śrī, whose sword is sharp—let Rādhā protect me; she is the incarnation who brings down serpent knowledge for masters of will who have their egos centered in Śiva." Also, from the same text:

राजशेखरकमलवन्धः

"Are you comfortable, Rādhā?" "Are you happy, Kaṁsa?"
"Kaṁsa?" "What is the difference between Kaṁsa and Rādhā?"
With these retorts of the cowherdess Pārī,
Hari triumphs in self-conscious laughter. (2.351)

As he tries repeatedly to lift
The raincloud-dark reflection of his own bright form,
Mistaking it for the black border of a garment
On the golden globe of Rādhā's breast,
Hari triumphs,
Laughing in shame as his love laughs at him. (3.110)

You left the house for the river to fetch water—you do not return.
Saying, "I shall bathe," you stop at bowers of vines on the Jumna bank.
Tethering the cows, you enter the thick woods of Mt. Govardhana.
Rādhā, didn't you catch sight of Krishna, Devakī's son? (4.177)

May the god who gracefully toys with Rādhā's cloth
On the surface of her breasts protect you!
Hari's hand is trembling
With sudden fear at their first encounter. (5.235)

"I have recently left Gokula, and the thought of Rādhā
Confounds me out of sleep—let it leave my bed and let 'Rādhā'
Stop coming in place of other names by day! I am afraid of this!"
May Hari's fatigue protect you!
He is spending sleepless nights, repeating Lakṣmī's name alone by day,
Trying to forget Rādhā, and delighting goddess Śrī. (5.448)

Seeing how thin Hari's arms were as he carelessly lifted Mt. Govardhana,
She rested her hand on Hari's shoulder and placed her feet on his,
Wanting to help him lift the mountain that was out of her reach—
Let the empty motions of Rādhā's hands in the sky triumph forever! (5.493)

From the *Daśāvatāracarita* of Kṣemendra (composed in A.D. 1066):[30]

While Krishna was kissing swarms of glowing nubile women,
Rādhā became most beloved for his joy—like jasmine for a bee. (83)

Then in the morning, having mounted the armed chariot,
Akrūra, Balarāma, and Krishna went to Mathurā with their retinue. (169)
"How could I have come here without bidding farewell to Rādhā?"
Mādhava sighed, felt discontent, languid, anxious at leaving. (170)
Going by way of hidden places in secret thickets of Gokula,
Krishna looked longingly, his face turned back,
The border of his garment held by his friend the forest earth—
He recalled Rādhā's "No! No! No!" while he loosened her skirt knot,

Her syllables marked by her confusion,
Her body wondrous in fear of love, her words barely intelligible. (171)
Filled with fire of Krishna's desertion when he left for Kaṁsa's city,
Like antelopes lying on smooth green banks in secret coves of the Godāvarī,
Secretly, in Gokula grass, cowherdesses passionately sang Krishna's virtues,
Heard by herds of cows standing ruminating, ears intimately erect. (172)
"His love is new and graced by shining youth,
Seductive to young women in the easy play of its gentle enchantment;
He subjugates the family of serpent Kāliya in turbulent Jumna waters,
Black as swarms of bees, cuckoos, dark lotuses, and kohl;
He is harsh in killing great demons like Keśi and his sons,
Tearing dangers from Gokula, upholding Mt. Govardhana—
Could anyone's eyes help drowning in him when he is addicted to passion,
A trembling wave of love, delighting delightful young women?" (173)
While each virtue in Krishna's ocean of virtues
Was sung with passionate feeling,
Passion rose secretly in the cowherd girls
And frenzy struck them again and again. (174)
Since Krishna had gone away without speaking
In his zeal to show deference in the presence of the elders,
Doe-eyed women who carelessly slept on cool ground under bakula trees,
When they met him in dream embraces,
Made their slender creeper bodies echo their words by writhing—
"Rogue, let go! Let go, cheat!" the young women loudly cried. (175)
With tears, flowing away like life in Mādhava's desertion,
Falling on her breasts' firm tips, Rādhā was like a laden kadamba tree
As tears were strewn by her endless sighing and trembling gait—
Darkened by the delusion that was bound to all her hopes,
She became like the new rainy season engulfed in darkness. (176)

From the *Subhāṣitaratnakoṣa* compiled by Vidyākara (latter half of eleventh century); [31] these three references have not been noted in earlier works:

"O Lakṣmaṇa, these clouds distress me who have lost my Sītā.
The cruel kadamba-scented breezes cut me to the quick."
So speaking, in his sleep, of separation
suffered in a former birth, may Hari,
glanced at jealously by Rādhā, bring you joy. (131)

"Go on ahead, milkmaids, taking home the pots already full.
Rādhā will follow later when the older cows are milked."
May Krishna, who by subterfuge thus made the cattle station

deserted but for Rādhā and for him,
the god, foster-son of Nanda,
steal away your ills. (139)

The pilgrims in the street have warded off the painful cold
with their broad quilts sewn of a hundred rags;
and now with voices clear and sweet
they break the morning slumber of the city folk
with songs of the secret love of Mādhava and Rādhā. (980)

From the *Vikramāṅkadevacarita* of Bilhaṇa (late eleventh century):[32]

Let Krishna's sword, "Delighter," reflecting joyful Lakṣmī
In its blade, hold out intense joy for you—
For demon Mura's enemy it perpetually revives
The memory of graceful Rādhā in the Jumna river's flow. (I.5)

[On his journey southward from Kashmir, Bilhaṇa stops at Brindaban.]

Broken by Rādhā's broad hips, which sway as she swings them,
Even now the trees in Krishna's playground have not recovered—
When the circle of Mathurā's sages was shaken by playful banter,
The poet spent several days in wandering around Brindaban. (XVIII.87)

From the *Siddhahemaśabdānuśāna* of Hemacandra (A.D. 1088–1172):[33]

Hari danced in the courtyard; the world was wonder-struck.
Let the glow of Rādhā's breasts endure! (4.420.2)

Though Hari sees every person with full regard,
Still his glance goes wherever Rādhā is—
Who can arrest eyes ensnared by love? (4.422.5)

From the *Naiṣadhīyacarita* of Śrīharṣa (latter half of twelfth century)[34] is a verse based on the double meaning of the names *Rādhā* and *Śrīvatsa.* The name *Rādhā* here refers to both Krishna's consort and Karṇa's foster mother in the *Mahābhārata;* the enemy of Rādhā's son Karṇa is Arjuna. *Śrīvatsa* means "Śrī's child" and the curl of hair on the chest of Vishnu or Krishna.

Rādhā is as dear to you as your life—
Your friendship with Arjuna, foe of Rādhā's son, is unfitting.
But is it fitting for Śrī's lover
To hold "the child of Śrī" on your own heart forever?

From the *Āryasaptaśatī* of Govardhana (late twelfth century):[35]

Friend, Tulasī, garland on the head of Madhu's foe,
Why compare yourself in vain with Rādhā?
All the outpouring of your fragrance
Is just to perfume her feet. (431)

When stories of how his head was washed
In royal ablution are told about Krishna,
Rādhā, her eyes slowed by the weight of pride,
Looks down at the lotus of her own feet. (488)

In order to shame demon Madhu's enemy,
Whose mind was drunk with all the cowherd girls,
Rādhā, feigning innocence, asked for the story of Śiva,
Who was satisfied with half his wife. (508)

Lovely women on shores of the milky sea
Eat balls of milk made thick
By hot winds of Lakṣmī's sighing,
And they sing the praises of Rādhā. (509)

When Krishna is wandering in search
Of Rādhā's impassioned quivering eyes,
The god of love is creating an arrow
Perfected to pierce the ten directions. (530)

To complement Krishna's role as the dramatic hero (*nāyaka*) and the embodiment of erotic mood (*śṛṅgāramūrtiman*), Rādhā is the dramatic heroine (*nāyikā*) and is identified with passion (*rati*), the emotion (*bhāva*) through which erotic mood (*śṛṅgārarasa*) develops. As passion personified, she is also consort to Kāma. When Rādhā fulfills Krishna's passion, she provides the emotional means for a sympathetic audience (*rasikajana*) to enjoy the extraordinary experience of Krishna's springtime love. Through her suffering during Krishna's desertion, as described by her to her friend (*sakhī*) and by her friend to Krishna, she is transformed into a powerful consort, appropriate to share Krishna's divine love.[36]

Rādhā is referred to by the standard forms of address for a dramatic heroine. Among them are "foolish woman" (*mugdhavadhū*, I.38*; *mugdhā* V.17; X.11,12; XI.2*), "fiercely angry woman" (*caṇḍī*, X.11,13; XI.7),[37] "proud woman" (*māninī*, IX.2*), and "emotional woman" (*bhāvinī*, XII.6).

Rādhā plays the classical heroine in seven of the eight stylized psychological states of relation to the hero (*nāyikāvasthā*) that are delineated by theorists of Indian drama.[38] Each of the states is identified in the text by Jayadeva with reference to its technical name or to its characteristic sign. The increasing intensity of Rādhā's desolation is dramatized by concrete manifestations of her condition in the various states.[39] The culminating emotional intensity of her divine love with Krishna is not effected through psychological depth. It is effected through the accumulation of sensuous details expressing the chaos of feeling and fantasy a deserted woman suffers.

After their first night of love, Krishna deserts Rādhā to play with other cowherdesses. Her demand for Krishna's exclusive love, in the context of his common love (*sādhāraṇapraṇaya,* II.1) with the other cowherdesses, generates her state of envy (*īrṣyā*). A deserted cowherdess longing for love (*utkaṇṭhitagopavadhū,* II.18) is her basic condition throughout the night of the drama. The power of her longing makes Krishna reciprocate her love and suffer as much as she does in their separation. The longing is emotionally amplified by the other states. She waits in vain for Krishna, dressed and ornamented for love (*vāsakasajjā,* VI.8). She feels herself deceived (*vañcitā*) by her friends (VII.3*) and by Krishna (VIII.7,9).[40] She is jealously enraged (*khaṇḍitayuvati,* VIII.9), imagining the marks of love a rival has inflicted on Krishna. She is remorseful after quarreling (*kalahāntaritā,* IX.1). At her friend's urging, her modesty abandons her (*salajjā lajjā vyagamad iva,* XI.33) and she goes to meet her lover.[41] After their ecstatic reunion, she feels her lover in her power (*svādhīnabhartṛkā,* XII.11). The graceful intimacy of Rādhā's triumph gives Jayadeva's drama its unique flavor.

The character of Rādhā in the *Gītagovinda* established her as Krishna's consort within later traditions of the Krishna cult. Her relative obscurity in earlier literature encouraged the view that Jayadeva had invented "Rādhā." Although he clearly did not invent her, he did create a unique heroine for Indian devotional literature.[42]

NOTES

1 Jayadeva: The Wandering Poet

1. There exist other literary works whose authorship is also designated "Jayadeva," but there is no evidence to associate the author of the *Gītagovinda* with any of these works. The play on the life of Rāma, entitled *Prasannarāghava* (edited by S. M. Paranjpe; Poona: Shiralkar, 1894), bears little conceptual or stylistic resemblance to the *Gītagovinda.* It is first quoted in the anthology *Sūktimuktāvalī* of Bhagadatta Jalhaṇa (edited by E. Krishnamacharya, Gaekwad's Oriental Series, 82; Baroda: Central Library, 1938), dated A.D. 1257. The Sikh tradition that lists Jayadeva among the great saints of India is based on the sixteenth century *Bhaktamāl* legend (see note 2 below), but the two mixed Prākrit-Apabhraṁśa verses attributed to him in the *Guru Granth Sahib* are characterized by the kind of abstract devotionalism that is not present in the *Gītagovinda;* see M. A. Macauliffe, *The Sikh Religion* (1909; reprint, New Delhi: S. Chand, 1963), vol. VI, pp. 4–17. Jayadeva the author of the work on prosody entitled *Chandaḥśāstra* is referred to by the tenth-century critic Abhinavagupta in his *Abhinavabhāratī;* see P. K. Gode, *Studies in Indian Literary History* (Bombay: Bharatiya Vidya Bhavan, 1953), vol. I, pp. 138–43. The one-act Sanskrit drama *Pīyūṣalaharī* is attributed to the author of the *Gītagovinda* on the basis of similarity in content; see K. Kar, "Pīyūṣa-laharī: A One-act Drama of Poet Jayadeva," *Journal of the Kalinga Historical Research Society,* 1956, pp. 291–327. Many other derivative works are attributed to the author of the *Gītagovinda* with no better claim. The author of the *Candrāloka,* a work on poetics, is known as Jayadeva Pīyūṣavarṣa (see text edited by N. S. Khiste, Kashi Sanskrit Series 75; Varanasi: Chowkhamba Sanskrit Series Office, 1929); nothing in the text suggests identical authorship of it and the *Gītagovinda.*

2. The most widely known version of the legendry life of Jayadeva is in the Hindi *Bhaktamāl,* edited and rewritten by Nārāyaṇadāsa in the middle of the seventeenth century from old Hindi verses by Nābhājīdāsa (edited by S. B. Rupakala; Lucknow: Tejkumar Press, 1969), pp. 343–64; see G. Grierson, "Modern Vernacular Hindi Literature," *Journal of the Asiatic Society of Bengal,* 57 (1888), 27. On the Hindi version is based the Sanskrit *Bhaktamālā* of Candradatta; *sargas* 39–41, which give the life of Jayadeva, are quoted in the introduction to the Telang and Panshikar edition of the *Gītagovinda* with the commentaries of Kumbhakarṇa and Śaṅkaramiśra (Bombay: Nirṇayasāgara Press, 1899), pp. 1–19. The best-known Bengali version of the Jayadeva legend is Vanamālīdāsa's *Jayadevacarita* (edited by A. K. Goswami; Calcutta: Vangiya Sahitya Parishad, 1905, B.S. 1312). The legend is also related in the sixteenth-century *Śekhśubhodayā,* which centers on the life of a Muslim holy man who visited the court of Lakṣmaṇasena; see Sukumar Sen, ed., *Śekhśubhodayā,* Bibliotheca Indica, no. 286(Calcutta: Asiatic Society, 1963). Aspects of the legend are referred to in all the later commentaries.

A verse that names Jayadeva's parents as Bhojadeva and Rāmādevī is not found in all manuscripts of the *Gītagovinda,* but its presence in the most conservative version of the text justifies its inclusion in the present edition (XII.22). The legendary account of Jayadeva's life identifies Bhojadeva as a brahman of Kanauj who migrated to the village of Kindubilva.

3. S. N. Chatterji, *Jayadeva, Makers of Indian Literature* (New Delhi: Sahitya

Akademi, 1973); this is largely based on the material of Harekrishna Mukhopādhyāya that introduces his edition of the Bengali version of the *Gītagovinda,* with the commentary of Caitanyadāsa entitled *Bālabodhinī,* in *Kavijayadeva o śrīgītagovinda* (Calcutta: Gurudās Mukhopādhyāy, 1956, B.S. 1362). See also the introduction, in Latin, by C. Lassen to his edition and Latin translation of the *Gītagovinda* (Bonn, 1836); R. Pischel, "Die Hofdichter des Lakṣmanasena," *Abhandlungen der Königlichen Gesellschaft der Wissenschaften zu Göttigen,* philol.-histor. Klasse, 39 (1893), 1–39; K. N. Mahapatra, "New Light on Poet Jayadeva, The Author of the *Gitagovinda," The Orissa Historical Research Journal,* 7 (1959), 191–207; S. C. Mukherji, *A Study of Vaiṣṇavism in Ancient and Medieval Bengal* (Calcutta: Punthi Pustak, 1966), pp. 91–107; N. K. Sahu, editor, *Souvenir on Srijayadeva* (Bhubaneswar: The Jayadeva Sanskrutika Parishad, 1968), articles by S. N. Rajaguru, N. K. Sahu, and K. N. Mahapatra, pp. 1–41.

Richard and Carol Salomon have reminded me how similar the controversy about Jayadeva's place of origin is to the controversy surrounding the "Old Bengali" *Caryāpada* literature. The two cases suggest that the culture, as well as the language and literature, of eastern India was more or less uniform at this time. See note 13 to section 2 below.

4. See *Saduktikarṇāmṛta,* critical edition, edited by S. C. Banerji (Calcutta: K. L. Mukhopadhyay, 1965), author index, p. 8. For the best available account of the reign of Lakṣmaṇasena, see R. C. Majumdar, *History of Ancient Bengal* (Calcutta: G. Bharadwaj, 1971), pp. 231–50, 254–59.

5. *Skm.* 659 = *GG.* VI.11; *Skm.* 1144 = *GG.* XII.10. Three additional verses attributed to Jayadeva in the *Saduktikarṇāmṛta* are found in the text of the *Gītagovinda* on which Kumbhakarṇa commented (see edition of Telang and Panshikar) and which became the popular version after the sixteenth century. However, these are not found in conservative versions of the *Gitagovinda* and are included in the present critical edition only as variants: *Skm.* 294 = *GG* XI.33†; *Skm.* 1134 = *GG* XII.23† (a); *Skm.* 1160 = *GG* XII.23† (c). Many of the remaining verses show thematic and stylistic similarities to the *Gītagovinda* verses, but others attest the poet's ability to compose panegyrics to a king and descriptions of battle; see Chatterji, *Jayadeva,* pp. 20–28, for a collection of these verses.

6. Both Kumbhakarṇa, in whose text this is I.4, and the other early commentator, Mānāṅka (text and commentary edited by V. M. Kulkarni; Ahmedabad: L. D. Bharatiya Sanskriti Vidyamandira, 1965), interpret this verse with reference to Lakṣmaṇasena. Mānāṅka considers the king to be the author of the verse and Kumbhakarṇa considers the five, plus another named Śrutidhara, to be scholars at the court of Lakṣmaṇasena. If Jayadeva composed the verse, he is probably elaborating the preceding reference to the goddess of speech (*vāgdevatā,* I.2) with a comment on how some famous contemporary poets, including himself, use speech in their poetry.

7. *Pavanadūta of Dhoyī,* edited by C. Chakravarti (Calcutta: Sanskrit Sahitya Parishad, 1926). This is modeled on the *Meghadūta* of Kālidāsa; here Kuvalayavatī, a nymph from the Malaya hills, sends the wind (*pavana*), instead of a cloud (*megha*), as a messenger to Lakṣmaṇasena.

8. See Pischel, "Die Hofdichter"; Monmohan Chakravarti, "Sanskrit Literature during the Sena Rule," *Journal of the Asiatic Society of Bengal,* n.s., 2, no. 5 (1906),

157–76; S. C. Mukherji, *Vaiṣṇavism in Bengal,* pp. 71–83; D. K. Mukherji, "Identification of some Verses by Umāpatidhara found in Two Inscriptions of Lakṣmaṇasena," *Journal of the Asiatic Society of Bengal,* 4th ser., 9, nos. 3–4 (1967), 188–92. Some verses from the *Āryāsaptaśatī* of Govardhana are translated in section five of this study; texts are given in note 35 to that section. The following verse is quoted in the Durgāprasad and Parab edition of the text, Kāvyamālā, no. 1 (Bombay: Nirṇayasāgara Press, 1886), p. 1:

govardhanaś ca śaraṇo jayadeva umāpatiḥ |
kavirājaś ca ratnāni samitau lakṣmaṇasya ca ||

This is reported to have been seen by Caitanya's disciple Sanātana Gosvāmin in an inscription over the assembly hall at Lakṣmaṇasena's capital of Navadvipa. It is otherwise unnoticed.

9. Royal patronage of Sanskrit language and literature at the court of Lakṣmaṇasena was linked to a renaissance of Sanskrit in northern India during the tenth, eleventh, and twelfth centuries. The courts of Bengal, Orissa, Kashmir, Kanauj, and Dhāra were notable among centers of brahmanical scholarship and literary activity. Scholars and poets traveled extensively in the quest for patronage. Their philosophical, religious, and literary products were as complex and highly eclectic as the great Hindu temples that marked the style of the period. See K. K. Handiqui, *Yaśastilaka and Indian Culture* (Sholapur: Jaina Saṁskrti Saṁrakshaka Sangha, 1949); R. C. Majumdar, et al., *The Age of Imperial Kanauj* and *The Struggle for Empire,* vols. IV and V in *The History and Culture of the Indian People* (Bombay: Bharatiya Vidya Bhavan, 1955, 1957). Inscriptions of Vākpati-Muñja, the Paramāra ruler of Malwa at the end of the tenth century, make reference to the presence of brahmans who have migrated all the way from Bengal; see section five of this study, note 28. We also know from the poet's biographical sketch in his *Vikramāṅkadevacarita* that Bilhaṇa traveled from Kashmir in the latter part of the eleventh century to serve as the court poet of Vikramāditya VI, the Chalukya king of Kalyani (in modern Karnataka); see Barbara Stoler Miller, *Phantasies of a Love-Thief: The Caurapañcāśikā Attributed to Bilhaṇa* (New York: Columbia University Press, 1971), pp. 188–91; Helen Waddell, *The Wandering Scholars* (New York: Barnes and Noble, 1949).

10. N. G. Majumdar, ed., *Inscriptions of Bengal* (Rajshahi, Bengal: Varendra Research Society, 1929), vol. 3, pp. 81–172; for reference to other inscriptions, see R. C. Majumdar, *History of Ancient Bengal,* p. 231 and notes. It is notable that *auṁ namo nārāyaṇāya* is the principal mantra of the Śrīvaishnava cult. See Otto Schrader, *Introduction to the Pāñcarātra and the Ahirbudhnya Saṁhitā* (Madras: Adyar Library, 1916), pp. 141–43; see also S. N. Dasgupta, *A History of Indian Philosophy* (Cambridge: Cambridge University Press, 1961), vol. 3, pp. 12–21.

11. For a review of the accounts of Rāmānuja's life, see Dasgupta, *History of Indian Philosophy,* vol. 3, pp. 100–5. Dasgupta notes (p. 100*n*2): "Most of the details of Rāmānuja's life are collected from the account given in the *Prapannāmṛta* by Anantācārya, a junior contemporary of Rāmānuja."

12. J. F. Fleet, "Sanskrit and Old-Kanarese Inscriptions: Grants of Anantavarma-Choḍagaṅgadeva," *The Indian Antiquary,* 18 (1889), 161–76. The most detailed analysis of the reign of Choḍagaṅgadeva is in H. K. Mahtab, *History of Orissa* (Cuttack: Prajatantra Prachar Samity, 1959), pp. 196–211; a list of inscriptions by and referring to Choḍagaṅgadeva is given on pp. 209–211. See also Prabhat Mukherji, *The History of Medieval Vaishnavism in Orissa* (Calcutta: R. Chatterji,

1940); S. N. Rajaguru, *History of the Gaṅgas* (Bhubaneswar: State Museum, 1968), K. C. Miśra, *The Cult of Jagannātha* (Calcutta: K. L. Mukhopadhyay, 1971), pp. 40–42. In a late thirteenth century copper-plate inscription of the Gaṅga king Narasiṁhadeva II, the construction of the Jagannātha temple and a Lakṣmī temple is attributed to Choḍagaṅgadeva; N. N. Vasu, "Copper-plate inscription of Nṛsiṁhadeva II of Orissa, dated 1217 Śaka," *Journal of the Asiatic Society of Bengal*, 65, pt. 1 (1896), 240 (text), 261 (trans.), vv. 27–28.

13. See Miśra, *Cult of Jagannātha*.

14. Monmohan Chakravarti, "Uriya Inscriptions of the 15th and 16th Centuries," *Journal of the Asiatic Society of Bengal*, 62, pt. 1 (1894), 88–104; see Miśra, *Cult of Jagannātha*, pp. 54–55.

15. Relevant portions of the *Caitanyacaritāmṛta* are quoted by S. K. De in *The Early History of the Vaiṣṇava Faith and Movement in Bengal* (Calcutta: K. L. Mukhopadhyay, 1961), p. 112; see also E. C. Dimock, Jr., *The Place of the Hidden Moon: Erotic Mysticism in the Vaiṣṇava-sahajiyā Cult of Bengal* (Chicago: University of Chicago Press, 1966), p. 55.

16. The *Bālabodhinī* commentary of Caitanyadāsa, a Bengali Vaishnava scholar and devotee who lived in Vṛndāvana in the late sixteenth century, gives this interpretation to the text; it is followed by Harekrishna Mukhopādhyāya in his introduction to his edition of the text and commentary, as well as by most contemporary Vaishnava writers on the *Gītagovinda*.

17. See Dimock, *Place of the Hidden Moon*, pp. 56–57; Shashibhushan Dasgupta, *Obscure Religious Cults* (Calcutta: K. L. Mukhopadhyay, 1969), pp. 115, 118.

18. See Miśra, *Cult of Jagannātha*, p. 149. Kali Charan Patnaik, the Oriya poet who has composed an Oriya lyric version of the *Gītagovinda* (Cuttack: Das, 1970) and from whom I have learned much about Oriya traditions surrounding the poem and its performance, holds the title "Gītagovinda-sevaka" in the Jagannātha temple of Puri. This means that he is responsible for the singing of the *daśavatāra* song before the image at every evening worship and various other songs at night.

19. Cited from R. K. Majumdar, "A 15th Century Gītagovinda Ms. with Gujaratī Paintings," *Journal of the University of Bombay, Arts and Law*, 6, no. 11, pt. 6 (1937), 127, with plate. The significance of this inscription is discussed below in relation to the critical text of the *Gītagovinda*.

20. These manuscripts form the basis of my critical edition of the *Gītagovinda;* they are described and analyzed in detail in the critical apparatus in the clothbound edition of this book. Evidence of the poem's status by the fourteenth century is the citation of verse III.11 as an example of the poetic figure *niścaya*, "certainty," in the tenth *pariccheda* of the *Sāhityadarpaṇa* of Viśvanātha, edited with notes by P. V. Kane (Delhi: Motilal Banarsidass, 1965), X.39.

21. See Kulkarni's edition of the text and commentary and my analysis of the early dated manuscripts of the Shorter Recension of the *Gītagovinda;* see also Majumdar, "15th Century Gītagovinda Ms."

22. See Telang and Panshikar edition; also R. C. Majumdar, et al., *The Delhi Sultanate*, vol. V in *The History and Culture of the Indian People* (Bombay: Bharatiya Vidya Bhavan, 1960), pp. 332–38; the introduction to Premlata Sharma's edition of

Saṅgītarāja by Mahārāṇā Kumbhā (Varanasi: Hindu University Press, 1963), vol. 1, pp. 29–70.

2 The Lyrical Structure of Jayadeva's Poem

1. I. A. Richards, *Practical Criticism* (New York: Harcourt, Brace, Harvest paperback, 1958), p. 200.

2. Because Jayadeva's songs are characterized by long compounds in which the relations among words are fluid, any translation of the *Gītagovinda* is necessarily tentative.

3. See Daniel H. H. Ingalls, *An Anthology of Sanskrit Court Poetry*, Harvard Oriental Series, vol. 44 (Cambridge, Mass.: Harvard University Press, 1965); Barbara Stoler Miller, *Bhartrihari: Poems* (New York: Columbia University Press, 1967).

4. See A. B. Keith, *A History of Sanskrit Literature* (Oxford: Oxford University Press, 1920), pp. 191–92; S. N. Dasgupta, ed., *A History of Sanskrit Literature, Classical Period* (Calcutta: University of Calcutta, 1947), pp. 392–95, 509–10; E. Gerow and A. K. Ramanujan, "Indian Poetics" and "The Lyric Poem" in *The Literatures of India*, edited by E. C. Dimock, Jr., et al. (Chicago: University of Chicago Press, 1974), pp. 138–41, 155–56. V. Raghavan, in his study *Bhoja's Śṛṅgāra Prakāśa* (Madras: Punarvasu, 1963), pp. 549–51, suggests that the *Gītagovinda* is a kind of musical poem that Bhoja calls *citrarāgakāvya*, a poem meant to be sung in several melodic patterns (*rāga*) and to be interpreted in the language of gesture (*abhinaya*). The classification of poems that are to be sung as *rāgakāvya* is known from Abhinavagupta's *Abhinavabhāratī* on the *Nāṭyaśāstra*, edited by M. R. Kavi, Gaekwad's Oriental Series, 4 vols. (Baroda: Central Library, 1956), vol. 1, pp. 174–84. Both Abhinavagupta and Bhoja recognize a variety of "nonclassical" forms and attempt to codify them within the classical categories. Their recognition suggests the existence of a poetic genre similar to the form of the *Gītagovinda* by the tenth century, but no works survive for comparison. See A. K. Warder, *Indian Kāvya Literature* (Delhi: Motilal Banarsidass, 1972), vol. 1, pp. 163–65.

5. These sound patterns occur in earlier Sanskrit works, but only sporadically. See Keith, *Sanskrit Literature*, pp. 197–98; Edwin Gerow, *A Glossary of Indian Figures of Speech* (The Hague: Mouton, 1971), pp. 102–7; Warder, *Kāvya Literature*, vol. 2, pp. 174–76.

6. "Song cycle" is an attempt to put the terms *prabandha* and *padāvalī*, as Jayadeva uses them, in a meaningful relation.

7. For examples of alliteration in the verses, see I.1, 35, 36; III.15, 20; V.19. The *Rasikapriyā* commentary offers the most complete analyses of the standard figures employed in individual verses; see Gerow, *Glossary*.

8. I use the terms *akṣaravṛtta* and *tālavṛtta*, following the nomenclature most commonly found in commentaries on the *Gītagovinda*, but the term *chandas* is sometimes found in place of *vṛtta* as the general word for meter. Thus syllabic meters are designated *akṣarachandas* as well as *akṣaravṛtta; varṇavṛtta* is also used. Moric meters are designated *mātravṛtta* and *mātrachandas*, as well as *tālavṛtta; gaṇachandas* is used of moric meters where the beats are organized into measured units (*gaṇa*). The metrical analysis presented here draws on the following studies: C. Lassen, *Gītagovinda* (Bonn, 1836), pp. xxvii–xxxv; Sudhibhushan Bhattacarya in Harekrishna Mukhopādhyāya's *Kavijayadeva o śrīgītagovinda* (Calcutta: Gurudās Mukhopādhyāy,

1957, B.S. 1363, pp. 230–41; Edwin Gerow's unpublished paper on Jayadeva's meters, delivered at the annual meeting of the American Oriental Society in 1966, which the author generously made available to me. Detailed discussions of Sanskrit, Prākrit, and Apabhraṁśa moric meters include: H. Jacobi, "Ueber die Entwicklung d. indischen Metrik in nachvedischer Zeit," *Zeitschrift der Deutsche Morgenländische Gesellschaft*, 38, (1884), 590–617; H. D. Velanker, "Apabhraṁśa Meters," *Journal of the University of Bombay, Arts and Law*, 2, pt. 3 (1933), 32–62 and 5, pt. 3 (1936) 41–93; "Prākṛta and Apabhraṁśa Meters," *Journal of the Bombay Branch of the Royal Asiatic Society*, 22 (1947), 15–32, and 23 (1947), 1–11; Sivaprasad Bhattacaryya, *Jottings on Sanskrit Metrics* (Calcutta: Sanskrit College, 1963), pp. 15 ff.

9. With the exception of the meter Śloka, which allows of considerable variation, and Puṣpitāgrā, which is a syllabic meter with paired quarters of unequal length (*ardhasamacatuṣpadī*), the syllabic meters in the *Gītagovinda* have quarter-stanzas of identical length and form (*samacatuṣpadī*). The meters are noted here in order of their frequency within the text:

Śārdūlavikrīḍita (– – – ⏑ ⏑ – ⏑ – ⏑ ⏑ ⏑ –, – – ⏑ – – ⏑ –) I.1, 3, 16, 36, 46, 47; II.19; III.12, 13, 14; IV.10, 19, 21; V.7, 17, 18; VI.11; VII.11, 30; IX.10; X.13; XI.10, 11, 22; XII.10, 21.
Hariṇī (⏑ ⏑ ⏑ ⏑ ⏑ –, – – – –, ⏑ – ⏑ ⏑ – ⏑ –) II.1, 10; III.11; V.16, 19; VII.40; X.10, 12; XII.1, 20.
Vasantatilakā (– – ⏑ – ⏑ ⏑ ⏑ – ⏑ ⏑ – ⏑ – –) I.2, 25; III.15; VII.1, 41; X.1, 11; XI. 12, 13.
Śikhariṇī (⏑ – – – – –, ⏑ ⏑ ⏑ ⏑ ⏑ – – ⏑ ⏑ ⏑ –) I.26; II.20; VIII.10; XI.32, 33.
Śloka (a and c, X X X X ⏑ – – ⏑̲ [either heavy or light], b and d, X X X X ⏑ – ⏑ ⏑̲) III.1; IV.1; XI.23, XII.11.
Mālinī (⏑ ⏑ ⏑ ⏑ ⏑ ⏑ – –, – ⏑ – – ⏑ – –) I.35; VI.10; XI.1.
Puṣpitāgrā (*a* and *c*, ⏑ ⏑ ⏑ ⏑ ⏑ ⏑ – ⏑ – ⏑ – –, *b* and *d*, ⏑ ⏑ ⏑ ⏑ – ⏑ ⏑ – ⏑ – ⏑ – –) IV.22; V.1; VIII.1.
Vaṁśastha (⏑ – ⏑ – – ⏑ ⏑ – ⏑ – ⏑ –) I.37; III.2; VII.39.
Drutavilambita (⏑ ⏑ ⏑ – ⏑ ⏑ – ⏑ ⏑ – ⏑ –) I.4; VII.21.
Upendravajrā (⏑ – ⏑ – – ⏑ ⏑ – ⏑ – –) IV.20; VII.12.
Pṛthvī (⏑ – ⏑ ⏑ ⏑ – ⏑ –, ⏑ ⏑ ⏑ – ⏑ – – ⏑ –) X.14.
Upajāti (⏑̲ – ⏑ – – ⏑ ⏑ – ⏑ – ⏑̲) XII.22.

Five of the meters are named by punning in verses where they occur: Śikhariṇī (II.20); Śārdūlavikrīḍita (IV.10), Puṣpitāgrā (IV.22), Upendravajrā (IV.20), Pṛthvī (X.14). This punning is further evidence of Jayadeva's interest in the integration of sense and sound.

10. See examples from the *Sattasaī* of Hāla quoted in note 21 to section 5; see also G. L. Hart, III, *The Poems of Ancient Tamil* (Berkeley: University of California Press, 1975), appendix I, "An Analysis of the Meter and Rhyme of the First Twenty-five Poems of the *Sattasaī*," pp. 281–84.

11. Āryā is expressed in couplets of seven and one-half measures. Most measures (*gaṇa*) consists of four beats, with the standard exception of the sixth measure of the second line, which has a single beat, making the two lines asymmetrical. Further restrictions in the syllabic patterns of certain other measures give Āryā a fairly

fixed form. The opening verse of the sixth *sarga* (VI.1) is an example of how Sanskrit syllables may be ordered in terms of this form:

atha tāṁ gantum aśak̲tāṁ ciram anurak̲tāṁ latāgṛhe dṛṣṭvā |
taccaritaṁ govinde manasijamande sak̲hī prāha ||
⏑ ⏑ – | – ⏑ ⏑ | – – | ⏑ ⏑ ⏑ ⏑ | – – | ⏑ – ⏑ | – – | – |
– ⏑ ⏑ | – – | – – | ⏑ ⏑ ⏑ ⏑ | – – | ⏑ | – – | ⏑ ||

Four-beat measures in the forms ⏑ ⏑ ⏑ ⏑, – –, – ⏑ ⏑, or ⏑ ⏑ – occur freely. The syllabic sequence ⏑ – ⏑ is restricted to the second and fourth measures of both lines, and to the sixth measure of the first line, in which the sequence ⏑ ⏑ ⏑ ⏑ is its only alternative. The eighth measure of each line is conventionally a heavy or light monosyllable. The frequency and position of heavy syllables, including the spondaic sequence (– –), is notable in comparison with the meters of the songs; the amphibrach sequence (⏑ – ⏑) occurs only a few times in refrain verses of the songs.

12. In the terminology of classical Indian music theory (*saṅgītaśāstra*), the songs are called *prabandha* (the term Jayadeva uses at I.2) or *gītabandha.* See V. G. Apte, ed., *Saṅgītaratnāk̲ara,* Ānandāśrama Sanskrit Series, no. 35 (Poona: Ānandāśrama Press, 1942), chapter 4 (*prabandhādhyāya*), pp. 271–354. *Chandaḥprabandha* designates songs that are bound up in meter (*yati*), which provides their rhythmical component.

13. See note 3 to section 1 above—Pischel, p. 22; Chatterji, pp. 31–33. See also Louis Renou, et al., *L'Inde Classique* (Paris: Payot, 1949), vol. I, p. 443.

There is much confusion surrounding the use of the term "Apabhraṁśa." It is often broadly used to designate both forms and stages of Indo-Aryan language that differ from Sanskrit and the literary Prākrits. More specifically, it refers to a vernacular of western India that achieved literary form in the period ca. A.D. 600–1400. It was used by Jain writers in Gujarat and Rajasthan for the composition of poetry. A similar Prākrit, with its reduced inflections and increased postpositions, was used by Buddhist writers in Bengal and Orissa. See Richard Pischel, "Materialien zur Kenntnis des Apabhraṁśa," *Abhandlungen der K. Gesellschaft der Wissenschaften zu Göttigen,* n.s., 5, no. 4 (1902); Ludwig Alsdorf, "Apabhraṁśa Studien," *Deutsche Morgenländische Gesellschaft,* 22, no. 2 (1937); Sukumar Sen, "Charyageetikosh," *Indian Linguistics,* 9 (1944–48), 30–133; G. V. Tagare, *Historical Grammar of Apabhraṁśa* (Poona: Deccan College, 1948); S. K. Chatterji, *The Origin and Development of the Bengali Language* (1926; reprint, London: Allen and Unwin, 1970), vol. I, pp. 109–29; S. M. Katre, *Prak̲rit Languages and their Contribution to Indian Culture* (Poona: Deccan College, 1964), pp. 21, 24, 84–89; Shashibhusan Dasgupta, "The Buddhist Sahajiyā Cult," in *Obscure Religious Cults* (Calcutta: K. L. Mukhopadhyay, 1969), pp. 3–9 ff. It is worth noting that Jayadeva's rhyming moric meters, like the rhyming moric meters of the Caryā songs, are reflected in the meters of later Bengali and Oriya poetry, e.g., Payāra and Tripadī: see Sen, "Charyageetikosh," p. 125. The couplets of the *Gītagovinda* songs should also be compared with verses found in C. M. Ghose, ed., *Prāk̲rtapaingala.* (Calcutta: Asiatic Society of Bengal, 1902), a treatise on Prākrit and Apabhraṁśa versification. Examples are drawn from the floating mass of popular poetry of North India during the period ca. A.D. 900–1400; see vv. 334, 570, 576, 581, 586.

14. For example, the tenth-century Jain author Somadeva applied Prākrit and Apabhraṁśa meters to Sanskrit in his *Yaśastilak̲acampū* (edited by Śivadatta and

Parab, Kāvyamālā, no. 70; Bombay: Nirṇayasāgara Press, 1903). In the "Kṛṣṇāvatāra" chapter of Kṣemendra's *Daśāvatāracarita* (VIII.173, quoted below in note 30 to section 5), the narrative is interrupted by a song sung by the cowherdesses in four lines of long, end-rhymed compounds, set in a rhythm of ten four-beat measures followed by a heavy syllable, and so resembles the metrical structure of the *Gītagovinda* songs. It is notable that both of these works are among the scattered sources antedating Jayadeva that contain references to Rādhā (see section 5). If one accepts the convincing argument of H. D. Velankar in favor of the authenticity of the Apabhraṁśa stanzas in the fourth act of the *Vikramorvaśīya* of Kālidāsa, there is an even earlier example of Apabhraṁśa stanzas, and stanzas in a more conventional Prākrit, used in conjunction with Sanskrit forms; see H. D. Velankar, ed., *The Vikramorvaśīya of Kālidāsa* (Delhi: Sahitya Akademi, 1961), pp. lvi–lxxx, 61–91. See also W. Caland, "Een onbekend Indisch tooneelstuk (Gopālakelicandrikā)," *Verhandelingen der Koninklijke Akademie van Wetenschappen te Amsterdam*, 17, no. 3 (1917), 1–158; cf. review by Sten Konow in the *Indian Antiquary*, 49 (1920), 232–36; M. Winternitz, "Kṛṣṇa-dramen," *Zeitschrift der Deutschen Morgenländischen Gesellschaft*, 74 (1920), 137–44.

15: This meter is identified by the commentator Kumbhakarṇa as Layachandas; see Kumbha's *Saṅgītarāja*, edited by P. Sharma (Varanasi: Hindu University Press, 1963), I.3.21; see also, H. D. Velankar, "Hemacandra's *Chandonuśāsana*," *Journal of the Bombay Branch of the Royal Asiatic Society*, 20 (1944), 29 (VII.4). The same meter occurs in songs 4, 5, 6, 8, 11, 17, 20, 22, and 23. Several other meters patterned in four-beat measures are only variants of Layachandas. The meter of the first song has couplets in unequal lines of sixteen and twenty beats; it is identified by Kumbha as Kīrtidhavalachandas and is defined in the *Saṅgītarāja* (I.3.36). The meter of songs 9, 12, 14, and 18 has couplets of four four-beat measures. The meter of song 16 has three four-beat measures followed by a trochaic cadence (– ◡). The meter of song 15 has six four-beat measures followed by an iambic cadence (◡ –). The meter of song 24 has six four-beat measures followed by a cretic cadence (– ◡ –). The less regular meter of the second song, which Kumbha calls Maṅgalachandas and defines in the *Saṅgītarāja* (I.3.39), has couplets in unequal lines of twenty and eleven beats, the first line consisting of five four-beat measures and the second line of two four-beat measures followed by a trochaic cadence (– ◡).

16. The four-beat measures are expressed predominantly in two out of five possible syllabic combinations of groups of four beats: four light syllables (◡ ◡ ◡ ◡) or a heavy syllable followed by two light syllables (– ◡ ◡). Given the syllabic structure of Sanskrit, with the prominence of consonant clusters and heavy vowels, the control that Jayadeva exercises on the placement of heavy syllables is masterful. A measure of two heavy syllables (– –) normally occurs only in final position in a line of a couplet; a measure of two light syllables followed by a heavy syllable (◡ ◡ –) is rare; and no measure with a heavy syllable between two light syllables (◡ – ◡) occurs.

Of the remaining five songs in the *Gītagovinda*, three have meters based on measures of five beats, one has a meter that is best resolved into measures of seven beats, and another is entirely irregular. The five-beat meters generally show the same preference for light syllables and the same restriction of heavy syllables to initial position within a measure that characterize the four-beat meters. The combinations of five light syllables (◡ ◡ ◡ ◡ ◡) or a heavy syllable followed by three light syllables (– ⏑ ⏑ ⏑) are predominant. The meter of song 13 has couplets of four five-beat measures, the last of which is a cretic cadence (– ⏑ –). The meter of song 19 has couplets of six five-beat measures followed by a spondaic cadence (– –); the cretic pattern (– ⏑ –) in the fourth measure of almost every line gives this long meter a distinctive rhythm. The meter of song 21 has couplets of three five-beat measures, but the first line of each couple is lengthened by the addition of a final heavy syllable. The meter of song 7 divides into three seven-beat measures in the fixed sequence – ⏑ – ⏑ ⏑, followed by a trochaic cadence (– ⏑). Song 10 is expressed in five metrically identical verses of asymmetrical quarter-stanzas. The quarter-stanzas all differ in syllable sequence and moric length, while consistently rhyming in the pattern *a b/a b.* The first verse of the song shows the fixed pattern:

vahati malayasamīre madanam upanidhāya |
sphuṭati kusumanikare virahahṛdayadalanāya ||
⏑ ⏑ ⏑ ⏑ ⏑ ⏑ ⏑ – –, ⏑ ⏑ ⏑ ⏑ ⏑ ⏑ – ⏑ |
⏑ ⏑ ⏑ ⏑ ⏑ ⏑ ⏑ ⏑ –, ⏑ ⏑ ⏑ ⏑ ⏑ ⏑ ⏑ ⏑ – ⏑ ||

17. The Nepal manuscript dated A.D. 1447 and the Bombay manuscript dated A.D. 1515 omit *tāla* names. The frequent designation *yatitāla* in other manuscripts may perhaps be interpreted as "the *tāla* of the meter," meaning that the meter is the *tāla.* On *tāla,* see Alain Daniélou, *Northern Indian Music* (New York: Praeger, 1968), pp. 65–74; P. Sambamoorthy, *South Indian Music,* book II (Madras: Indian Music Publishing House, 1968), pp. 18–28; Ravi Shankar, *My Music, My Life* (New York: Simon and Schuster, 1968), pp. 29–30.

18. The refrains whose measured unit differs from the *gaṇa* organization of the couplets in the song may be resolved as follows:

SONG 9: two measures of seven beats, followed by a light syllable; cf. song 7, which also seems to follow a *saptagaṇa* pattern, a rarity in Indian prosody.
SONG 10: four measures of four beats, followed by two light syllables.
SONG 14: four measures of five beats, followed by a heavy syllable.
SONG 15: four measures of six beats, followed by a heavy syllable.
SONG 18: begins with a trochaic unit of heavy-light (– ⏑), followed by four measures of four beats, like the meter of the couplets.
SONG 22: one line has five measures of four beats, the second line begins with a unit of eight beats (– ⏑ – ⏑ ⏑ ⏑), followed by five measures of four beats.

19. There are more heavy syllables in the four-beat measures of the refrains: the spondaic unit of two heavy syllables (– –) and the anapestic unit of two light syllables followed by a heavy syllable (⏑ ⏑ –) occur in the interior of lines, e.g. song 16 (VII.31, refrain). The amphibrach unit of a heavy syllable between two light syllables, which is nowhere used in the four-beat meters of the couplets, occurs in the refrains of songs 1, 4, 7, 17, 20, and 24.

20. See Gerow, *Glossary,* pp. 102–7. It should be noted that the repetition of consonant clusters is minimal in the *Gītagovinda,* suggesting comparison with Prākrit and Apabhraṁśa, where the clusters are normally reduced; see Gerow on *grāmyānuprāsa, Glossary,* p. 103.

21. For example, II.5:

vipulapu | *lakabhuja* | *pallava* | *valayita* | *ballava* | *yuvatisa* | *hasram* |
⏑ ⏑ ⏑ ⏑ | ⏑ ⏑ ⏑ ⏑ | – ⏑ ⏑ | ⏑ ⏑ ⏑ ⏑ | – ⏑ ⏑ | ⏑ ⏑ ⏑ ⏑ | – – |
karacara | *ṇorasi* | *maṇigaṇa* | *bhūṣaṇa* | *kiraṇavi* | *bhinnata* | *masram* ||
⏑ ⏑ ⏑ ⏑ | – ⏑ ⏑ | ⏑ ⏑ ⏑ ⏑ | – ⏑ ⏑ | ⏑ ⏑ ⏑ ⏑ | – ⏑ ⏑ | – – ||

22. An early instance of the use of *antānuprāsa* is the sixth *sarga* of *Sundarakāṇḍa* in the *Vālmīkirāmāyaṇa*. Though the date of this section is debated by scholars, it is accepted in the critical edition; see G. C. Jhala, ed., *Vālmīkirāmāyaṇa* (Baroda: Oriental Institute, 1966), vol. 5, pp. 76–80.

23. See K. Krishnamoorthy, ed., *Dhvanyāloka* (Dharwar: Karnatak University, 1974), II.14–15.

24. See, e.g., Daṇḍin, *Kāvyadarśa,* edited by V. N. Ayer (Madras: Ramaswamy Sastrulu, 1964) I.51–60; Daṇḍin discusses *anuprāsa* in the context of delineating the differences between the two major styles of poetry, called *vaidarbhī-rīti* and *gauḍī-rīti* (I.40–54). The *gauḍī* style was located in eastern India; its exponents were noted for their love of *anuprāsa.* See also Bhoja, *Sarasvatīkaṇṭhābharaṇa* (Bombay: Nirṇayasāgara Press, 1934) II.76, 77, 106; Jagannātha, *Rasagaṅgadhāra* (Bombay: Nirṇayasāgara Press, 1939), p. 89.

25. See note 9 above.

26. See section 4 below. For other examples of Jayadeva's word-play, see *rasana, rasa, rasita* in song 14 (VII.16, 17); and *hari, hara, hāra* in song 20 (XI.6). Song 19, which begins the climax of the poem, has rich word-play on various levels. Puns in verse I.36, in the long compound *dhyānāvadhānakṣaṇaprāptaprāṇasamāsamāgamarasollāsa* which modifies *pathika,* relate yogic meditation to lonely travelers' evocation of erotic union.

27. See Gerow, *Glossary,* on *anuprāsa* (pp. 102–7), *citra* (pp. 175–89), *yamaka* (pp. 223–38).

28. See Stella Kramrisch, *The Hindu Temple,* 2 vols. (Calcutta, 1946). The interplay of "surface beauty" and underlying structure is also characteristic of Indian dance and music.

29. My initial appreciation of the music of the *Gītagovinda* came from many hours of listening to singers in various regions of India render their versions of the songs. A deeper appreciation is based on formal study under the tutelage of Vasant Rai, Director of the Alam School of Indian Music in New York, who belongs to the tradition of Allaudin Khan, and under V. Deshikachar at the Mysore College of Fine Arts. This attempt to define the *rāga* draws on Ravi Shankar's exposition in *My Music, My Life.* See also Daniélou, *Northern Indian Music,* pp. 20–63, 75–96ff.; N. A. Jairazbhoy, *The Rāgs of North Indian Music: Their Structure and Evolution* (London: Faber and Faber, 1971); Walter Kaufmann, *The Ragas of North India* (Bloomington: Indiana University Press, 1968); Sambamoorthy, *South Indian Music,* books I–V; V. G. Apte, ed., *Saṅgītaratnākara* (Poona: Ānandāśrama Press, 1942), 2 vols.

30. The northern versions of the songs, as I heard them in Orissa and Bengal, follow the *rāga* designations most commonly found in the manuscripts; these differ from those of Kumbhakarṇa, which are defined in his *Saṅgītarājā.* In articles written for the "Geet Govind Celebrations" held at the Sangeet Natak Akademi in Delhi (March 18–20, 1967), Premlata Sharma and C. S. Pant both suggest that the *rāgas* and *tālas* Kumbha prescribes were associated with his own compositions. The South Indian versions of the songs, as I heard them in Madras, Mysore, and Guruvayor (Kerala), accord with the *rāgas* given by Semmangudi R. Sreenivasa Iyer in *Gītagovindam with Musical Notations* (Tripunithura: Sanskrit College, 1962). The

designations in the present text of the *Gītagovinda* are those common to the oldest manuscripts; significant variants are noted in the critical apparatus in the clothbound edition of this book. For a comparison of the musical characteristics associated with different *rāgas* of the Hindusthani and Karnatak systems, see B. Subba Rao, *Rāganidhi* (Madras: Music Academy, 1964–66), vols. I–IV.

3 Jayadeva's Language for Love

1. The background for this analysis is provided by the *rasa* theory of dramatic esthetics in its general form. The relation between esthetic experience and religious experience that is central to the *Gītagovinda* encouraged me to search for evidence of Jayadeva's direct reference to the special theories of Abhinavagupta or Bhoja, but the vocabulary of esthetics that Jayadeva uses is drawn directly from the *Nāṭyaśāstra.* The technical terminology of *dhvani* theory and *śṛṅgāra* theory is notably absent; individual terms are analyzed in the glossary to the hardcover edition. For a general introduction to basic notions of Indian literary esthetics, see Edward C. Dimock, Jr., et al., *The Literatures of India* (Chicago: The University of Chicago Press, 1974), chapter 3. Within Sanskrit literature, the *rasa* theory is summarized in book 4 of Dhanaṁjaya's *Daśarūpa,* translated, with Sanskrit text and notes, by G. C. O. Haas (reprint, Delhi: Motilal Banarsidass, 1962), pp. 106–48. The summary is based on book 7 of Bharata's *Nāṭyaśāstra,* edited, with the commentary of Abhinavagupta, by M. R. Kavi, Gaekwad's Oriental Series, 4 vols. (Baroda: Central Library, 1926), vol. I, pp. 343–86.

2. Bhoja, in his *Śṛṅgāraprakāśa,* concentrated on *rati* and the *śṛṅgāra* developing from it. He expanded and further universalized *śṛṅgāra* into an absolute *rasa* called *ahaṁkāraśṛṅgāra,* a rarefication of ordinary love which is for him the universal of existence; see V. Raghavan, *Bhoja's Śṛṅgāra Prakāśa* (Madras: Punarvasu, 1963), pp. 425–532. Earlier, Rudraṭa had expressed the more general view of the importance of *rati* and *śṛṅgāra* by raising the question of how any other *rasa* except *śṛṅgāra* could be truly relished and how the name *rasa* could apply to any sentiment but *śṛṅgāra; Kāvyālaṁkāra* XIV.38 says:

anusarati rasānaṁ rasyatāmasya nānyaḥ
sakalam idam anena vyāptam ābālavṛddham.

See S. K. De, *Ancient Indian Erotics and Erotic Literature* (Calcutta: K. L. Mukhopadhyay, 1959).

3. A conventionalized blending of the two modes is made in the *adyāpi smarāmi* formula that dominates the *Caurapañcāśikā* attributed to Bilhaṇa; see my *Phantasies of a Love-Thief* (New York: Columbia University Press, 1971). The interplay of the two modes is dominant in Indian literature from the epic period, as well as later. Outstanding examples include the *Nalopakhyāna* of the *Mahabhārata,* the *Vālmīkirāmāyaṇa,* and Kālidāsa's *Kumārasaṁbhava,* as well as his plays.

4. See the introduction to my translation *Bhartrihari: Poems* (New York: Columbia University Press, 1967). It seems significant to me that the esthetic presentation of emotion in the *Gītagovinda* can be characterized by the same generalizations that I applied to the Bhartṛhari collection.

5. The earliest known critic to contrast what is vulgar (*grāmya*) from what is conducive to *rasa* was Daṇḍin, in his *Kāvyadarśa,* edited and translated by V. N.

Ayer (Madras: Ramaswamy Sastrulu, 1964), I.62–64. Abhinavagupta used the example of the breasts of a woman exciting most profoundly when they are only half revealed; in the *Dhvanyālokalocana* (edited with the *Bālapriyā;* Varanasi: Kashi Sanskrit Series, 1940), p. 138, he says:

. . . gopyamānaṁ sannāyikākucayugalam
iva mahārghatam upayad dhvanyate ||

The material is taken from J. L. Masson, "Obscenity in Sanskrit Literature," *Mahfil,* 7, nos. 3–4 (1971), pp. 197–207.

6. See J. L. Masson and M. V. Patwardhan, *Śāntarasa and Abhinavagupta's Philosophy of Aesthetics* (Poona: Bhandarkar Oriental Research Institute, 1969), pp. 56 ff.

7. The perspective of the friend is later codified into the elaborate esthetic theory of *sakhībhāva* in Bengali Vaishnavism; for the relevance of this theory to the *Gītagovinda,* see Shashibhusan Dasgupta, *Obscure Religious Cults* (Calcutta: K. L. Mukhopadhyay, 1969), pp. 125–26.

8. The technical term for such an opening verse is *vastunirdeśa.* It is possible that the much-debated phrase *nanda-nideśataḥ* is Jayadeva's pun on the type of this verse, referring to the fact that the subject of the poem is *nanda,* "joy," which is experienced as Krishna himself in the final song of the *Gītagovinda,* where he is addressed by the two epithets *Yadunandana* and *Hṛdayānandana.*

9. In his *Kavijayadeva o śrīgītagovinda* (Calcutta: Gurudās Mukhopādhyāy, 1957, B.S. 1362), Harekrishna Mukhopādhyāya devotes an entire chapter (15) to the analysis of this verse. Each of the commentators gives it detailed consideration.

10. Kumbhakarṇa gives an elaborate statement on poetic propriety in support of this interpretation. He glosses *nandanideśataḥ* with *nandasamīpāt.* He points to the combination of *śṛṅgāra* and *bhayanaka* here.

11. Mānāṅka interprets the speech as the *svagatam* of Rādhā, spoken from excessive love, as an alternative to understanding Nanda as the speaker.

12. This is the most frequent interpretation. It is related to the story that the child Krishna followed Nanda into the woods one evening at dusk and became afraid. Śankaramiśra gives this story in its simplest form. See Suniti Kumar Chatterji, *Jayadeva, Makers of Indian Literature* (New Delhi: Sahitya Akademi, 1973), pp. 15–18.

13. Caitanyadāsa explains that the words spoken by Rādhā's friend are intended to bring joy (*nanda*); Krishna's foster father is thus removed from any involvement with the erotic relationship between Rādhā and Krishna and is replaced by the conventional figure of the *sakhī.*

14. Cf. *Bṛhadāraṇyaka Upaniṣad* I.4.2:

so' bibhet tasmād ekākī bibheti sa hāyam īkṣāṁ cakre yan mad anyan nāsti kaṣmān nu bibhemīti tata evāsya bhayaṁ vīyāya kasmād hy abheṣyat dvitīyād vai bhayaṁ bhavati.

He was afraid. Therefore one who is alone is afraid. This one then thought to himself, "since there is nothing else than myself, of what am I afraid?" Thereupon his fear, verily, passed away, for of what should he have been afraid? Assuredly it is from a second that fear arises.

Text and translation quoted from S. Radhakrishnan, *The Principal Upaniṣads* (New York: Harper, 1953), pp. 163–64. Although there is no evidence that Jayadeva consciously refers to this analysis of fear in the creative process, the dynamic role of fear in connecting isolation with pairing seems suggestive in interpreting the opening verse of the *Gītagovinda.*

15. In the second half of the poem it is increasingly clear that Krishna himself is the mysterious power of darkness, the essence of night in which Rādhā's love develops through various stages of desertion to consummation.

16. Mānāṅka makes the point, which is followed by other commentators, that the word order of the dual compound is irregular in its priority (*pūrvanipāta*), like *naranārāyaṇau, umāmaheśvarau, kākamayūrau,* etc.

17. See section I above, notes 15–17. The subject of allegory, with reference to the *Gītagovinda,* is treated by Lee Siegel in "Sacred and Profane Dimensions of Love in Indian Traditions as Exemplified in the *Gītagovinda* of Jayadeva" (unpublished Ph.D. thesis, Oxford University, 1975), pp. 209–25; also in the short essay by Ranajit Sarkar, "*Gītagovinda:* Towards a Total Understanding," *Publikaties van het Instituut voor Indische talen en culturen,* no. 2, Rijksuniversiteit te Gronigen, 1974.

4 Krishna: Cosmic Cowherd Lover

1. A selected bibliography of references relevant to interpreting Jayadeva's treatment of Krishna includes: R. G. Bhandarkar, *Collected Works,* vol. IV: *Vaiṣṇavism, Śaivism, and Minor Religious Systems,* edited by N. B. Utgikar (Poona: Bhandarkar Oriental Research Institute, 1929); Shashibhusan Dasgupta, *Obscure Religious Cults* (1946; 2d ed., Calcutta: K. L. Mukhopadhyay, 1962—references throughout are to this edition); S. K. De, *Vaiṣṇava Faith and Movement in Bengal* (Calcutta: K. L. Mukhopadhyay, 1961); Franklin Edgerton, *The Bhagavad Gītā,* part 2, Harvard Oriental Series, vol. 39 (Cambridge, Mass.: Harvard University Press, 1952); Jan Gonda, *Aspects of Early Viṣṇuism* (1954; reprint, Delhi: Motilal Banarsidass, 1969); idem., *Viṣṇuism and Śivaism: A Comparison* (London: Athlone Press, 1970); E. Washburn Hopkins, *Epic Mythology* (1915; reprint, New York: Biblo and Tannen, 1969); Daniel H. H. Ingalls, "The Harivaṁśa as a Mahākāvya," in *Mélanges d'Indianisme à la mémoire de L. Renou* (Paris: Boccard, 1968), pp. 381–94; Hermann Jacobi, "Incarnation," *Encyclopedia of Religion and Ethics,* edited by James Hastings (Edinburgh, 1908–26), vol. VII, pp. 193–97; D. D. Kosambi, "The Avatāra Syncretism and Possible Sources of the Bhagavad-gītā," *Journal of the Bombay Branch of the Royal Asiatic Society,* n.s., 24 (1949), 121–34; idem., *Myth and Reality* (Bombay: Popular Prakashan, 1962), pp. 12–41; B. Majumdar, *Kṛṣṇa in History and Legend* (Calcutta: University of Calcutta, 1969); J. L. Masson, "The Childhood of Kṛṣṇa," *Journal of the American Oriental Society,* 94 (1974), 454–59; K. C. Miśra, *The Cult of Jagannātha* (Calcutta: K. L. Mukhopdhyay, 1971); Walter Ruben, *Krishna: Konkordanz und Kommentar der Motives seines Heldenlebens*(Istanbul, 1944); Milton Singer, ed., *Krishna: Myths, Rites, and Attitudes* (Honolulu: East-West Center, 1966); S. N. Tadpatrikar, "The Kṛṣṇa Problem," *Annals of the Bhandarkar Oriental Research Institute,* 10, (1931), 296–344; Charlotte Vaudeville, "Aspects du mythe de Kṛṣṇa-Gopāla dans l'Inde ancienne,". in *Mélanges L. Renou,* pp. 737–61.

Most of the major Indian mythological themes are woven into Krishna's total legend, with the exception of asceticism. The absence of asceticism in Krishna's legend is focal to the contrast between him and Śiva; see Wendy O'Flaherty, *Asceticism and Eroticism in the Mythology of Śiva* (London: Oxford University Press, 1973).

2. The main sources for Krishna's legend in early Sanskrit literature are the *Mahābhārata* and certain Purāṇas, but the origins of many of his epithets and characteristics are found in Vedic literature. The following texts are referred to throughout this section in the editions cited:

Atharva Veda. Atharvaveda Saṁhitā, edited by W. D. Whitney and R. Roth (Berlin: F. Dummler, 1856); translated by W. D. Whitney (1905; reprint, Delhi: Motilal Banarsidass, 1962).

Bhāgavata Purāṇa. Gita Press edition (Gorakhpur, 1962); translated into French by Eugène Burnouf, 5 vols. (Paris: Imprimerie Royale, 1840–98) and into English by J. M. Sanyal, 5 vols. (Calcutta: Oriental Publishing and Datta Bose, 1930–34).

Harivaṁśa. Critical edition, edited by P. L. Vaidya, 2 vols. (Poona: Bhandarkar Oriental Research Institute, 1969); translated into French by S. A. Langlois (London: Parbury, Allen, 1834–35).

Mahābhārata. Critical edition, edited by V. S. Sukthankar, et al. (Poona: Bhandarkar Oriental Research Institute, 1933–66); translated by J.A.B. van Buitenen (Chicago: University of Chicago Press, 1973–), vols. 1 and 2, books 1–3.

Matsya Purāṇa. Edited by H. N. Apte, Ānandāśrama Sanskrit Series, no. 54 (Poona: Ānandāśrama Press, 1907); translated in the Sacred Books of the Hindus, vol. 17 (Allahabad: Pāṇini Office, 1916–17; reprint, New York, 1973).

Ṛg Veda. The Hymns of the Rig-Veda, edited by Max Müller, 2 vols. (London: Trübner, 1877); translated into German by K. F. Geldner, 3 vols., Harvard Oriental Series, vols. 33–35 (Cambridge, Mass.: Harvard University Press, 1951).

Śatapatha Brāhmaṇa. Edited by Albrecht Weber (1855; reprint, Varanasi: Chowkhamba Sanskrit Series Office, 1964); translated by Julius Eggeling, Sacred Books of the East, vols. 12, 26, 41, 43, 44 (1882; reprint, Delhi: Motilal Banarsidass, 1964).

Viṣṇu Purāṇa. Gita Press edition (Gorakhpur, 1962); translated by H. H. Wilson, 5 vols. (1840; reprint, Calcutta, 1961).

3. *Mahābhārata* VI.33.30 = *Bhagavadgītā* 11.30.

4. See Gonda, *Aspects of Viṣṇuism,* p. 159; Hopkins, *Epic Mythology,* p. 213.

5. See *Viṣṇu P.* VI.2.17, where it says that singing of Keśava is the way of the Kali Yuga.

6. See J. Gonda, *Epithets in the Ṛgveda* (The Hague: Mouton, 1959).

7. The contrast between the conception of Krishna in the *Gītagovinda* and in the *Bhāgavata P.* is striking in terms of vocabulary and devotional attitude; see Thomas J. Hopkins, "The Social Teaching of the *Bhāgavata Purāṇa*" and J.A.B. van Buitenen, "On the Archaism of the *Bhāgavata Purāṇa,*" both in Singer, *Krishna,* pp. 3–40; also Tadpatrikar, "Kṛṣṇa Problem."

8. See section 5 below.

9. Daniel H. H. Ingalls, *An Anthology of Sanskrit Court Poetry,* Harvard Oriental Series, vol. 44 (Cambridge, Mass.: Harvard University Press, 1965), intr. 6.2, p. 93.

10. *Śatapatha Brāhmaṇa* XI.5.4.18; cf. the "honey-doctrine" of the *Bṛhadāraṇyaka Upaniṣad* II.5.16–19. In classical Hindu law a celibate student (*brahmacārin*) is ordered to abstain from "honey, meat, perfumes, garlands, condiments, women, etc.," *Manusmṛti* II.177; see *The Laws of Manu,* translated by G. Bühler, Sacred Books of the East, vol. 25 (Oxford: Clarendon Press, 1886), p. 62.

11. See Claude Lévi-Strauss, *From Honey to Ashes, Introduction to a Science of Mythology,* (New York: Harper and Row, 1973), vol. 2, pp. 122–23. In Indian literature, spring itself is considered an aphrodisiac; see, e.g., Kālidāsa's *Kumārasaṁbhava,* critical edition, edited by Suryakanta (New Delhi: Sahitya Akademi, 1962), III.21–34.

12. *Mādhava* and *Madhusūdana* are both commonly used of Krishna throughout the *Mahābhārata* and after; e.g., *Mahābhārata* I.213.20, 30 ff., 214.15 ff.; cf. Gonda, *Aspects of Viṣṇuism,* pp. 16 ff., 237; Hopkins, *Epic Mythology,* pp. 192–93, 203; G. Dumézil, *The Destiny of a King* (Chicago: The University of Chicago Press, 1973), pp. 81–83. A legend given in the *Nāṭyaśāstra,* edited and translated by M. Ghosh (Calcutta: Granthalaya, 1967), XXII.1–16, attributes the origin of drama to Krishna's battle with the demons Madhu and Kaitabha.

13. See, e.g., *Harivaṁśa* 48.1 ff.;. *Mahābhārata* I.1.60.

14. See, e.g., *Ṛg Veda* X.96; Gonda, *Aspects of Viṣṇuism,* p. 107.

15. Cf. *Mahābhārata* I.1.20–22, VI.33.9 (= *Bhagavadgītā* 11.9), VI.40.77 (= *BG* 18.77).

16. See, e.g., *Bhāgavata P.* X.37.

17. See Krishna as *Jagannivāsa, Mahābhārata* VI.33.25, 37 (= *BG* XI.25, 37); see Miśra, *Cult of Jagannātha,* pp. 57–58; section 1, note 14 above.

18. See *Mahābhārata* VI.26.5–9 (= *BG* IV.5–9); *Matsya P.* 47.8 ff.; *Viṣṇu P.* V.17.10 ff.; *Bhāgavata P.* II.6.41. Earlier references to the ten incarnations include: *Matsya P.* 285.6–7 (*matsyaḥ kurmo varāhaś ca narasiṁho 'tha vāmanaḥ rāmo rāmaś ca kṛṣṇaś ca buddhaḥ kalkīti ca kramāt*); Kṣemendra, *Daśāvatāracarita,* Kāvyamālā, no. 26 (Bombay: Nirṇayasāgara Press, 1891); see also H. K. Sastri, "Two Statues of Pallava Kings and Five Pallava Inscriptions in a Rock-Temple at Mahabalipuram," *Memoirs of the Archaeological Survey of India,* no. 26, plate I, C, p. 5; "An Ajmer Stone Inscription," *Epigraphica Indica,* vol. 29, pp. 179 ff. The *Harivaṁśa* list (ch. 31) differs somewhat. In the list of twenty-two incarnations in the *Bhāgavata P.,* the pair Balarāma and Krishna are nineteenth and twentieth (I.3.23; cf. II.7). See Gonda, *Aspects of Viṣṇuism,* pp. 124–64; Hopkins, *Epic Mythology,* pp. 209–19; Jacobi, "Incarnation," pp. 193–97; Kosambi, "Avatāra Syncretism"; also Otto Schrader, *Introduction to the Pāñcarātra and the Ahirbudhnya Saṁhitā* (Madras: Adyar Library, 1916), pp. 35–59.

19. Cf. Edward C. Dimock, Jr., *The Place of the Hidden Moon* (Chicago: University of Chicago Press, 1966), pp. 192–95.

20. See the glossary in the clothbound edition, s.v. *adbhuta, śṛṅgāra.*

21. Cf. *Matsya P.* I.29 ff.; *Bhāgavata P.* VIII.24. See Hopkins, *Epic Mythology,* pp. 201–2.

22. Cf. *Gītagovinda* I.23; *Mahābhārata* I.16.10–11; *Bhāgavata P.* XII.13.2. See Gonda, *Aspects of Viṣṇuism,* pp. 126–29; Klaus Rüping, *Amṛtamanthana und Kūrma-Avatāra* (Weisbaden: Harrassowitz, 1970).

23. Cf. *Atharva Veda* XII.1.48 (*sūkara*); *Viṣṇu P.* V.29.23 (*śūkara*); *Bhāgavata P.*

III.18–19 (*śūkara*). See Gonda, *Aspects of Viṣṇuism*, pp. 129–45; V. S. Agrawala, *Solar Symbolism of the Boar: Yajña-varāha—An Interpretation* (Varanasi: Prithivi Prakashan, 1963).

24. Cf. *Viṣṇu P.* I.17–21; *Bhāgavata P.* VII.2–8.

25. See *Ṛg Veda* I.154.1–6, 155.3–5; *Śatapatha Brāhmaṇa* I.9.3.8 ff.; Gonda, *Aspects of Viṣṇuism*, pp. 55–72, 145–46; F.B.J. Kuiper, "The Three Strides of Viṣṇu," in *Indological Studies in Honor of W. Norman Brown* (New Haven: American Oriental Society, 1962), pp. 137–51; Wendy O'Flaherty, *Hindu Myths* (London: Penguin, 1975), Bibliographical Notes, pp. 328–29.

26. See *Bhāgavata P.* VIII.19–23.

27. See *Mahābhārata* III.115–17; *Bhāgavata P.* IX.15–17; Hopkins, *Epic Mythology*, pp. 184, 211.

28. See *Bhāgavata P.* IX.10–11.

29. See *Mahābhārata* I.189.31; *Viṣṇu P.* V.1.59–63.

30. See *Viṣṇu P.* V.25; *Bhāgavata P.* X.65; Hopkins, *Epic Mythology*, p. 212.

31. See, e.g., *Matsya P.* 47.247; and *Agni Purāṇa*, Ānandāśrama Sanskrit Series, no. 41 (Poona: Ānandāśrama Press, 1900) ch. 16; cf. *Bhāgavata P.* I.3.24; Sastri, "Pallava Statues," pp. 5–7.

32. See Dimock, *Hidden Moon*, pp. 26–29.

33. See *Mahābhārata* III.188–89; *Bhāgavata P.* I.3.25; Gonda, Aspects of *Viṣṇuism*, pp. 149–50.

34. See *Harivaṁśa* 50–64; *Viṣṇu P.* V.6–14; *Bhāgavata P.* X.5–37; *Bālacarita* in *Plays Ascribed to Bhāsa*, edited by C. R. Devadhar (Poona: Oriental Book Agency, 1962), pp. 511–60. See also Gonda, *Aspects of Viṣṇuism*, pp. 154–64; Ruben, *Krishna*, pp. 45 ff.

35. The more common reading of the refrain as *jaya jaya deva hare* ignores the word play and the significance of *Jayadeva* as an epithet.

36. A reference to the *Mahābhārata* as *jaya*, which comes at the beginning of the epic (I.1.1), may not be relevant to the meaning of Jayadeva's signature and his epithet for Krishna, but it seems worth noting:

nārāyaṇaṁ namaskṛtya naraṁ caiva narottamam |
devīṁ sarasvatīṁ caiva tato jayam udīrayet ||

37. See Hopkins, *Epic Mythology*, pp. 215, 217.

38. See *Mahābhārata* III.194.15; *Harivaṁśa* 52.2; *Bhāgavata P.* VIII.17.4; X.32.2.

39. See *Harivaṁśa* 52.4.

40. See Pāṇini, *Aṣṭādhyāyī* III.1.138, *vārt.* 2: *gāvādiṣu vinde saṁjñāyas.* In the form of Varāha, the Boar, Govinda is *gāṁ vindatṛ*, "finder of earth"; *Mahābhārata* I.19.11.

41. See *Mahābhārata* I.59.22.

42. See *Mahābhārata* II.13.33, V.126.37f.; *Harivaṁśa* 27, 44–48, 65–78; *Bhāgavata P.* X.1–4, 36–44.

43. See Ruben, *Krishna*, pp. 107–8.

44. See, e.g., *Mahābhārata* I.15; Hopkins, *Epic Mythology*, pp. 206, 208, 213–14.

45. Discussed in section 3; cf. *Harivaṁśa* 49; *Viṣṇu P.* 6.4 ff.; *Bhāgavanta P.* X .5.1 ff.

46. See *Mahābhārata* I.31.10; *Harivaṁśa* 55–56; *Bhāgavata P.* X.16–17.

47. See *Harivaṁśa* 50.20–23.

48. See *Mahābhārata* I.20–30; Gonda, *Aspects of Viṣṇuism*, pp. 101–3.

49. See Ruben, *Krishna*, pp. 112 ff.

50. See, e.g., Lévi-Strauss, *Honey to Ashes;* Yolanda and Robert Murphy, *Women of the Forest* (New York: Columbia University Press, 1975).

51. The Jumna has its confluence with the Ganges at Allahabad. It flows through Brindaban. It is also called *Kalindanandinī* (*GG* III.2), "daughter of Mt. Kalinda." Cf. *Harivaṁśa* 55.27 ff.

52. Cf. *Harivaṁśa* 63.18–35; *Viṣṇu P.* V.13.47–55; *Bhāgavata P.* III.2.14; X.33; *Bālacarita* III.1–3. See V. Raghavan, *Bhoja's Śṛṅgāra Prakāśa* (Madras: Punarvasu, 1963), pp. 561–73.

53. See O'Flaherty, *Mythology of Śiva*, pp. 141–72; also the glossary in the clothbound edition of this book, s.v. *anaṅga, kāma, rati,* and related references.

54. See the glossary in the clothbound edition of this book, s.v. *kānta, dayita, priya.*

55. Cf. *Bhāgavata P.* VII.20.3. Also *kaitava,* "deceitful," *GG* VIII.2*; cf. *Kumārasaṁbhava,* edited by Suryakanta (New Delhi: Sahitya Akademi, 1962), VIII.3.

56. This is given as a way to angrily address a *nāyaka;* see *Nāṭyaśāstra,* XXIV.310.

5 Rādhā: Consort of Krishna's Springtime Passion

1. Much of this material has been published in a more technical form in an article entitled, "Rādhā: Consort of Krishna's Vernal Passion," *Journal of the American Oriental Society,* 95, no. 4 (1975), 655–71.

In my attempt to describe the nature of Rādhā's relation to Krishna in literature antedating the *Gītagovinda,* I have drawn on the work of several scholars. See Śaśibhuṣan Dasgupta, *Śrīrādhār kramabikāśa—darśane o sāhitye* (Calcutta: E. Mukherji, 1953, B.S. 1359); A. K. Majumdar, "A Note on the Development of the Rādhā Cult," *Annals of the Bhandarkar Institute,* 36 (1955), pp. 231–57; Harekrishna Mukhopādhyāya, *Kavijayadeva śrīgītagovinda* (Calcutta: Gurudās Mukhopādhyāy, 1956, B.S. 1362); B. Majumdar, *Kṛṣṇa in History and Legend* (Calcutta: University of Calcutta, 1969), pp. 165–232; S. L. Katre, "Kṛṇṣa, Gopas, Gopīs, and Rādhā," in *P. K. Gode Commemoration Volume,* edited by H. L. Hariyappa and M. M. Patkar (Poona: Oriental Book Agency, 1960), pp. 83–92. In the Vaishnava literature that postdates the *Gītagovinda,* Rādhā is a ubiquitous figure in relation to Krishna; since some excellent studies of these works exist, I do not deal with the material here. See Shashibhusan Dasgupta, *Obscure Religious Cults* (Calcutta: K. L. Mukhopadhyay, 1962), pp. 113–46; S. K. De, *Vaiṣṇava Faith and Movement in Bengal* (Calcutta: K. L. Mukhopadhyay, 1961); Edward C. Dimock, Jr., *The Place of the Hidden Moon: Erotic Mysticism in the Vaishnava Sahajiyā Cult of Bengal* (Chicago: University of Chicago Press, 1966); Norvin Hein, *The Miracle Plays of Mathurā* (New Haven: Yale University Press, 1972), pp. 163–271; Milton Singer, ed., *Krishna: Myths, Rites and Attitudes* (Honolulu: East-West Center Press, 1966). I have also omitted references from two works that make some claim for inclusion. Original verses on Rādhā quoted in *Saduktikarṇāmṛta* (edited by S. K. Banerji; Calcutta: K. L. Mukhopadhyay, 1965) are attributed to Jayadeva's contemporaries Umāpatidhara and Śaraṇa (I.53.5, I.55.3, I.61.2); another (I.58.4) is quoted below from *Vakroktijīvita* (2.56). Verses on Rādhā in the *Kṛṣṇakarṇāmṛta* of Līlāśuka Bilvamaṅgala are numerous, but the dating of the work remains problematic (it is variously assigned to periods ranging from the ninth to the fifteenth century). See S. K. De, *The Kṛṣṇā-karṇāmṛta,* University of Dacca Oriental Publication Series, no. 5 (Dacca: University of Dacca, 1938), Francis Wilson, *The Love of Krishna: The Kṛṣṇakarṇāmṛta of Līlāśuka Bilvamaṅgala* (Philadelphia: University of Pennsylvania Press, 1975).

2. H. Grassman, *Wörterbuch zum Rig-Veda* (1872; reprint, Wiesbaden: Otto Harrassowitz, 1955), 1160–62; *Bhāgavata Purāṇa* (Gorakhpur: Gita Press, 1962) II.4.14; IV.7.57, 24.18, 31.11; IX.21.17; X.65.6.

3. Max Müller, ed., *The Hymns of the Rig-Veda,* 2 vols. (London: Trübner, 1877) VIII.61.14; cf. I.30.5, etc; related epithets *vasupati, vasudā,* etc.

4. See J. Gonda, *Aspects of Early Viṣṇuism* (1954; reprint, Delhi: Motilal Banarsidass, 1969), pp. 224–25; see also *The Mahābhārata,* critical edition, edited by V. S. Sukthankar, et al. (Poona: Bhandarkar Oriental Research Institute, 1933–36), I:16.

5. E.g., R. C. Artal, "A Note on Kṛṣṇa and His Consort Rādhā," *Anthropological Society of Bombay,* 8, no. 5 (1907–9), 356–60; Sukumar Sen, "Etymology of the Name Rādhā," *Indian Linguistics,* 8 (1943), 434. Sen speculates that the word *rādhā* must have been a common noun with the meaning of "beloved, desired woman." He supports his argument with reference to the Vedic *rādhas* meaning "a desired object" and its masculine cognate in Avestan *rāδa,* meaning "lover" in Yasna 9.23. My colleague Professor Dale Bishop informs me that the passage is problematic, but if it is taken with a Gāthic passage (Yasna 29.9) where the only other reference to *rāδa* occurs, the contexts suggest that the word could mean something like "satisfaction" as an abstract; in any case, most scholarly interpretations indicate something or someone that "fulfills a need."

6. A. A. Macdonell and A. B. Keith, *Vedic Index* (1912, reprint, Delhi: Motilal Banarsidass, 1967), vol. I, p. 417. *Atharva Veda* XIX.7.3(c–d):

rā́dhe viśā́khe suhávānurā́dhā *jyeṣṭā sunákṣatram áriṣṭaṁ mū́lam* ||

Atharvaveda Saṁhitā, edited by W. D. Whitney and R. Roth (Berlin: F. Dummler, 1856), p. 356. Although Whitney reports all manuscripts examined to read *rā́dhe* (fem. dual) and commentaries to explain this as meaning that *rādhā* is another name for *viśākhā,* he feels that it is an interpolation based on a later misunderstanding of *anurādhā* as meaning "the one after (*anu*) or following *rādhā.*" He therefore changes the reading to *rā́dho* and translates it "be the two Viśākhās bestowal (*rā́dhas*)." W. D. Whitney, trans., *Atharva-veda Saṁhitā* (1905; reprint, Delhi: Motilal Banarsidass, 1962), vol. II, p. 908. If one follows the manuscript evidence and reads *rā́dhe,* it can be understood that the two stars called *Viśākhā* are identified with a dual *rādhā.* The identification is supported by the fifth century lexical work *Amarakoṣa,* I.3.22: *rādhā viśākhā puṣye tu sidhyatiṣyau śraviṣṭhayā,* etc. Amarasiṁha, *The Nāmaliṅgānuśāsanam* (*Amarakoṣa*), edited by Pandit Śivadatta (Bombay: Nirṇayasāgara Press, 1944), p. 38.

7. Rajendra Mittra, ed., Taittirīya Brāhmaṇa Bibliotheca Indica, no. 125 (Calcutta: Asiatic Society of Bengal, 1855), p. 4.

8. *Taittirīya Saṁhitā,* translated by A. B. Keith, Harvard Oriental Series, vols. 18–19 (Cambridge, Mass.: Harvard University Press, 1914).

9. *Mahābhārata* XIII.135.60(c), *nakṣatranemir nakṣatrī;* in the episode of the burning of Khāṇḍava forest (I.214 ff.) Krishna is repeatedly addressed as *Mādhava,* and also *Madhusūdana;* see section 4, notes 9–12 above, esp. Gonda, *Aspects of Viṣṇuism,* pp. 16 ff., 237.

10. F. E. Pargiter, *Ancient Indian Historical Tradition* (London: Oxford University Press, 1922), p. 135.

11. *Amarakośa,* I.3.22; the authors of the *Brahmavaivarta P.* incorporate Rādhā's *nakṣatrā* associations into the story of her heavenly birth and descent; see Walter Ruben, "The Kṛṣṇacarita in the Harivaṁśa and Certain Purāṇas," *Journal of the American Oriental Society,* 61 (1941), 126–27.

12. This Rādhā has no apparent connection with the epic figure named Rādhā, who is the wife of the charioteer Adhiratha and the foster-mother of Kuntī's son Karṇa. *Mahābhārata* I.104.14(b) and 181.28(a):

tam utsṛṣṭaṁ tadā garbhaṁ rādhābhartā mahāyaśaḥ |
putratve kalpayāmāsa sabhāryaḥ sūtanandaḥ ||

Rādhā's renowned husband [Adhiratha], son of a charioteer,
Rescued the abandoned child and he and his wife made him their own son.

ko hi rādhāsutaṁ karṇaṁ śakto yodhayituṁ raṇe |
anyatra rāmād droṇād vā kṛpād vāpi śaradvataḥ ||

Who can fight in battle with Rādhā's son Karṇa
Other than Paraśurāma, Droṇa, Kṛpa, or Śaradvat?

13. See Dimock, *Place of the Hidden Moon,* pp. 32–35; B. Majumdar, *Kṛṣṇa in History and Legend,* pp. 171–91.

14. References to Rādhā in these Purāṇas are given in tentative chronological order.

Matsya Purāṇa, edited by H. N. Apte, Ānandāśrama Sanskrit Series, no. 54 (Poona: Ānandāśrama Press, 1907), XIII.38. In verses 24–53 of this section, Devī ennumerates her various names at different holy places in response to Dakṣa's question as to what names are to be invoked at the *tīrthas.* Verse 38 is quoted by Jīva Gosvāmin in his commentary on *Bhāgavata* X.21.17.

śivakuṇḍe śivānandā nandinī devikātaṭe |
rukmiṇī dvāravatyāṁ tu rādhā vṛndāvane vane || 38 ||

At Śivakuṇḍa she is Śivānandā; at Devikātaṭe she is Nandinī;
At Dvāravatī she is Rukmiṇī; in the forest at Vṛndāvana she is Rādhā.

Liṅga Purāṇa, edited by P. J. Vidyasagara (Calcutta: Valmiki Press, 1885), *Uttarārdhe* 48.14. The verse is one of a series of mantras (48.5–26) in imitation of the Gāyatrī, all ending *pracodayāt,* in which various gods and goddesses are invoked; 48.12 invokes Vishnu, 48.13 Lakṣmī.

samuddhṛtāyai vidmahe viṣṇunaikena dhīmahi |
tan no rādhā pracodayāt || 14 ||

We know about one whom Vishnu himself redeems, we meditate on her—
Then let Rādhā inspire us!

Varāha Purāṇa, edited by Hṛshikeśa Śāstrī, Bibliotheca Indica, no. 109 (Calcutta: Asiatic Society of Bengal, 1887), 164.33–35. Krishna's encounter with Rādhā here follows his slaying of the demon Ariṣṭa. Note that *Ariṣṭa* appears in apposition to the *nakṣatra Mūla* in the *Atharva Veda* passage quoted above in note 7.

> *tatra rādhā samāśliṣya kṛṣṇam akliṣṭakāraṇam* |
> *svanāmnā viditaṁ kuṇḍaṁ kṛtaṁ tīrtham adūrataḥ* || 33 ||
> *rādhākuṇḍam iti khyātaṁ sarvapāpaharaṁ śubham* |
> *ariṣṭarādhākuṇḍābhyāṁ snānāt phalam avāpnuyāt* |
> *rājasūyāśvamedhānāṁ nātra kāryyā vicāraṇā* |
> *gohatyābrahmahatyāyāḥ pāpaṁ kṣipraṁ vinaśyati* || 34|35 ||

> Since Rādhā embraced tireless Krishna there,
> The tank was known by her name and a holy place was created nearby.
> It was known as "Rādhā's tank," removing all sins, auspicious.
> With ablution from the Ariṣṭa tank and the Rādhā tank
> One may doubtless attain the reward of Rājasūya and Aśvamedha rites—
> It quickly destroys the sin of cow killing and even Brahman killing.

Brahmavaivarta Purāṇa, edited by V. G. Apte, Ānandāśrama Sanskrit Series, no. 102 (Poona: Ānandāśrama Press, 1935), translated by Rajendra Nath Sen, Sacred Books of the Hindus, vol. 24 (Allahabad: Pāṇini Office, 1922); *Kṛṣṇa-janma-khaṇḍa, adhyāyas* 2–5, 15, 17, 27–30, 52, 53, 57, 58, 66–68, 92–98, 110, 111, 123–28. Rādhā occupies a leading position in the section devoted to Krishna's birth. This elaborate section seems to be as late as the sixteenth century in its present form, but since it is an obvious compilation of various strands of the Rādhā legend it furnishes many relevant suggestions about the nature of the figure and her relationship to Krishna. See Cheever MacKenzie Brown, *God as Mother: A Feminine Theology in India* (Hartford, Vt.: Claude Stark, 1974).

An older version of this Purāṇa may be as early as the eighth century; see A. J. Rawal, "Some Problems Regarding the Brahmavaivartapurāṇa," *Purāṇa*, 14, no. 2 (1972), 107–24.

Padma Purāṇa, edited with Hindi paraphrase by S. S. Śarma (Bareli: Saṃskṛti-saṃsthāna, 1968); *Pātāla-khaṇḍa* (IV), 52, *Śrīrādhā-janmāṣṭamī-mahātmya*. This section is noted several times in the attempts of the Gosvāmins to fix Rādhā's place in established textual traditions, but the section itself seems to me to be a crude interpolation aimed at elevating Rādhā's position in a more orthodox Vishnu cult. Rādhā's lowly birth as a cowherdess is rationalized by explaining that she is called *gopī* ("cow-protectress") because she conserves energy; she is one of the chief deities, the *hlādinī-śakti* of Krishna; she is Mahālakṣmī and Krishna Nārāyaṇa, etc.

The Gosvāmin commentators quote this with reference to *Kārttikamahātmya*, of Pātāla-khaṇḍa; see A. K. Majumdar, "Note on the Rādhā Cult," pp. 245–46.

For discussions of Purāṇic chronology, see A. D. Pusalker, *Studies in the Epics and Purāṇas* (Bombay: Bharatiya Vidya Bhavan, 1963), pp. 205–30; R. C. Hazra, "Studies in the Purāṇic Records on Hindu Rites and Customs," *University of Dacca Bulletin*, no. 20 (Dacca, 1940); M. Winternitz, *Geschichte der indischen Litterature* (Leipzig: C. F. Amelangs Verlag, 1909), vol. I, pp. 440–83. In *The Purana Index* (Madras: University of Madras, 1951–55) under "Rādhā" V.R.R. Dikshitar lists additional references to Rādhā in *Brahmāṇḍa Purāṇa* (III.36.56; 42.21, 47–48; 43.21 and 29; 44.29) and *Vāyu Purāṇa* (105.52), but these could not be located in editions available to me. The late date and derivative nature of treatments of Rādhā in *Devībhāgavata* (translated by Swami Vijñānanda in Sacred Books of the Hindus, vol. 23; Allahabad: Pāṇini Office, 1922, chapter IX, pp. 797–1008) and *Mahābhāgavata* (edited by M. I. Desai; Bombay: Gujarati Printing Press, 1913) has made me omit them from the list; see A. K. Majumdar, "Note on the Rādhā Cult," pp. 246–47; also, R. D. Hazra, "The Mahābhāgavata-purāṇa," *Indian Historical Quarterly,* 28 (1952), 17–28.

15. *Bhāgavata Purāṇa* (Gita Press edition) X.30.28:

> *anayārādhito nūnam bhāgavan harir īśvaraḥ |*
> *yan no vihāya govindaḥ prīto yām anayad rahaḥ ||*
>
> Lord Hari, God, was certainly satisfied by her—
> For, leaving us, Govinda, the lover, led her in secret.

16. *Bhāgavata Purāṇa,* Murshidabad edition, with the commentaries of Śrīdhara-svāmin, Sanātana Gosvamin, Jīva Gosvāmin, and Viśvanātha Cakravartī (Berhampur: Rādhāraman Press, 1888, B.S. 1294). Later commentators identify the figure of the solitary *gopī* with *hlādinī-śakti,* the means by which Krishna gives bliss to his devotees; see Dimock, *Place of the Hidden Moon,* pp. 134, 203–4. It is worth noting again that in the *Bhāgavata,* the *rāsa* dance is an autumnal rite where the emphasis is on Krishna's ability to love all the cowherdesses simultaneously, whereas Krishna's love with Rādhā is an erotic duet enacted in springtime. Following the *Bhāgavata* identification, other commentators claim reference to Rādhā in similar passages in other texts, e.g., *Harivaṁśa,* critical edition, edited by P. L. Vaidya (Poona: Bhandarkar Oriental Research Institute, 1969), 6.33:

> *hāheti kurvatas tasya prahṛṣṭās tā varāṅganāḥ |*
> *jagṛhur niḥsṛtāṁ vāṇiṁ sāmnā dāmodareritām ||*

The seventeenth-century Maharastrian commentator Nīlakaṇṭha explains the verse as Krishna's call for Rādhā; see the edition of R. Kinjawadekar (Poona: Citraśāla Press, 1936), II.20.33. Also, *Viṣṇu Purāṇa* (Gorakhpur: Gita Press, 1962) V.13.33–46; commenting on *Bhāgavata* X.32.8, Sanātana Gosvāmin refers to this passage.

17. Charlotte Vaudeville, "Evolution of Love-Symbolism in Bhagavatism," *Journal of the American Oriental Society,* 82 (1962), 31–40; see also Jean Filliozat, "Les Dates du Bhāgavatapurāṇa et du Bhāgavatamāhātmya," in *Indological Studies in Honor of W. Norman Brown,* American Oriental Series, vol. 47 (New Haven; American Oriental Society, 1962), pp. 70–77; Thomas J. Hopkins, "The Social Teaching of the *Bhāgavata Purāṇa,*" and J.A.B. van Buitenen, "On the Archaism of the *Bhāgavata Purāṇa,*" in Milton Singer, ed., *Krishna: Myths, Rites, and Attitudes* (Honolulu: East-West Center, 1966), pp. 3–40.

18. The *Harivaṁśa* episode of Krishna's marriage to Nīlā is not known in the Northern Recension and is given by Vaidya as Appendix I, no. 12. Local traditions contribute many variants to events and figures in the Krishna story; see Walter Ruben, *Krishna: Konkordanz und Kommentar der Motive Seines Heldenlebens,* Istanbuler Schriften, no. 17 (Istanbul, 1944).

19. See J.S.M. Hooper, *Hymns of the Ālvārs* (Calcutta: Association Press, 1929), pp. 55, 62; V.V.R. Dikshitar, *Śilappadikāram* (London: Oxford University Press, 1939), p. 229.

20. Occurrences of the name Rādhā in prose portions of *Lalitavistara* (*tena khalu punar bhikṣavaḥ samayena sujātāyā grāmikaduhiturdāsī rādhā nāma kālagatābhūt*),

edited by P. L. Vaidya (Darbhanga, 1958) and the vulgate of *Pañcatantra* (*kiṁ paraṁ tu rādhā nāma me bhāryā gopakulaprasūtā prathamam āsīt sā tvam atrāvatīrṇā*) edited by K. P. Parab (Bombay: Nirṇayasāgara Press, 1950, p. 54) are difficult to date.

21. On dating, see A. B. Keith, *History of Sanskrit Literature* (1920; reprint, London: Oxford University Press, 1956), pp. 223–24. For *Sattasaī*, see vulgate, entitled *Gāthasaptaśatī*, edited with the commentary of Gangādharabhatta by P. Durgāprasād and K. P. Parab, Kāvyamālā, no. 21 (Bombay: Nirṇayasāgara Press, 1933), I.89; and critical text, *Saptaśatakam des Hāla*, edited with German translation by Albrecht Weber, *Abhandlungen für die Kunde des Morgenländes*, 5, no. 3 (1870; reprint, Nendeln, Liechtenstein: Kraus Reprint, 1966), I.86:

muhamāruena taṁ kaṇha goraaṁ rāhiāĕ avaṇento |
etāṇaṁ vallavīṇaṁ annānaṁ vi goraaṁ harasi || I.89 (Weber I.86) ||

The Sanskrit version would be:

mukhamārutena tvaṁ kṛṣṇa gorajo rādhikāyā apanayan |
etāsāṁ ballavīnām anyāsām api gauravaṁ harasi ||

In another verse (2.28; Weber, 131) an unnamed *gopī* is singled out and associated with singing and spring; the alliterative pattern of the verse also makes it relevant to *Gītagovinda*.

mahumāsamāruāhaamahuarajhaṁkāraṇibbhare raṇṇe |
gāaï virahakkharavaddhapahiamaṇamohaṇaṁ govī ||

"In woods full of humming bees attacked by winds of the honeyed month of spring, a *gopī* sings a seductive chant to bind a traveler's heart with words of her neglected love."

22. Dated according to the dating of Vākpati's patron, Yaśovarma of Kanauj, by Kalhaṇa in the *Rājataraṅginī*. *Gaüḍavaho: A Historical Poem in Prākṛt*, edited by S. P. Pandit, Bombay Sanskrit Series, no. 34 (Bombay: Central Book Depot, 1887), v. 22:

ṇaha-rehā rāhā-kāraṇā oṁ karuṇaṁ harantu vo sarasā |
vaccha-tthalammi kotthuha-kiraṇāantī oṁ kaṇhassa ||

Pandit's Sanskrit version reads *nakharekhā rādhākaraṇā* (*rādhayā gopyā nirmitāḥ karajaprahārāḥ*) *karuṇānimittaṁ* (*saṁsāraduḥkhaṁ*) *harantu* (*nāśayantu*) *sarasā* (*ārdrā*) *vakṣaḥsthale kaustubhakiraṇāyamānāḥ kṛṣṇasya.*

23. Bhaṭṭa Nārāyaṇa is dated to the first half of the seventh century by D. D. Kosambi in his introduction to *Subhāṣitaratnakoṣa*, edited by Kosambi and V. V. Gokhale, Harvard Oriental Series, no. 42 (Cambridge, Mass: Harvard University Press, 1957), p. lxxxiii, but the only basis for dating is the citations to his work by Vāmana and Ānandavardhana, which places him before the ninth century; see A. B. Keith, *The Sanskrit Drama* (1924, reprint London: Oxford University Press, 1959), p. 212.

Veṇīsaṁhāra of Bhaṭṭa Nārāyaṇa, edited by Julius Grill (Leipzig: Fues's Verlag, 1871), *nāndī* 2:

kālindyāḥ pulineṣu kelikupitām utsṛjya rāse rasaṁ
gacchantīm anugacchato 'srukaluṣāṁ kaṁsadviṣo rādhikām |
tatpādapratimāniveśitapadasyodbhūtaromodgater
akṣuṇṇo'nunayaḥ prasannadayitādṛṣṭasya puṣṇātu vaḥ ||

This *nāndī,* like the two others accompanying it in most editions, could have been added to the text at any time, but the subject of Rādhā's sulking and Krishna's pacifying her is sufficiently relevant to the theme of Draupadī's insults and Bhīma's soothing her with revenge to be part of the original play. It is noteworthy too that after the three *nāndī* verses, the *sūtradhāra* goes on to praise Vishnu and to inform the audience that Krishna has undertaken to act as mediator between the Kauravas and Pāṇḍavas.

24. *Dhvanyāloka* of Ānandavardhana, edited, with the commentary of Abhinavagupta, by P. Durgāprasād and K. P. Parab, Kāvyamālā, no. 25 (Bombay: Nirṇayasāgara Press, 1891), 2.6, 3.41, critical text and translation by K. Krishnamoorthy (Dharwar: Karnatak University, 1974), 2.5, 3.40.

teṣāṁ gopavadhūvilāsasuhṛdāṁ rādhārahaḥsākṣiṇāṁ
kṣemaṁ bhadra kalindaśailatanayātīre latāveśmanām |
vicchinne smaratalpakalpanamṛducchedopayoge 'dhunā
te jāne jaraṭhībhavanti vigalannīlatviṣaḥ pallavāḥ || 2.6 ||

This verse is attributed to the poetess Vidyā in the *Subhāṣitaratnakoṣa* (808). The translation and all others from Vidyākara's anthology cited here are by Daniel H. H. Ingalls, quoted from his *Sanskrit Court Poetry,* Harvard Oriental Series, vol. 44 (Cambridge, Mass.: Harvard University Press, 1965).

durārādhā rādhā subhaga yad anenāpi mṛjatas
tavaitat prāṇeśājaghanavasanenāśru patitam |
kaṭhoraṁ strīcetas tad alam upacārair virama he
kriyāt kalyāṇaṁ vo harir anunayeṣv evam uditaḥ || 3.41 ||

It seems significant that Ānandavardhana is the earliest writer to illustrate his theories with examples from existing Sanskrit and Prākrit literature rather than composing his own. Abhinavagupta, in commenting on these two verses, attributes the first to Krishna after he has left Mathurā for Dvārakā; he says the second is Rādhā's words to Krishna.

25. *Dhvanyālokalocana* of Abhinavagupta, commentary on the two *Dhvanyāloka* verses quoted in note 24; another reference to Rādhā quoted in the *Locana* on 1.4 (Kāvyamālā ed., p. 25).

yāte dvāravatīṁ tadā madhuripau taddattakampānatāṁ
kālindītaṭarūḍhavañjulalatām āliṅgya sotkaṇṭhayā |
tadgītaṁ gurubāṣpagadgadagalattārasvaraṁ rādhayā
yenāntarjalacāribhir jalacarair apy utkam utkūjitam ||

V. Raghavan notes that in his *Abhinavabhāratī,* Abhinavagupta quotes from a work, now lost, entitled *Rādhāvipralambha;* Bhoja categorizes the work as a *rāsakāṅka.* See V. Raghavan, *Bhoja's Śṛṅgāra Prakāśa* (Madras: Punarvasu, 1963), p. 567; idem., "Writers Quoted in the Abhinavabhāratī," *Journal of Oriental Research, Madras,* 6 (1932).

See also the *Vakroktijīvita* of Kuntaka, dated mid tenth to eleventh century (edited by S. K. De, 3d ed.; Calcutta: K. L. Mukhopadhyay, 1961), chapters 1–3.

The verse *teṣām gopavadhūo,* quoted from *Dhvanyāloka* (2.6), is cited illustratively in the *svopajñavṛtti* on 3.3–4; the verse *yāte dvaravatīm,* quoted from the *Locana,* is cited in the *svopajñavṛtti* on 2.59, with the variants (a) *taddattasaṁpādanāṁ* (b) *kālindījalakelivañjulalatām ālambya.*

26. *Kāvyamimāṁsa* of Rājaśekhara, edited by C. D. Dalal and R. A. Shastry, Gaekwad's Oriental Series, no. 1 (Baroda: Central Library, 1916), p. 71. Two verses comparing the breaths of Śiva and Hari are quoted in *adhyāya* 13 following the comment *atha tulyadehitulyasya bhidāḥ. . . . tasyaiva vastuno viṣayāntarayojanād anyarūpāpattir viṣayaparivartaḥ.*

ye sīmantitagātrabhasmarajaso ye kumbhakadveṣiṇo
ye līḍhāḥ śravaṇāśrayeṇa phaṇinā ye candraśaityadruhaḥ |
te kupyadgirijāvibhaktavapuṣaś cittavyathāsākṣiṇaḥ
sthāṇor dakṣiṇanāsikāpuṭabhuvaḥ śvāsānilāḥ pāntu vaḥ ||
ye kīrṇakvathitodarābjamadhavo ye mlāpitoraḥsrajo
ye tāpāt taralena talpaphaṇinā pītapratāpojjhitāḥ |
te rādhāsmṛtisākṣiṇaḥ kamalayā sāsūyam ākarṇitā
gāḍhāntardavathoḥ prataptasaralāḥ śvāsā hareḥ pāntu vaḥ ||

See *Subhāṣitaratnakoṣa* 136, with variants.

27. *Damayantīkathā* is the oldest extant *campū-kāvya;* Keith, *History of Sanskrit Literature,* pp. 332–33. *Damayantīkathā* (also called *Nalacampū*) of Trivikrama Bhaṭṭa, edited by N. B. Parvaṇīkar, P. Durgāprasād, and P. Śivadatta, with the commentary of Caṇḍapāla (Bombay: Nirṇayasāgara Press, 1931), p. 108 (chapter 4).

kevalam anavarataśikṣitavaidagdhyakalāparādhātmikātrapāparāparihṛtya guṇino gurūn parapuruṣe māyāvini kṛtakeśivadhe dhṛtamandarāge rāgaṁ badhnāti |

The sense of this passage is based on a series of puns: "She being not very much taught [or, "not newly taught in sexual pleasures"] in the arts of cunning [or, "passion"] and committing a fault of giving up modesty [*aparādhā-ātmika; rādhā-ātmikā* means "as Radha did"], ignoring the virtuous elders, set her passion on the highest man [or, "a stranger, other than her husband"], Krishna [*māyāvin* also means "trickster"], slayer of demon Keśi [*kṛta-keśi-vadhe; kṛtake 'śivadhe* means "who is artificial, who confers evil"], upholder of Mt. Mandara [or, "whose passion was inactive"]."

For the *Yaśastilakacampūkāvya* the dating is firm; at the end of the text itself Somadeva says that he composed the work in *śāka* 881 (A.D. 959); verse from *Yaśastilakacampūkāvya* of Somadeva, edited, with the commentary of Śrutadeva Sūri, by M. P. Śivadatta and K. P. Parab, Kāvyamālā, no. 70 (Bombay: Nirṇayasāgara Press, 1903), p. 142. The example of Rādhā is cited in chapter 4, while the king is narrating the love of Amṛtamati:

tathā hi—purāpi kiṁ na reme gaṅgā saha maheśvareṇa, rādhā nārāyaṇena, bṛhaspatipatnī dvijarājena, tārā ca vālinā |

See K. K. Handiqui, *Yaśastilaka and Indian Culture* (Sholapur: Jaina Samskrti Samrakshaka Sangha, 1949), pp. 1–21.

28. Three copper-plate inscriptions of Vākpati-Muñja, dated v.s. 1031 (A.D. 974), v.s. 1038 (A.D. 982), v.s. 1043 (A.D. 986); v.s. 1031 plate: N. J. Kirtane, "On Three Mālwā Inscriptions," *Indian Antiquary,* 6 (1877), 48–53; v.s. 1038, 1043 plates: K. N.

Dikshit, "Three Copper-Plate Inscriptions from Gaonri," *Epigraphica Indica,* 23, no. 17, (1935), 108, 109, 112.

yal lakṣmīvadanendunā na sukhitaṁ yan nārdritaṁ vāridher
vārā yan na nijena nābhisarasīpadmena śāntiṁ gatam |
yac cheṣāhiphaṇāsahasramadhuraśvāsair na cāśvāsitaṁ
tad rādhāvirahāturaṁ muraripor velladvapuḥ pātu vaḥ ||

On the relation between Vākpati-Muñja and Bhoja, see Kirtane, pp. 49–50. Dikshit notes, "The most important information contained in these plates is regarding the migration of Brāhmaṇas from various parts of the country to Mālwā where they were recipients of donations at the hands of the Paramāra prince. In several instances the donees seem to have migrated all the way from Bengal. . . ." (p. 103).

29. *Sarasvatīkaṇṭhābharaṇa* of Bhoja, edited, with the commentary of Rāmasiṁha on I–III and of Jagaddhara on IV, by K. Durgāprasād and W. L. S. Pansikar, Kāvyamālā, no. 94 (Bombay: Nirṇayasāgara Press, 1934).

rātāvadyādhirājyā visarararasavidvyājavākkṣmāpakārā
rākā pakṣmābhaśeṣā nayanananayanasvā(sā)khayā stavyamārā |
rāmā vyastasthiratvā tuhinananahituḥ śrīḥ karakṣāradhārā
rādhā rakṣāstu mahyaṁ śivamamamavaśivyālavidyāvatārā || 2.294 ||

kuśalaṁ rādhe sukhito 'si kaṁsa kaṁsaḥ kva nu sā rādhā |
iti pārīprativacanair vilakṣahāso harir jayati || 2.351 ||

kanakakalaśasvacche rādhāpayodharamaṇḍale
navajaladharaśyāmām ātmadyvtiṁ pratibimbitām |
asitasicayaprāntabhrāntyā muhur muhur utkṣipañ
jayati janitavrīḍāhāsaḥ priyāhasito hariḥ || 3.110 ||

This verse is cited again as 5.17; same as *Subhāṣitaratnakoṣa,* 147 (Kosambi and Gokhale ed., p. 29); Hemacandra's *Kāvyānuśāsana* 2.110, with variants (Parikh and Kulkarni ed. cited in note 31, p. 115).

gehād yātā saritam udakaṁ hārikā nājihīṣe
maṅkṣyāmīti śrayasi yamunātīravīrudgṛhāṇi |
gosaṁdāyī viśasi vipināny eva govardhanādrer
na tvaṁ rādhe dṛśi nipatitā devakīnandanasya || 4.177 ||

līlāio ṇiasaṇe rakkhiu taṁ rāhiāi thaṇavaṭṭhe |
hariṇo paḍhamasamāgamasajjhasavasarehiṁ veviro hattho || 5.235 ||

The Sanskrit version reads: *līlāyito nivasane rakṣatu tvāṁ rādhikāyāḥ stanapṛṣṭhe* | *hareḥ prathamasamāgamasādhvasaprasarair vepanaśīlo hastaḥ* ||

pratyagrojjhitagokulasya śayanād utsvapnamūḍhasya me
sā gotraskhalanād apaitu ca divā rādheti bhīror iti |
rātrāv asvapato divā ca vijane lakṣmīti cābhyasyato
rādhāṁ prasmarataḥ śriyaṁ ramayataḥ khedo hareḥ pātu vaḥ || 5.448 ||

helodastamahīdharasya tanutām ālokya doṣno harer
hastenāṁsataṭe 'valambya caraṇāv āropya tatpādayoḥ |
śailoddhārasahāyatāṁ jigamiṣor aspṛṣṭagovardhanā
rādhāyāḥ suciraṁ jayanti gagane vandhyāḥ karabhrāntayaḥ || 5.493 ||

30. *Daśāvatāracarita* by Kṣemendra, edited by P. Durgāprasād and K. P. Parab, Kāvyamālā, no. 26 (Bombay: Nirṇayasāgara Press, 1891), VIII.83, 170, 171, 176. Be-

cause the context seems important, the entire passage VIII.169–76 is quoted following VIII.83. It is this passage which Sukumar Sen considers to be the prototype of the *Gītagovinda;* see *History of Bengali Literature* (Delhi: Sāhitya Akademi, 1960), pp. 15–16.

prītyai babhūva kṛṣṇasya śyāmānicayacumbinaḥ |
jātī madhukarasyeva rādhevādhikavallabhā || 83 ||
tataḥ prabhāte saṁnaddhaṁ ratham āruhya sānugāḥ |
mathurāṁ yayur akrūrasaṁkarṣaṇajanārdanāḥ || 169 ||
kathaṁ rādhām anāmantryāgato 'ham iti mādhavaḥ |
aratiṁ mlānatāṁ cintāṁ vrajan bheje viniḥśvasan || 170 ||
gacchan gokulagūḍhakuñjagahanāny ālokayan keśavaḥ
sotkaṇṭhaṁ valitānano vanabhuvā sakhyeva ruddhāñcalaḥ |
rādhāyā na na neti nīviharaṇe vaiklavyalakṣyākṣarāḥ
sasmāra smarasādhvasādbhutatano rāvokti[?]*riktā giraḥ* || 171 ||
govindasya gatasya kaṁsanagarīṁ vyāptā viyogāgninā
snigdhaśyāmalakūlalīnahariṇī godāvarīgahvare[?] |
romanthasthitagogaṇaiḥ paricayād utkarṇam ākarṇitaṁ
guptaṁ gokulapallave guṇagaṇaṁ gopyaḥ sarāgā jaguḥ || 172 ||
lalitavilāsakalāsukhakhelanalalanālobhanaśobhanayauvanamānitanavamadane |
alikulakokilakuvalayakajjalakālakalindasutāvivalajjalakāliyakuladamane |
keśikiśoramahāsuramāraṇadāruṇagokuladuritavidāraṇagovardhanadharaṇe |
kasya na nayanayugaṁ ratisajje majjati manasijataralataraṅge vararamaṇīramaṇe || 173 ||
udgīyamāne guṇasāgarasya guṇe guṇe rāgarasena śaureḥ |
gopāṅganā gūḍharasānurāgā muhur muhur mohahatā babhūvuḥ || 174 ||
govinde gurusaṁnidhau paravaśāveśād anuktvā gate
suptānāṁ bakulasya śītalatale svairaṁ kuraṅgīdṛśām |
svapnāliṅganasaṁgate 'ṅgalatikāvikṣepalakṣyā muhur
mugdhā vañcaka muñca muñca kitavety uccerur uccair giraḥ || 175 ||
rādhā mādhavaviprayogavigalajjīvopamānair muhur
bāṣpaiḥ pīnapayodharāgragalitaiḥ phullatkadambākulā |
acchinnaśvasanena vegagatinā vyākīryamāṇaiḥ puraḥ
sarvāśāpratibaddhamohamalinā prāvṛṇnavevābhavat || 176 ||

31. *Subhāṣitaratnakoṣa* compiled by Vidyākara (cited in note 23). Verses 131; 136 = *Kāvyamimāṁsa* verse quoted above, with variants in the first and second *padas* (a) *ye saṁtāpitanābhipadmamadhavo ye snāpitoraḥsrajo* (b) *prītapratīpojjhatāḥ*) 139; 147 = *Sarasvatīkaṇṭhābharaṇa* 3.11 quoted above, with variant in the fourth *pada:* (d) *janitavrīḍānamrapriyāhasito*); 808 = *Dhvanyāloka* 2.6 quoted above, with variants in the second and third *padas:* (b) *kalindarāja*°, (c) *smaratalpakalpanavidhi*°: 980. Translations are by Ingalls, quoted from *Sanskrit Court Poetry.*

ete lakṣmaṇa jānakīvirahiṇaṁ māṁ khedayanty ambudā
marmāṇīva ca ghaṭṭayanty alam amī krūrāḥ kadambānilāḥ |
itthaṁ vyāhṛtapūrvajanaviraho yo rādhayā vīkṣitaḥ
serṣyaṁ śaṅkitayā sa vaḥ sukhayatu svapnāyamāno hariḥ || 131 ||

agre gacchata dhenudugdhakalaśānādāyagopye gṛhaṁ
dugdhe vaskayaṇīkule punar iyaṁ rādhā śanair yāsyati |
ity anyavyapadeśaguptahṛdayaḥ kurvan viviktaṁ vrajaṁ
devaḥ kāraṇanandasūnur aśivaṁ kṛṣṇaḥ sa muṣṇātu vaḥ || 139 ||

rathyākārpaṭikaiḥ paṭaccaraśatasyūtorukanthābala-
pratyādiṣṭahimāgamārtiviśadaprasnigdhakaṇṭhodaraiḥ |
gīyante nagareṣu nāgarajanapratyūṣanidrānudo
rādhāmādhavayoḥ parasparaRahaḥprastāvanāgītayaḥ || 980 ||

Verse 980 is attributed to the Bengali poet Ḍimboka, who, like Jayadeva, is quoted in *Saduktikarṇāmṛta;* see D.H.H. Ingalls, "A Sanskrit Poetry of Village and Field: Yogeśvara and His Fellow Poets," *Journal of the American Oriental Society,* 74 (1954), 119–31.

32. Dated fourth quarter of the eleventh century, according to the dates of Vikramāditya VI, the Chalukya king whom Bilhaṇa served as *vidyāpati* and in whose honor *Vikramāṅkadevacarita* was composed. *Vikramāṅkadevacarita* of Bilhaṇa, edited by Georg Bühler, Bombay Sanskrit Series, no. 14 (Bombay: Central Book Depot, 1875), I.5, XVIII.87.

sāndrāṁ mudaṁ yacchatu nandako vaḥ sollāsalakṣmīpratibimbagarbhaḥ |
kurvann ajasraṁ yamunāpravāhasalīlarādhāsmaraṇaṁ murāreḥ || I.5 ||

dolāloladghanajaghanayā rādhayā yatra bhagnāḥ
kṛṣṇakrīḍāṅgaṇaviṭapino nādhunāpy ucchvasanti |
jalpakrīḍāmathitamathurāsūricakreṇa kecit
tasmin vṛndāvanaparisare vāsarā yena nītāḥ || XVIII.87 ||

See Barbara Stoler Miller, *Phantasies of a Love-Thief: The Caurapañcāśika Attributed to Bilhaṇa* (New York: Columbia University Press, 1971), pp. 188–91, which outline Bilhaṇa's travels.

33. In P. L. Vaidya, *Prakrit Grammar of Hemacandra, Revised Edition,* Bombay Sanskrit and Prakrit Series, no. 60 (Poona: Bhandarkar Oriental Research Institute, 1958), Appendix, pp. 190–91, 271–72; illustrative verses from Hemacandra are included in section describing characteristics of Apabhraṁśa: *adhyāya* 8, 4.420.2, 4.22.5.

hari naccāviu paṅgaṇai vimhai pāḍiu lou |
emvahiṁ rāha-paoharahaṁ jaṁ bhāvai taṁ hou || 4.420.2||

The Sanskrit version reads: *hariḥ nartitaḥ prāṅgane vismaye pātitaḥ lokaḥ* | *idānīṁ rādhāpayodharayoḥ yat (prati) bhāti tad bhavatu* ||.

ekamekvauṁ jai vi joedi hari suṭṭhu savvāyareṇa |
to vi drehi jahiṁ kahim vi rāhī |
ko sakkai saṁvareṁ vi daḍḍha-nayaṇā nehiṁ paluṭṭā || 4.422.5||

The Sanskrit version reads: *ekaikaṁ yadyapi paśyati hariḥ suṣṭu sarvādareṇa* | *tathāpi dṛṣṭḥ yatra kvāpi rādhā* | *kaḥ śaknoti saṁvarītuṁ nayane snehena paryaste* ||.

In another work attributed to Hemacandra, the *Kāvyānuśasana* (edited, with *Alaṁkāracūḍāmaṇi* and *Viveka,* by R. C. Parikh and V. M. Kulkarni; Bombay: Śrī Mahāvīra Jaina Vidyālaya, 1964), 2.8 (example 107) is the verse *teṣām gopavadhu°* . . . quoted from the *Dhvanyāloka,* 2.6; occurring also in *Vakroktijīvita,* 2.56 and *Subhāṣitaratnakoṣa,* 808; 2.11 (example 110) is the verse *kanakakalaśa°* quoted from *Sarasvatīkaṇṭhābharaṇa,* 3.110; 2.29 (example 131) is the verse *ete lakṣmaṇa* . . . quoted from *Subhāṣitaratnakoṣa,* 131.

34. *Naiṣadhīyacarita* of Śrīharṣa, edited, with the commentary of Nārāyaṇa, by P. Śivadatta and W.L.S. Pansikar (9th ed., Bombay: Nirṇayasāgara Press, 1952), 21.83.

5 *Rādhā: Consort of Krishna's Springtime Passion (cont.)*

prāṇavatpraṇayirādha na rādhāputraśatrusakhitā sadṛśī te |
śrīpriyasya sadṛg eva tava śrīvatsam ātmahṛdi dhartum ajasram ||

35. Dated according to dating of Govardhana's patron Lakṣmaṇasena of Bengal (ca. A.D. 1185–1205); in *Gītagovinda* I.4, Jayadeva praises him for his erotic compositions. *Āryasaptaśatī* of Govardhana, edited, with the commentary of Anantapaṇḍita, by P. Durgāprasād and K. P. Parab, Kāvyamālā, no. 1 (Bombay: Nirṇayasāgara Press, 1886).

madhumathanamaulimāle sakhi tulayasi tulasi kiṁ mudhā rādhām |
yat tava padam adaśīyaṁ surabhayituṁ saurabhodbhedaḥ || 431 ||
rājyābhiṣekasalilakṣālitamauleḥ kathāsu kṛṣṇasya |
garvabharamantharākṣī paśyati padapaṅkajaṁ rādhā |
lajjayitum akhilagopīnipītamanasaṁ madhudviṣaṁ rādhā |
ajñeva pṛcchati kathāṁ śambhor dayitārdhatuṣṭasya || 508 ||
lakṣmīniḥśvāsānilapiṇḍīkṛtadugdhajaladhisārabhujaḥ |
kṣīranidhitīrasudṛśo yaśāṁsi gāyanti rādhāyāḥ || 509 ||
vicarati paritaḥ kṛṣṇe rādhāyāṁ rāgacapalanayanāyām |
daśadigvedhaviśuddhaṁ viśikhaṁ vidadhāti viṣameṣuḥ || 530 ||

36. Jayadeva certainly knew Kālidāsa's *Kumārasaṁbhava,* and his conception of the significance of Rādhā's suffering may have been influenced by the image of Pārvatī's austerities preceding her union with Śiva.

37. *Caṇḍī* is also an epithet of Devī, the great goddess, with whom comparison is implied in the use of the term.

38. See Bharata's *Nāṭyaśāstra,* edited and translated by M. Ghosh (Calcutta: Granthalaya, 1967), XXIV.210–24; see also Dimock, *Place of the Hidden Moon,* pp. 215–20. Each state is defined in quotations from the *Nāṭyaśastra* in the glossary to the Sanskrit text in the clothbound edition. The eighth of the classical states, that of a *proṣitabhartṛkā,* one whose lover is away in a distant place, is inappropriate to the context of the *Gītagovinda* and is not ascribed to Rādhā.

39. A detailed discussion of the significance of external manifestations of emotion in Indian esthetic theory is found in the introduction to my *Phantasies of a Love-Thief,* pp. 10–11.

40. *Vañcitā* is a variant designation for the state more usually called *vipralabdhā.*

41. Although Jayadeva does not use the term *abhisārikā,* he clearly refers to it in his use of the defining characteristic of this state, which is abandoned modesty.

42. See Dimock, *Place of the Hidden Moon,* pp. 33–35.

Gītagovinda Translation

THE FIRST PART

Joyful Krishna

"Clouds thicken the sky.
Tamāla trees darken the forest.
The night frightens him.
Rādhā, you take him home!"
They leave at Nanda's order,
Passing trees in thickets on the way,
Until secret passions of Rādhā and Mādhava
Triumph on the Jumna riverbank. 1

Jayadeva, wandering king of bards
Who sing at Padmāvatī's lotus feet,
Was obsessed in his heart
By rhythms of the goddess of speech,
And he made this lyrical poem
From tales of the passionate play
When Krishna loved Śrī. 2

Umāpatidhara is prodigal with speech,
Śaraṇa is renowned for his subtle flowing sounds,
But only Jayadeva divines the pure design of words.
Dhoyī is famed as king of poets for his musical ear,
But no one rivals master Govardhana
For poems of erotic mood and sacred truth. 3

If remembering Hari enriches your heart,
If his arts of seduction arouse you,
Listen to Jayadeva's speech
In these sweet soft lyrical songs. 4

The First Song, sung with Rāga "Mālava"

In seas that rage as the aeon of chaos collapses,
You keep the holy Veda like a ship straight on course.
You take form as the Fish, Krishna.
Triumph, Hari, Lord of the World! 5

Where the world rests on your vast back,
Thick scars show the weight of bearing earth.
You take form as the Tortoise, Krishna.
Triumph, Hari, Lord of the World! 6

The earth clings to the tip of your tusk
Like a speck of dust caught on the crescent moon.
You take form as the Boar, Krishna.
Triumph, Hari, Lord of the World! 7

Nails on your soft lotus hand are wondrous claws
Tearing the gold-robed body of black bee Hiraṇyakaśipu.
You take form as the Man-lion, Krishna.
Triumph, Hari, Lord of the World! 8

Wondrous dwarf, when you cheat demon Bali with wide steps,
Water falls from your lotus toenails to purify creatures.
You take form as the Dwarf, Krishna.
Triumph, Hari, Lord of the World! 9

You wash evil from the world in a flood of warriors' blood,
And the pain of existence is eased.
You take form as the axman Priest, Krishna.
Triumph, Hari, Lord of the World! 10

Incited by gods who guard the directions in battle,
You hurl Rāvaṇa's ten demon heads to the skies.
You take form as the prince Rāma, Krishna.
Triumph, Hari, Lord of the World! 11

The robe on your bright body is colored with rain clouds,
And Jumna waters roiling in fear of your plow's attack.
  You take form as the plowman Balarāma, Krishna.
  Triumph, Hari, Lord of the World! 12

Moved by deep compassion, you condemn the Vedic way
That ordains animal slaughter in rites of sacrifice.
  You take form as the enlightened Buddha, Krishna.
  Triumph, Hari, Lord of the World! 13

You raise your sword like a fiery meteor
Slashing barbarian hordes to death.
  You take form as the avenger Kalki, Krishna.
  Triumph, Hari, Lord of the World! 14

Listen to the perfect invocation of poet Jayadeva,
Joyously evoking the essence of existence!
  You take the tenfold cosmic form, Krishna.
  Triumph, Hari, Lord of the World! 15

For upholding the Vedas,
For supporting the earth,
For raising the world,
For tearing the demon asunder,
For cheating Bali,
For destroying the warrior class,
For conquering Rāvaṇa,
For wielding the plow,
For spreading compassion,
For routing the barbarians,
Homage to you, Krishna,
In your ten incarnate forms! 16

The Second Song, sung with Rāga "Gurjarī"

You rest on the circle of Śrī's breast,
Wearing your earrings,
Fondling wanton forest garlands.
Triumph, God of Triumph, Hari! 17

The sun's jewel light encircles you
As you break through the bond of existence—
A wild Himalayan goose on lakes in minds of holy men.
Triumph, God of Triumph, Hari! 18

You defeat the venomous serpent Kāliya,
Exciting your Yadu kinsmen
Like sunlight inciting lotuses to bloom.
Triumph, God of Triumph, Hari! 19

You ride your fierce eagle Garuḍa
To battle demons Madhu and Mura and Naraka,
Leaving the other gods free to play.
Triumph, God of Triumph, Hari! 20

Watching with long omniscient lotus-petal eyes,
You free us from bonds of existence,
Preserving life in the world's three realms.
Triumph, God of Triumph, Hari! 21

Janaka's daughter Sītā adorns you.
You conquer demon Dūṣaṇa.
You kill ten-headed Rāvaṇa in battle.
Triumph, God of Triumph, Hari! 22

Your beauty is fresh as rain clouds.
You hold the mountain to churn elixir from the sea.
Your eyes are night birds drinking from Śrī's moon face.
Triumph, God of Triumph, Hari! 23

Poet Jayadeva joyously sings
This song of invocation
In an auspicious prayer.
  Triumph, God of Triumph, Hari! 24

As he rests in Śrī's embrace,
On the soft slope of her breast,
The saffroned chest of Madhu's killer
Is stained with red marks of passion
And sweat from fatigue of tumultuous loving.
May his broad chest bring you pleasure too! 25

When spring came, tender-limbed Rādhā wandered
Like a flowering creeper in the forest wilderness,
Seeking Krishna in his many haunts.
The god of love increased her ordeal,
Tormenting her with fevered thoughts,
And her friend sang to heighten the mood. 26

The Third Song, sung with Rāga "Vasanta"

Soft sandal mountain winds caress quivering vines of clove.
Forest huts hum with droning bees and crying cuckoos.
When spring's mood is rich, Hari roams here
To dance with young women, friend—
A cruel time for deserted lovers. 27

Lonely wives of travelers whine in love's mad fantasies.
Bees swarm over flowers clustered to fill mimosa branches.
When spring's mood is rich, Hari roams here
To dance with young women, friend—
A cruel time for deserted lovers. 28

Tamāla trees' fresh leaves absorb strong scents of deer musk.
Flame-tree petals, shining nails of Love, tear at young hearts.
When spring's mood is rich, Hari roams here
To dance with young women, friend—
A cruel time for deserted lovers. 29

Gleaming saffron flower pistils are golden scepters of Love.
Trumpet flowers like wanton bees are arrows in Love's quiver.
When spring's mood is rich, Hari roams here
To dance with young women, friend—
A cruel time for deserted lovers. 30

Tender buds bloom into laughter as creatures abandon modesty.
Cactus spikes pierce the sky to wound deserted lovers.
When spring's mood is rich, Hari roams here
To dance with young women, friend—
A cruel time for deserted lovers. 31

Scents of twining creepers mingle with perfumes of fresh garlands.
Intimate bonds with young things bewilder even hermit hearts.
When spring's mood is rich, Hari roams here
To dance with young women, friend—
A cruel time for deserted lovers. 32

Budding mango trees tremble from the embrace of rising vines.
Brindaban forest is washed by meandering Jumna river waters.
When spring's mood is rich, Hari roams here
To dance with young women, friend—
A cruel time for deserted lovers. 33

Jayadeva's song evokes the potent memory of Hari's feet,
Coloring the forest in springtime mood heightened by Love's presence.
When spring's mood is rich, Hari roams here
To dance with young women, friend—
A cruel time for deserted lovers. 34

Wind perfumes the forests with fine pollen
Shaken loose from newly blossomed jasmine
As it blows Love's cactus-fragrant breath
To torture every heart it touches here. 35

Crying sounds of cuckoos, mating on mango shoots
Shaken as bees seek honey scents of opening buds,
Raise fever in the ears of lonely travelers—
Somehow they survive these days
By tasting the mood of lovers' union
In climaxing moments of meditation. 36

Pointing to Mura's defeater nearby
Delighting in his seductive game
Of reveling in many women's embraces,
Her friend sang to make Rādhā look back. 37

The Fourth Song, sung with Rāga "Rāmakarī"

Yellow silk and wildflower garlands lie on dark sandaloiled skin.
Jewel earrings dangling in play ornament his smiling cheeks.
Hari revels here as the crowd of charming girls
Revels in seducing him to play. 38

One cowherdess with heavy breasts embraces Hari lovingly
And celebrates him in a melody of love.
Hari revels here as the crowd of charming girls
Revels in seducing him to play. 39

Another simple girl, lured by his wanton quivering look,
Meditates intently on the lotus face of Madhu's killer.
Hari revels here as the crowd of charming girls
Revels in seducing him to play. 40

A girl with curving hips, bending to whisper in his ear,
Cherishes her kiss on her lover's tingling cheek.
Hari revels here as the crowd of charming girls
Revels in seducing him to play. 41

Eager for the art of his love on the Jumna riverbank, a girl
Pulls his silk cloth toward a thicket of reeds with her hand.
Hari revels here as the crowd of charming girls
Revels in seducing him to play. 42

Hari praises a girl drunk from dancing in the rite of love,
With beating palms and ringing bangles echoing his flute's low tone.
Hari revels here as the crowd of charming girls
Revels in seducing him to play. 43

He hugs one, he kisses another, he caresses another dark beauty.
He stares at one's suggestive smiles, he mimics a willful girl.
Hari revels here as the crowd of charming girls
Revels in seducing him to play. 44

The wondrous mystery of Krishna's sexual play in Brindaban forest
Is Jayadeva's song. Let its celebration spread Krishna's favors!
Hari revels here as the crowd of charming girls
Revels in seducing him to play. 45

When he quickens all things
To create bliss in the world,
His soft black sinuous lotus limbs
Begin the festival of love
And beautiful cowherd girls wildly
Wind him in their bodies.
Friend, in spring young Hari plays
Like erotic mood incarnate. 46

Winds from sandalwood mountains
Blow now toward Himalayan peaks,
Longing to plunge in the snows
After weeks of writhing
In the hot bellies of ground snakes.
Melodious voices of cuckoos
Raise their joyful sound
When they spy the buds
On tips of smooth mango branches. 47

"Joyful Krishna" is the first part in *Gītagovinda*

THE SECOND PART

Careless Krishna

While Hari roamed in the forest
Making love to all the women,
Rādhā's hold on him loosened,
And envy drove her away.
But anywhere she tried to retreat
In her thicket of wild vines,
Sounds of bees buzzing circles overhead
Depressed her—
She told her friend the secret. 1

The Fifth Song, sung with Rāga "Gurjarī"

Sweet notes from his alluring flute echo nectar from his lips.
His restless eyes glance, his head sways, earrings play at his cheeks.
My heart recalls Hari here in his love dance,
Playing seductively, laughing, mocking me. 2

A circle of peacock plumes caressed by moonlight crowns his hair.
A rainbow colors the fine cloth on his cloud-dark body.
My heart recalls Hari here in his love dance,
Playing seductively, laughing, mocking me. 3

Kissing mouths of round-hipped cowherd girls whets his lust.
Brilliant smiles flash from the ruby-red buds of his sweet lips.
My heart recalls Hari here in his love dance,
Playing seductively, laughing, mocking me. 4

Vines of his great throbbing arms circle a thousand cowherdesses.
Jewel rays from his hands and feet and chest break the dark night.
  My heart recalls Hari here in his love dance,
  Playing seductively, laughing, mocking me. 5

His sandalpaste browmark outshines the moon in a mass of clouds.
His cruel heart is a hard door bruising circles of swelling breasts.
  My heart recalls Hari here in his love dance,
  Playing seductively, laughing, mocking me. 6

Jeweled earrings in sea-serpent form adorn his sublime cheeks.
His trailing yellow cloth is a retinue of sages, gods, and spirits.
  My heart recalls Hari here in his love dance,
  Playing seductively, laughing, mocking me. 7

Meeting me under a flowering tree, he calms my fear of dark time,
Delighting me deeply by quickly glancing looks at my heart.
  My heart recalls Hari here in his love dance,
  Playing seductively, laughing, mocking me. 8

Jayadeva's song evokes an image of Madhu's beautiful foe
Fit for worthy men who keep the memory of Hari's feet.
  My heart recalls Hari here in his love dance,
  Playing seductively, laughing, mocking me. 9

My heart values his vulgar ways,
Refuses to admit my rage,
Feels strangely elated,
And keeps denying his guilt.
When he steals away without me
To indulge his craving
For more young women,
My perverse heart
Only wants Krishna back.
What can I do? 10

The Sixth Song, sung with Rāga "Mālava"

I reach the lonely forest hut where he secretly lies at night.
My trembling eyes search for him as he laughs in a mood of passion.
Friend, bring Keśi's sublime tormentor to revel with me!
I've gone mad waiting for his fickle love to change. 11

I shy from him when we meet; he coaxes me with flattering words.
I smile at him tenderly as he loosens the silken cloth on my hips.
Friend, bring Keśi's sublime tormentor to revel with me!
I've gone mad waiting for his fickle love to change. 12

I fall on the bed of tender ferns; he lies on my breasts forever.
I embrace him, kiss him; he clings to me drinking my lips.
Friend, bring Keśi's sublime tormentor to revel with me!
I've gone mad waiting for his fickle love to change. 13

My eyes close languidly as I feel the flesh quiver on his cheek.
My body is moist with sweat; he is shaking from the wine of lust.
Friend, bring Keśi's sublime tormentor to revel with me!
I've gone mad waiting for his fickle love to change. 14

I murmur like a cuckoo; he masters love's secret rite.
My hair is a tangle of wilted flowers; my breasts bear his nailmarks.
Friend, bring Keśi's sublime tormentor to revel with me!
I've gone mad waiting for his fickle love to change. 15

Jewel anklets ring at my feet as he reaches the height of passion.
My belt falls noisily; he draws back my hair to kiss me.
Friend, bring Keśi's sublime tormentor to revel with me!
I've gone mad waiting for his fickle love to change. 16

I savor passion's joyful time; his lotus eyes are barely open.
My body falls like a limp vine; Madhu's foe delights in my love.
Friend, bring Keśi's sublime tormentor to revel with me!
I've gone mad waiting for his fickle love to change. 17

Jayadeva sings about Rādhā's fantasy of making love with Madhu's killer.
Let the story of a lonely cowherdess spread joy in his graceful play.
Friend, bring Keśi's sublime tormentor to revel with me!
I've gone mad waiting for his fickle love to change. 18

The enchanting flute in his hand
Lies fallen under coy glances;
Sweat of love wets his cheeks;
His bewildered face is smiling—
When Krishna sees me watching him
Playing in the forest
In a crowd of village beauties,
I feel the joy of desire. 19

Wind from a lakeside garden
Coaxing buds on new aśoka branches
Into clusters of scarlet flowers
Is only fanning the flames to burn me.
This mountain
Of new mango blossoms
Humming with roving bumblebees
Is no comfort to me now, friend. 20

"Careless Krishna" is the second part in *Gītagovinda*

THE THIRD PART

Bewildered Krishna

Krishna, demon Kaṁsa's foe,
Feeling Rādhā bind his heart with chains
Of memories buried in other wordly lives,
Abandoned the beautiful cowherd girls. 1

As he searched for Rādhikā in vain,
Arrows of love pierced his weary mind
And Mādhava repented as he suffered
In a thicket on the Jumna riverbank. 2

The Seventh Song, sung with Rāga "Gurjarī"

She saw me surrounded in the crowd of women,
And went away.
I was too ashamed,
Too afraid to stop her.
  Damn me! My wanton ways
  Made her leave in anger. 3

What will she do, what will she say to me
For deserting her this long?
I have little use for wealth or people
Or my life or my home.
  Damn me! My wanton ways
  Made her leave in anger. 4

I brood on her brow curving
Over her anger-shadowed face,
Like a red lotus
Shadowed by a bee hovering above.
  Damn me! My wanton ways
  Made her leave in anger. 5

In my heart's sleepless state
I wildly enjoy her loving me.
Why do I follow her now in the woods?
Why do I cry in vain?
  Damn me! My wanton ways
  Made her leave in anger. 6

Frail Rādhā, I know jealousy
Wastes your heart.
But I can't beg your forgiveness
When I don't know where you are.
  Damn me! My wanton ways
  Made her leave in anger. 7

You haunt me,
Appearing, disappearing again.
Why do you deny me
Winding embraces you once gave me?
  Damn me! My wanton ways
  Made her leave in anger. 8

Forgive me now!
I won't do this to you again!
Give me a vision, beautiful Rādhā!
I burn with passion of love.
  Damn me! My wanton ways
  Made her leave in anger. 9

Hari's state is painted
With deep emotion by Jayadeva—
The poet from Kindubilva village,
The moon rising out of the sea.
Damn me! My wanton ways
Made her leave in anger. 10

Lotus stalks garland my heart,
Not a necklace of snakes!
Blue lily petals circle my neck,
Not a streak of poison!
Sandalwood powder, not ash,
Is smeared on my lovelorn body!
Love-god, don't attack, mistaking me for Śiva!
Why do you rush at me in rage? 11

Don't lift your mango-blossom arrow!
Don't aim your bow!
Our games prove your triumph, Love.
Striking weak victims is empty valor.
Rādhā's doe eyes broke my heart
With a volley of glances
Impelled by love—
Nothing can arouse me now! 12

Glancing arrows your brow's bow conceals
May cause pain in my soft mortal core.
Your heavy black sinuous braid
May perversely whip me to death.
Your luscious red berry lips, frail Rādhā,
May spread a strange delirium.
But how do breasts in perfect circles
Play havoc with my life? 13

Her joyful responses to my touch,
Trembling liquid movements of her eyes,
Fragrance from her lotus mouth,
A sweet ambiguous stream of words,
Nectar from her red berry lips—
Even when the sensuous objects are gone,
My mind holds on to her in a trance.
How does the wound of her desertion deepen? 14

Her arched brow is his bow,
Her darting glances are arrows,
Her earlobe is the bowstring—
Why are the weapons guarded
In Love's living goddess of triumph?
The world is already vanquished. 15

"Bewildered Krishna" is the third part in *Gītagovinda*

THE FOURTH PART

Tender Krishna

In a clump of reeds on the Jumna riverbank
Where Mādhava waited helplessly,
Reeling under the burden of ardent love,
Rādhikā's friend spoke to him. 1

The Eighth Song, sung with Rāga "Karṇāṭa"

She slanders sandalbalm and moonbeams—weariness confuses her.
She feels venom from nests of deadly snakes in sandal mountain winds.
Lying dejected by your desertion, fearing Love's arrows,
She clings to you in fantasy, Mādhava. 2

Trying to protect you from the endless fall of Love's arrows,
She shields her heart's soft mortal core with moist lotus petals.
Lying dejected by your desertion, fearing Love's arrows,
She clings to you in fantasy, Mādhava. 3

She covets a couch of Love's arrows to practice her seductive art.
She makes her flower bed a penance to win joy in your embrace.
Lying dejected by your desertion, fearing Love's arrows,
She clings to you in fantasy, Mādhava. 4

She raises her sublime lotus face, clouded and streaked with tears,
Like the moon dripping with nectar from cuts of the eclipse's teeth.
Lying dejected by your desertion, fearing Love's arrows,
She clings to you in fantasy, Mādhava. 5

She secretly draws you with deer musk to resemble the god of love,
Riding a sea monster, aiming mango-blossom arrows—she worships you.
Lying dejected by your desertion, fearing Love's arrows,
She clings to you in fantasy, Mādhava. 6

She cries out the words, "Mādhava, I fall at your feet!
When your face turns away, even moonlight scorches my body."
Lying dejected by your desertion, fearing Love's arrows,
She clings to you in fantasy, Mādhava. 7

She evokes you in deep meditation to reach your distant form.
She laments, laughs, collapses, cries, trembles, utters her pain.
Lying dejected by your desertion, fearing Love's arrows,
She clings to you in fantasy, Mādhava. 8

If your heart hopes to dance to the haunting song of Jayadeva,
Study what her friend said about Rādhā suffering Hari's desertion.
Lying dejected by your desertion, fearing Love's arrows,
She clings to you in fantasy, Mādhava. 9

Her house becomes a wild jungle,
Her band of loving friends a snare.
Sighs fan her burning pain
To flames that rage like forest fire.
Suffering your desertion,
She takes form as a whining doe
And turns Love into Death
Disguised as a tiger hunting prey. 10

The Ninth Song, sung in Rāga "Deśākhya"

An exquisite garland lying on her breasts
Is a burden to the frail wasted girl.
  Krishna, Rādhikā suffers in your desertion. 11

Moist sandalbalm smoothed on her body
Feels like dread poison to her.
  Krishna, Rādhikā suffers in your desertion. 12

The strong wind of her own sighing
Feels like the burning fire of love.
  Krishna, Rādhikā suffers in your desertion. 13

Her eyes shed tears everywhere
Like dew from lotuses with broken stems.
  Krishna, Rādhikā suffers in your desertion. 14

Her eyes see a couch of tender shoots,
But she imagines a ritual bed of flames.
  Krishna, Rādhikā suffers in your desertion. 15

She presses her palm against her cheek,
Wan as a crescent moon in the evening.
  Krishna, Rādhikā suffers in your desertion. 16

"Hari! Hari!" she chants passionately,
As if destined to die through harsh neglect.
Krishna, Rādhikā suffers in your desertion. 17

May singing Jayadeva's song
Give pleasure to the worshipper at Krishna's feet!
Krishna, Rādhikā suffers in your desertion. 18

She bristles with pain, sucks in breath,
Cries, shudders, gasps,
Broods deep, reels, stammers,
Falls, raises herself, then faints.
When fevers of passion rage so high,
A frail girl may live by your charm.
If you feel sympathy, Krishna,
Play godly healer! Or Death may take her. 19

Divine physician of her heart,
The love-sick girl can only be healed
With elixir from your body.
Free Rādhā from her torment, Krishna—
Or you are crueler
Than Indra's dread thunderbolt. 20

While her body lies sick
From smoldering fever of love,
Her heart suffers strange slow suffocation
In mirages of sandalbalm, moonlight, lotus pools.
When exhaustion forces her to meditate on you,
On the cool body of her solitary lover,
She feels secretly revived—
For a moment the feeble girl breathes life. 21

She found your neglect in love unbearable before,
Despairing if you closed your eyes even for a moment.
How will she live through this long desertion,
Watching flowers on tips of mango branches? 22

"Tender Krishna" is the fourth part in *Gītagovinda*

THE FIFTH PART

Lotus-eyed Krishna Longing for Love

"I'll stay here, you go to Rādhā!
Appease her with my words and bring her to me!"
Commanded by Madhu's foe, her friend
Went to repeat his words to Rādhā. 1

The Tenth Song, sung with Rāga "Deśavarāḍī"

Sandalwood mountain winds blow,
Spreading passion.
Flowers bloom in profusion,
Tearing deserted lovers' hearts.
  Wildflower-garlanded Krishna
  Suffers in your desertion, friend. 2

Cool moon rays scorch him,
Threatening death.
Love's arrow falls
And he laments his weakness.
  Wildflower-garlanded Krishna
  Suffers in your desertion, friend. 3

Bees swarm, buzzing sounds of love,
Making him cover his ears.
Your neglect affects his heart,
Inflicting pain night after night.
  Wildflower-garlanded Krishna
  Suffers in your desertion, friend. 4

He dwells in dense forest wilds,
Rejecting his luxurious house.
He tosses on his bed of earth,
Frantically calling your name.
  Wildflower-garlanded Krishna
  Suffers in your desertion, friend. 5

Poet Jayadeva sings
To describe Krishna's desolation.
When your heart feels his strong desire,
Hari will rise to favor you.
  Wildflower-garlanded Krishna
  Suffers in your desertion, friend. 6

Mādhava still waits for you
In Love's most sacred thicket,
Where you perfected love together.
He meditates on you without sleeping,
Muttering a series of magical prayers.
He craves the rich elixir that flows
From embracing your full breasts. 7

The Eleventh Song, sung with Rāga "Gurjarī"

He ventures in secret to savor your passion, dressed for love's delight.
Rādhā, don't let full hips idle! Follow the lord of your heart!
In woods on the wind-swept Jumna bank,
Krishna waits in wildflower garlands. 8

He plays your name to call you on his sweet reed flute.
He cherishes breeze-blown pollen that touched your fragile body.
In woods on the wind-swept Jumna bank,
Krishna waits in wildflower garlands. 9

When a bird feather falls or a leaf stirs, he imagines your coming.
He makes the bed of love; he eyes your pathway anxiously.
In woods on the wind-swept Jumna bank,
Krishna waits in wildflower garlands. 10

Leave your noisy anklets! They clang like traitors in love play.
Go to the darkened thicket, friend! Hide in a cloak of night!
In woods on the wind-swept Jumna bank,
Krishna waits in wildflower garlands. 11

Your garlands fall on Krishna's chest like white cranes on a dark cloud.
Shining lightning over him, Rādhā, you rule in the climax of love.
In woods on the wind-swept Jumna bank,
Krishna waits in wildflower garlands. 12

Loosen your clothes, untie your belt, open your loins!
Rādhā, your gift of delight is like treasure in a bed of vines.
  In woods on the wind-swept Jumna bank,
  Krishna waits in wildflower garlands. 13

Hari is proud. This night is about to end now.
Speed my promise to him! Fulfill the desire of Madhu's foe!
  In woods on the wind-swept Jumna bank,
  Krishna waits in wildflower garlands. 14

While Jayadeva sings his enticing song to worship Hari,
Bow to Hari! He loves your favor—his heart is joyful and gentle.
  In woods on the wind-swept Jumna bank,
  Krishna waits in wildflower garlands. 15

Sighing incessantly, he pours out his grief.
He endlessly searches the empty directions.
Each time he enters the forest thicket,
Humming to himself, he gasps for breath.
He makes your bed of love again and again,
Staring at it in empty confusion.
Lovely Rādhā, your lover suffers
Passion's mental pain. 16

Your spitefulness ebbed
As the hot-rayed sun set.
Krishna's mad desire
Deepened with the darkness.
The pitiful cry of lonely cuckoos
Keeps echoing my plea,
"Delay is useless, you fool—
It is time for lovers to meet!" 17

Two lovers meeting in darkness
Embrace and kiss
And claw as desire rises
To dizzying heights of love.
When familiar voices reveal
That they ventured into the dark
To betray each other,
The mood is mixed with shame. 18

As you cast your frightened glance
On the dark path,
As you stop at every tree,
Measuring your steps slowly,
As you secretly move
With love surging through your limbs,
Krishna is watching you, Rādhā!
Let him celebrate your coming! 19

"Lotus-eyed Krishna Longing for Love" is the fifth part in *Gītagovinda*

THE SIXTH PART

Indolent Krishna

Seeing Rādhā in her retreat of vines,
Powerless to leave, impassioned too long,
Her friend described her state
While Krishna lay helpless with love. 1

The Twelfth Song, sung with Rāga "Naṭa"

In her loneliness she sees you everywhere
Drinking springflower honey from other lips.
  Lord Hari,
  Rādhā suffers in her retreat. 2

Rushing in her haste to meet you,
She stumbles after a few steps and falls.
  Lord Hari,
  Rādhā suffers in her retreat. 3

Weaving bracelets from supple lotus shoots
As symbols of your skillful love, she keeps alive.
  Lord Hari,
  Rādhā suffers in her retreat. 4

Staring at her ornaments' natural grace,
She fancies, "I am Krishna, Madhu's foe."
  Lord Hari,
  Rādhā suffers in her retreat. 5

"Why won't Hari come quickly to meet me?"
She incessantly asks her friend.
Lord Hari,
Rādhā suffers in her retreat. 6

She embraces, she kisses cloud-like forms
Of the vast dark night. "Hari has come," she says.
Lord Hari,
Rādhā suffers in her retreat. 7

While you idle here, modesty abandons her,
She laments, sobs as she waits to love you.
Lord Hari,
Rādhā suffers in her retreat. 8

May poet Jayadeva's song
Bring joy to sensitive men!
Lord Hari,
Rādhā suffers in her retreat. 9

Her body bristling with longing,
Her breath sucking in words of confusion,
Her voice cracking in deep cold fear—
Obsessed by intense thoughts of passion,
Rādhā sinks in a sea of erotic mood,
Clinging to you in her meditation, cheat! 10

She ornaments her limbs
When a leaf quivers or a feather falls.
Suspecting your coming,
She spreads out the bed
And waits long in meditation.
Making her bed of ornaments and fantasies,
She evokes a hundred details of you
In her own graceful play.
But the frail girl will not survive
Tonight without you. 11

"Indolent Krishna" is the sixth part in *Gītagovinda*

THE SEVENTH PART

Cunning Krishna

As night came
The mood displayed cratered stains,
Seeming to flaunt its guilt
In betraying secret paths
Of adulterous women,
Lighting depths of Brindaban forest
With moonbeam nets—
A spot of sandalwood powder
On the face of a virgin sky. 1

While the moon rose
And Mādhava idled,
Lonely Rādhā
Cried her pain aloud
In pitiful sobbing. 2

The Thirteenth Song, sung with Rāga "Mālava"

Just when we promised to meet, Hari avoided the woods.
The flawless beauty of my youth is barren now.
  Whom can I seek for refuge here?
  My friend's advice deceives me. 3

I followed him at night to depths of the forest.
He pierced my heart with arrows of love.
  Whom can I seek for refuge here?
  My friend's advice deceives me. 4

Death is better than living in my barren body.
Why do I blankly endure love's desolating fire?
Whom can I seek for refuge here?
My friend's advice deceives me. 5

The sweet spring night torments my loneliness—
Some other girl now enjoys Hari's favor.
Whom can I seek for refuge here?
My friend's advice deceives me. 6

Every bangle and jewel I wear pains me,
Carrying the fire of Hari's desertion.
Whom can I seek for refuge here?
My friend's advice deceives me. 7

Even a garland strikes at the heart of my fragile body
With hard irony, like Love's graceful arrow.
Whom can I seek for refuge here?
My friend's advice deceives me. 8

I wait among countless forest reeds;
Madhu's killer does not recall me, even in his heart.
Whom can I seek for refuge here?
My friend's advice deceives me. 9

Jayadeva's speech takes refuge at Hari's feet.
Keep it in your heart like a tender girl skillful in love.
Whom can I seek for refuge here?
My friend's advice deceives me. 10

Has he waylaid some loving girl?
Do his friends hold him by clever tricks?
Is he roaming blindly near the dark forest?
Or does my lover's anguished mind so tangle the path
That he cannot come into this thicket of vines
And sweet swamp reeds where we promised to meet? 11

When Rādhā saw her friend come back
Without Mādhava,
Downcast and tongue-tied,
Suspicion raised a vision of some girl
Delighting Krishna,
And she told her friend. 12

The Fourteenth Song, sung with Rāga "Vasanta"

She is richly arrayed in ornaments for the battle of love;
Tangles of flowers lie wilted in her loosened hair.
Some young voluptuous beauty
Revels with the enemy of Madhu. 13

She is visibly excited by embracing Hari;
Her necklaces tremble on full, hard breasts.
Some young voluptuous beauty
Revels with the enemy of Madhu. 14

Curling locks caress her moon face;
She is weary from ardently drinking his lips.
Some young voluptuous beauty
Revels with the enemy of Madhu. 15

Quivering earrings graze her cheeks;
Her belt sounds with her hips' rolling motion.
Some young voluptuous beauty
Revels with the enemy of Madhu. 16

She laughs bashfully when her lover looks at her;
The taste of passion echoes from her murmuring.
Some young voluptuous beauty
Revels with the enemy of Madhu. 17

Her body writhes with tingling flesh and trembling.
The ghost of Love expands inside with her sighing.
Some young voluptuous beauty
Revels with the enemy of Madhu. 18

Drops of sweat wet the graceful body
Fallen limp on his chest in passionate battle.
Some young voluptuous beauty
Revels with the enemy of Madhu. 19

May Hari's delight in Jayadeva's song
Bring an end to this dark time.
Some young voluptuous beauty
Revels with the enemy of Madhu. 20

The lonely moon,
Like the lotus face of Mura's foe,
Wan in love's desolation,
Is calming the surface of my mind.
But the moon is Love's friend—
It still inflicts his torments
On my heart. 21

The Fifteenth Song, sung with Rāga "Gurjarī"

Her rapt face shows the passion her lips feel kissing him;
With deer musk he draws the form of a stag on the moon.
In woods behind a sandbank on the Jumna river,
Mura's foe makes love in triumph now. 22

He lays an amaranth blossom in clouds of hair massed on her soft face—
A shimmer of lightning shines in the forest where Love goes hunting.
In woods behind a sandbank on the Jumna river,
Mura's foe makes love in triumph now. 23

He smears the domes of her swelling breasts with shining deer musk,
He makes star clusters with pearls and a moonmark with his nail.
In woods behind a sandbank on the Jumna river,
Mura's foe makes love in triumph now. 24

The dark sapphire bangle he slips over each lotus-petal hand
Encircles her arm's cool pale supple stalk like a swarm of bees.
In woods behind a sandbank on the Jumna river,
Mura's foe makes love in triumph now. 25

Her broad hips are a temple of passion holding Love's golden throne;
He lays a girdle of gemstones there to mark the gate of triumph.
In woods behind a sandbank on the Jumna river,
Mura's foe makes love in triumph now. 26

He applies a shining coat of lac to feet lying on his heart
Like tender shoots tipped with pearls to honor Lakṣmī's place inside.
  In woods behind a sandbank on the Jumna river,
  Mura's foe makes love in triumph now. 27

While Balarāma's fickle brother is delighting some pretty girl,
Why does barren disgust haunt my bower of branches, tell me friend?
  In woods behind a sandbank on the Jumna river,
  Mura's foe makes love in triumph now. 28

Jayadeva, king of poets, echoes Hari's merit in the mood of his song.
Let evil dark-age rhythms cease at the feet of Madhu's foe!
  In woods behind a sandbank on the Jumna river,
  Mura's foe makes love in triumph now. 29

Friend, if the pitiless rogue won't come,
Why should it pain my messenger?
He wantonly delights in loving many women.
Why is this your fault?
See! His tenderness in love
Draws my heart to meet him.
It is trying to break away
From the pain of longing for him. 30

The Sixteenth Song, sung with Rāga "Deśākhya"

His eyes flirt like blue night lilies in the wind.
The bed of tender shoots won't burn her.
  Wildflower-garlanded Krishna
  Caresses her, friend. 31

His soft mouth moves like an open lotus.
Arrows of love won't wound her.
  Wildflower-garlanded Krishna
  Caresses her, friend. 32

His mellow speech is elixir of honey.
Sandal mountain winds won't scorch her.
  Wildflower-garlanded Krishna
  Caresses her, friend. 33

His hands and feet gleam like hibiscus blossoms.
Cold moon rays won't make her writhe.
  Wildflower-garlanded Krishna
  Caresses her, friend. 34

His color deepens like rain-heavy thunderheads.
Long desertion won't tear at her heart.
  Wildflower-garlanded Krishna
  Caresses her, friend. 35

His bright cloth shines gold on black touchstone.
Her servants' teasing won't make her sigh.
Wildflower-garlanded Krishna
Caresses her, friend. 36

His tender youth touches all creatures.
She won't feel the pain of terrible pity.
Wildflower-garlanded Krishna
Caresses her, friend. 37

Through words that Jayadeva sings
May Hari possess your heart!
Wildflower-garlanded Krishna
Caresses her, friend. 38

Sandalwood mountain wind,
As you blow southern breezes
To spread the bliss of love,
Soothe me! End the paradox!
Lifebreath of the world,
If you bring me Mādhava
For a moment,
You may take my life! 39

Friends are hostile,
Cool wind is like fire,
Moon nectar is poison,
Krishna torments me in my heart.
But even when he is cruel
I am forced to take him back.
Women with night-lily eyes feel love
In a paradox of passion-bound infinity. 40

Command my torment, sandal mountain wind!
Take my lifebreath with arrows, Love!
I will not go home for refuge again!
Jumna river, sister of Death,
Why should you be kind?
Drown my limbs with waves!
Let my body's burning be quenched! 41

"Cunning Krishna" is the seventh part in *Gītagovinda*

THE EIGHTH PART

Abashed Krishna

After struggling through the night,
She seemed wasted by the arrows of love.
She denounced her lover bitterly
As he bowed before her, pleading forgiveness. 1

The Seventeenth Song, sung with Rāga "Bhairavī"

Bloodshot from a sleepless night of passion, listless now,
Your eyes express the mood of awakened love.
Damn you, Mādhava! Go! Keśava, leave me!
Don't plead your lies with me!
Go after her, Krishna!
She will ease your despair. 2

Dark from kissing her kohl-blackened eyes,
At dawn your lips match your body's color, Krishna.
Damn you, Mādhava! Go! Keśava, leave me!
Don't plead your lies with me!
Go after her, Krishna!
She will ease your despair. 3

Etched with scratches of sharp nails in the battle of love,
Your body tells the triumph of passion in gold writing on sapphire.
Damn you, Mādhava! Go! Keśava, leave me!
Don't plead your lies with me!
Go after her, Krishna!
She will ease your despair. 4

Drops of red lac from her lotus feet wet your sublime breast.
They force buds from the tree of love to bloom on your skin.
  Damn you, Mādhava! Go! Keśava, leave me!
  Don't plead your lies with me!
  Go after her, Krishna!
  She will ease your despair. 5

The teethmark she left on your lip creates anguish in my heart.
Why does it evoke the union of your body with mine now?
  Damn you, Mādhava! Go! Keśava, leave me!
  Don't plead your lies with me!
  Go after her, Krishna!
  She will ease your despair. 6

Dark Krishna, your heart must be baser black than your skin.
How can you deceive a faithful creature tortured by fevers of Love?
  Damn you, Mādhava! Go! Keśava, leave me!
  Don't plead your lies with me!
  Go after her, Krishna!
  She will ease your despair. 7

Why am I shocked that you roam in the woods to consume weak girls?
The fate of Pūtanā shows your cruel childhood bent for killing women.
  Damn you, Mādhava! Go! Keśava, leave me!
  Don't plead your lies with me!
  Go after her, Krishna!
  She will ease your despair. 8

Jayadeva sings the lament of a jealous girl deceived by passion.
Listen, sages! Heaven rarely yields such sweet elixir.
  Damn you, Mādhava! Go! Keśava, leave me!
  Don't plead your lies with me!
  Go after her, Krishna!
  She will ease your despair. 9

The red stains her lac-painted feet
Lovingly left on your heart
Look to me like fiery passion
Exposing itself on your skin.
Cheat, the image I have of you now
Flaunting our love's break
Causes me more shame
Than sorrow.

"Abashed Krishna" is the eighth part in *Gītagovinda*

THE NINTH PART

Languishing Krishna

Then, when she felt wasted by love,
Broken by her passion's intensity,
Despondent, haunted by Hari's
Response to her quarreling,
Her friend spoke to her. 1

The Eighteenth Song, sung with Rāga "Gurjarī"

Hari comes when spring winds, bearing honey, blow.
What greater pleasure exists in the world, friend?
Don't turn wounded pride on Mādhava!
He is proud too, sullen Rādhā. 2

Your swollen breasts are riper than palm fruits.
Why do you waste their rich flavor?
Don't turn wounded pride on Mādhava!
He is proud too, sullen Rādhā. 3

How often must I repeat the refrain?
Don't recoil when Hari longs to charm you!
Don't turn wounded pride on Mādhava!
He is proud too, sullen Rādhā. 4

Why do you cry in hollow despair?
Your girlfriends are laughing at you.
Don't turn wounded pride on Mādhava!
He is proud too, sullen Rādhā. 5

See Hari on his cool couch of moist lotuses!
Reward your eyes with this fruit!
  Don't turn wounded pride on Mādhava!
  He is proud too, sullen Rādhā. 6

Why conjure heavy despair in your heart?
Listen to me tell how he regrets betraying you.
  Don't turn wounded pride on Mādhava!
  He is proud too, sullen Rādhā. 7

Let Hari come! Let him speak sweet words!
Why condemn your heart to loneliness?
  Don't turn wounded pride on Mādhava!
  He is proud too, sullen Rādhā. 8

May Jayadeva's lilting song
Please sensitive men who hear Hari's story!
  Don't turn wounded pride on Mādhava!
  He is proud too, sullen Rādhā. 9

When he is tender you are harsh,
When he is pliant you are rigid,
When he is passionate you are hateful,
When he looks expectant you turn away,
You leave when he is loving.
Your perverseness justly
Turns your sandalbalm to poison,
Cool moon rays to heat, ice to fire,
Joys of loveplay to torments of hell. 10

"Languishing Krishna" is the ninth part in *Gītagovinda*

THE TENTH PART

Four Quickening Arms

As night came, he approached Rādhā,
Finding the force of her anger softened,
Her face weak from endless sighing.
At dusk she stared in shame at her friend's face
As Hari stammered his blissful words. 1

The Nineteenth Song, sung with Rāga "Deśavarāḍī

If you speak, moonlight gleaming on your teeth
Dispels the dread darkness of fear.
Let your moon face lure my nightbird eyes
To taste nectar from your quivering lips!
  Rādhā, cherished love,
  Abandon your baseless pride!
  Love's fire burns my heart—
  Bring wine in your lotus mouth! 2

If you feel enraged at me, Rādhā,
Inflict arrow-wounds with your sharp nails!
Bind me in your arms! Bite me with your teeth!
Or do whatever excites your pleasure!
  Rādhā, cherished love,
  Abandon your baseless pride!
  Love's fire burns my heart—
  Bring wine in your lotus mouth! 3

You are my ornament, my life,
My jewel in the sea of existence.
Be yielding to me forever,
My heart fervently pleads!
  Rādhā, cherished love,
  Abandon your baseless pride!
  Love's fire burns my heart—
  Bring wine in your lotus mouth! 4

Frail Rādhā, even with dark lotus pupils,
Your angry eyes are like scarlet lilies.
As your arrows of love arouse emotion,
My black form responds with red passion.
  Rādhā, cherished love,
  Abandon your baseless pride!
  Love's fire burns my heart—
  Bring wine in your lotus mouth! 5

Let pearls quivering on full breasts
Move the depths of your heart!
Let a girdle ringing on round hips
Proclaim the command of Love!
  Rādhā, cherished love,
  Abandon your baseless pride!
  Love's fire burns my heart—
  Bring wine in your lotus mouth! 6

Your hibiscus-blossom foot colors my heart
As your beauty fills the stage of love.
Speak, soft voiced Rādhā! Let me dye your feet
With the rich liquid of gleaming red lac!
  Rādhā, cherished love,
  Abandon your baseless pride!
  Love's fire burns my heart—
  Bring wine in your lotus mouth! 7

Place your foot on my head—
A sublime flower destroying poison of love!
Let your foot quell the harsh sun
Burning its fiery form in me to torment Love.
  Rādhā, cherished love,
  Abandon your baseless pride!
  Love's fire burns my heart—
  Bring wine in your lotus mouth! 8

This graceful loving coaxing
Mura's foe spoke to Rādhikā
Triumphs in the joy Jayadeva sings
To delight his muse Padmāvatī.
  Rādhā, cherished love,
  Abandon your baseless pride!
  Love's fire burns my heart—
  Bring wine in your lotus mouth! 9

Fretful Rādhā, don't suspect me!
A rival has no place
When your voluptuous breasts and hips
Always occupy my heart.
Only the ghost of Love is potent enough
To penetrate my subtle core.
When I start to press your heavy breasts,
Fulfill our destined rite! 10

Punish me, lovely fool!
Bite me with your cruel teeth!
Chain me with your creeper arms!
Crush me with your hard breasts!
Angry goddess, don't weaken with joy!
Let Love's despised arrows
Pierce me to sap my life's power! 11

Your useless silence tortures me, frail Rādhā.
Sing sweet lyrics in the mode of love!
Tender girl, destroy my pain with your eyes!
Beautiful Rādhā, don't be indifferent!
Don't elude me! I am deeply devoted to you.
Lovely fool, I am here as your lover. 12

Your moist lips glow
Like crimson autumn blossoms;
The skin of your cheek
Is a honey-colored flower.
Fierce Rādhā, your eyes glower
Like gleaming dark lotuses;
Your nose is a sesame flower;
Your teeth are white jasmine.
Love's flower arms conquer worlds
By worshipping your face. 13

Your eyes are lazy with wine, like Madālasā.
Your face glows like the moonlight nymph Indumatī.
Your gait pleases every creature, like Manoramā.
Your thighs are plantains in motion, like Rambhā.
Your passion is the mystic rite of Kalāvatī.
Your brows form the sensual line of Citralekhā.
Frail Rādhā, as you walk on earth,
You bear the young beauty of heavenly nymphs. 14

"Four Quickening Arms" is the tenth part in *Gītagovinda*

THE ELEVENTH PART

Blissful Krishna

Soothing Rādhā with his pleas,
Keśava dressed elaborately
And went to lie on his thicket bed.
As night fell to blind prying eyes,
Rādhā dressed in gleaming ornaments
And one woman urged her to move quickly. 1

The Twentieth Song, sung with Rāga "Vasanta"

He made himself soothe you with flattery.
He made himself fall limp at your feet.
Now he waits for sensual play in his bed
On a bank of sweet swamp reeds.
Madhu's tormentor
Is faithful to you, fool.
Follow him, Rādhikā! 2

Your full hips and breasts are heavy to bear.
Approach with anklets ringing!
Their sound inspires lingering feet.
Run with the gait of a wild goose!
Madhu's tormentor
Is faithful to you, fool.
Follow him, Rādhikā! 3

Listen to enticing sounds of honey bees
Buzzing to bewilder tender women!
Sympathize when a flock of cuckoos
Sing Love's commands like bards.
Madhu's tormentor
Is faithful to you, fool.
Follow him, Rādhikā! 4

A mass of vines with thickly clustered shoots
Quivering in the wind like a hand
Seems to be gesturing to your tapering thighs
To quicken your pace. Stop loitering here!
Madhu's tormentor
Is faithful to you, fool.
Follow him, Rādhikā! 5

Strong waves of love throbbing in you
Suggest that you feel Hari's embrace.
Ask your rounded breasts if they wear
Seductive pearls or drops of pure water!
Madhu's tormentor
Is faithful to you, fool.
Follow him, Rādhikā! 6

Your friends know your armed body is ready
For passionate battle, fierce Rādhā,
By the war-drum beat of your clanging girdle.
Meet his rich mood without shame!
Madhu's tormentor
Is faithful to you, fool.
Follow him, Rādhikā! 7

As you cling to your friend in graceful play,
Nails on your hand are arrows of love—
Let your ringing bangles go to him!
Wake Hari! Claim his intimacy!
Madhu's tormentor
Is faithful to you, fool.
Follow him, Rādhikā! 8

Jayadeva's singing devalues necklaces;
It solves the paradox of beauty.
May it always adorn the throats
Of men who devote their hearts to Hari!
Madhu's tormentor
Is faithful to you, fool.
Follow him, Rādhikā! 9

"She will look at me, tell me a tale of love,
Feel pleasure in every limb from my embraces,
Delight in meeting me, friend," he says anxiously.
Your lover looks for you, trembles, bristles,
Rejoices, sweats, advances, falls faint
In the thicket buried in darkness. 10

Night is putting black kohl on their eyes,
Tamāla-flower clusters on their ears,
Dark lotus wreaths on their heads,
Leaf designs of musk on their breasts.
In every thicket, friend,
The night's dark cherished cloak
Embraces limbs of beautiful adulteresses
Whose hearts rush to meet their lovers. 11

As saffron-bright bodies
Of women rushing to meet lovers
Streak the night
With clusters of light,
Night spreads darkness as dense
As tamāla leaves,
Making a touchstone
To test the gold of love. 12

Seeing Hari light the deep thicket
With brilliant jewel necklaces, a pendant,
A golden rope belt, armlets, and wrist bands,
Rādhā modestly stopped at the entrance,
But her friend urged her on. 13

The Twenty-first Song, sung with Rāga "Varāḍī"

Revel in wild luxury on the sweet thicket floor!
Your laughing face begs ardently for his love.
Rādhā, enter Mādhava's intimate world! 14

Revel in a thick bed of red petals plucked as offerings!
Strings of pearls are quivering on your rounded breasts.
Rādhā, enter Mādhava's intimate world! 15

Revel in a bright retreat heaped with flowers!
Your tender body is flowering.
Rādhā, enter Mādhava's intimate world! 16

Revel in the fragrant chill of gusting sandal-forest winds!
Your sensual singing captures the mood.
Rādhā, enter Mādhava's intimate world! 17

Revel where swarming bees drunk on honey buzz soft tones!
Your emotion is rich in the mood of love.
Rādhā, enter Mādhava's intimate world! 18

Revel where cries of flocking cuckoos sweetly sound!
Your teeth glow like seeds of ripe pomegranate.
Rādhā, enter Mādhava's intimate world! 19

Revel in tangles of new shoots growing on creeping vines!
Your voluptuous hips have languished too long.
Rādhā, enter Mādhava's intimate world! 20

Consecrate your joyful union with Padmāvatī!
Enemy of Mura, grant a hundred holy blessings
While poet-king Jayadeva is singing!
  Rādhā, enter Mādhava's intimate world! 21

Bearing you in his mind so long
Has wearied him, inflamed him with love.
He longs to drink your sweet berry lips' nectar.
Ornament his body with yours now!
He worships your lotus feet—a slave bought
With Śrī's flashing glance. Why are you afraid? 22

Her restless eyes were on Govinda
With mixed alarm and bliss
As she entered his place
To the sweet sound of ringing anklets. 23

The Twenty-second Song, sung with Rāga "Varāḍī"

All his deep-locked emotions broke when he saw Rādhā's face,
Like sea waves cresting when the full moon appears.
She saw her passion reach the soul of Hari's mood—
The weight of joy strained his face; Love's ghost haunted him. 24

He toyed with ropes of clear pearls lying on his chest,
Like the dark Jumna current churning shining swells of foam.
She saw her passion reach the soul of Hari's mood—
The weight of joy strained his face; Love's ghost haunted him. 25

The soft black curve of his body was wrapped in fine silk cloth,
Like a dark lotus root wrapped in veils of yellow pollen.
She saw her passion reach the soul of Hari's mood—
The weight of joy strained his face; Love's ghost haunted him. 26

Her passion rose when glances played on his seductive face,
Like an autumn pond when wagtails mate in lotus blossom hollows.
She saw her passion reach the soul of Hari's mood—
The weight of joy strained his face; Love's ghost haunted him. 27

Earrings caressing his lotus face caught the brilliant sunlight.
Flushed lips flashing a smile aroused the lust of passion.
She saw her passion reach the soul of Hari's mood—
The weight of joy strained his face; Love's ghost haunted him. 28

Flowers tangled his hair like moonbeams caught in cloudbreaks.
His sandal browmark was the moon's circle rising in darkness.
She saw her passion reach the soul of Hari's mood—
The weight of joy strained his face; Love's ghost haunted him. 29

His body hair bristled to the art of her sensual play.
Gleaming jewels ornamented his graceful form.
  She saw her passion reach the soul of Hari's mood—
  The weight of joy strained his face; Love's ghost haunted him. 30

Jayadeva's singing doubles the power of Krishna's adornments.
Worship Hari in your heart and consummate his favor!
  She saw her passion reach the soul of Hari's mood—
  The weight of joy strained his face; Love's ghost haunted him. 31

Her eyes transgressed their bounds—
Straining to reach beyond her ears,
They fell on him with trembling pupils.
When Rādhā's eyes met her lover,
Heavy tears of joy
Fell like streaming sweat. 32

She neared the edge of his bed,
Masking her smile by pretending to scratch
As her friends swarmed outside—
When she saw her lover's face
Graced by arrows of Love,
Even Rādhā's modesty left in shame. 33

"Blissful Krishna" is the eleventh part in *Gītagovinda*

THE TWELFTH PART

Ecstatic Krishna

When her friends had gone,
Smiles spread on Rādhā's lips
While love's deep fantasies
Struggled with her modesty.
Seeing the mood in Rādhā's heart,
Hari spoke to his love;
Her eyes were fixed
On his bed of buds and tender shoots. 1

The Twenty-third Song, sung with Rāga "Vibhāsa"

Leave lotus footprints on my bed of tender shoots, loving Rādhā!
Let my place be ravaged by your tender feet!
  Nārāyaṇa is faithful now. Love me, Rādhikā! 2

I stroke your foot with my lotus hand—You have come far.
Set your golden anklet on my bed like the sun.
  Nārāyaṇa is faithful now. Love me, Rādhikā! 3

Consent to my love; let elixir pour from your face!
To end our separation I bare my chest of the silk that bars your breast.
  Nārāyaṇa is faithful now. Love me, Rādhikā! 4

Throbbing breasts aching for loving embrace are hard to touch.
Rest these vessels on my chest! Quench love's burning fire!
  Nārāyaṇa is faithful now. Love me, Rādhikā! 5

Offer your lips' nectar to revive a dying slave, Rādhā!
His obsessed mind and listless body burn in love's desolation.
Nārāyaṇa is faithful now. Love me, Rādhikā! 6

Rādhā, make your jeweled girdle cords echo the tone of your voice!
Soothe the long torture my ears have suffered from cuckoo's shrill cries!
Nārāyaṇa is faithful now. Love me, Rādhikā! 7

Your eyes are ashamed now to see me tortured by baseless anger;
Glance at me and end my passion's despair!
Nārāyaṇa is faithful now. Love me, Rādhikā! 8

Each verse of Jayadeva's song echoes the delight of Madhu's foe.
Let emotion rise to a joyful mood of love in sensitive men!
Nārāyaṇa is faithful now. Love me, Rādhikā! 9

Displaying her passion
In loveplay as the battle began,
She launched a bold offensive
Above him
And triumphed over her lover.
Her hips were still,
Her vine-like arm was slack,
Her chest was heaving,
Her eyes were closed.
Why does a mood of manly force
Succeed for women in love? 10

Then, as he idled after passionate love,
Rādhā, wanting him to ornament her,
Freely told her lover,
Secure in her power over him. 11

The Twenty-fourth Song, sung with Rāga "Rāmakarī"

Yādava hero, your hand is cooler than sandalbalm on my breast;
Paint a leaf design with deer musk here on Love's ritual vessel!
She told the joyful Yadu hero, playing to delight her heart. 12

Lover, draw kohl glossier than a swarm of black bees on my eyes!
Your lips kissed away the lampblack bow that shoots arrows of Love.
She told the joyful Yadu hero, playing to delight her heart. 13

My ears reflect the restless gleam of doe eyes, graceful Lord.
Hang earrings on their magic circles to form snares for love.
She told the joyful Yadu hero, playing to delight her heart. 14

Pin back the teasing lock of hair on my smooth lotus face!
It fell before me to mime a gleaming line of black bees.
She told the joyful Yadu hero, playing to delight her heart. 15

Make a mark with liquid deer musk on my moonlit brow!
Make a moon shadow, Krishna! The sweat drops are dried.
She told the joyful Yadu hero, playing to delight her heart. 16

Fix flowers in shining hair loosened by loveplay, Krishna!
Make a flywhisk outshining peacock plumage to be the banner of Love.
She told the joyful Yadu hero, playing to delight her heart. 17

My beautiful loins are a deep cavern to take the thrusts of love—
Cover them with jeweled girdles, cloths, and ornaments, Krishna!
She told the joyful Yadu hero, playing to delight her heart. 18

Make your heart sympathetic to Jayadeva's splendid speech!
Recalling Hari's feet is elixir against fevers of this dark time.
She told the joyful Yadu hero, playing to delight her heart. 19

"Paint a leaf on my breasts!
Put color on my cheeks!
Lay a girdle on my hips!
Twine my heavy braid with flowers!
Fix rows of bangles on my hands
And jeweled anklets on my feet!"
Her yellow-robed lover
Did what Rādhā said. 20

His musical skill, his meditation on Vishnu,
His vision of reality in the erotic mood,
His graceful play in these poems,
All show that master-poet Jayadeva's soul
Is in perfect tune with Krishna—
Let blissful men of wisdom purify the world
By singing his *Gītagovinda.* 21

Bhojadeva's heir, Rāmadevī's son, Jayadeva,
Expresses the power of poetry
In the *Gītagovinda.*
Let his poem be in the voice
Of devotees like sage Parāśara. 22

"Ecstatic Krishna" is the twelfth part in *Gītagovinda*

Gītagovinda Sanskrit Text

श्रीजयदेवकविविरचितम्

गीतगोविन्दम्

॥ प्रथमः सर्गः ॥

। सामोददामोदरः ।

मेघैर्मेदुरमम्बरं वनभुवः श्यामास्तमालद्रुमैर्
नक्तं भीरुरयं त्वमेव तदिमं राधे गृहं प्रापय ।
इत्थं नन्दनिदेशतश्चलितयोः प्रत्यध्वकुञ्जद्रुमं
राधामाधवयोर्जयन्ति यमुनाकूले रहःकेलयः ॥ १ ॥

वाग्देवताचरितचित्रितचित्तसद्मा
पद्मावतीचरणचारणचक्रवर्ती ।
श्रीवासुदेवरतिकेलिकथासमेतम्
एतं करोति जयदेवकविः प्रबन्धम् ॥ २ ॥

वाचः पल्लवयत्युमापतिधरः सन्दर्भशुद्धिं गिरां
जानीते जयदेव एव शरणः श्लाघ्यो दुरूहद्रुते ।
शृङ्गारोत्तरसत्प्रमेयरचनैराचार्यगोवर्धन-
स्पर्धी कोऽपि न विश्रुतः श्रुतिधरो धोयी कविक्ष्मापतिः ॥ ३ ॥

यदि हरिस्मरणे सरसं मनो यदि विलासकलासु कुतूहलम् ।
मधुरकोमलकान्तपदावलीं शृणु तदा जयदेवसरस्वतीम् ॥ ४ ॥

मालवरागेण गीयते ॥ गीतम् १ ॥

प्रलयपयोधिजले धृतवानसि वेदम् ।
विहितवहित्रचरित्रमखेदम् ॥
केशव धृतमीनशरीर जय जगदीश हरे ॥ ५ ॥

क्षितिरतिविपुलतरे तव तिष्ठति पृष्ठे ।
धरणिधरणकिणचक्रगरिष्ठे ॥
केशव धृतकच्छपरूप जय जगदीश हरे ॥ ६ ॥

वसति दशनशिखरे धरणी तव लग्ना ।
शशिनि कलङ्ककलेव निमग्ना ॥
केशव धृतशूकररूप जय जगदीश हरे ॥ ७ ॥

तव करकमलवरे नखमद्भुतशृङ्गम् ।
दलितहिरण्यकशिपुतनुभृङ्गम् ॥
केशव धृतनरहरिरूप जय जगदीश हरे ॥ ८ ॥

छलयसि विक्रमणे बलिमद्भुतवामन ।
पदनखनीरजनितजनपावन ॥
केशव धृतवामनरूप जय जगदीश हरे ॥ ९ ॥

क्षत्रियरुधिरमये जगदपगतपापम् ।
स्नपयसि पयसि शमितभवतापम् ॥
केशव धृतभृगुपतिरूप जय जगदीश हरे ॥ १० ॥

वितरसि दिक्षु रणे दिक्पतिकमनीयम् ।
दशमुखमौलिबलिं रमणीयम् ॥
केशव धृतरामशरीर जय जगदीश हरे ॥ ११ ॥

वहसि वपुषि विशदे वसनं जलदाभम् ।
हलहतिभीतिमिलितयमुनाभम् ॥
केशव धृतहलधररूप जय जगदीश हरे ॥ १२ ॥

निन्दसि यज्ञविधेरहह श्रुतिजातम् ।
सदयहृदयदर्शितपशुघातम् ॥
केशव धृतबुद्धशरीर जय जगदीश हरे ॥ १३ ॥

म्लेच्छनिवहनिधने कलयसि करवालम् ।
धूमकेतुमिव किमपि करालम् ॥
केशव धृतकल्किशरीर जय जगदीश हरे ॥ १४ ॥

श्रीजयदेवकवेरिदमुदितमुदारम् ।
शृणु सुखदं शुभदं भवसारम् ॥
केशव धृतदशविधरूप जय जगदीश हरे ॥ १५ ॥

वेदानुद्धरते जगन्निवहते भूगोलमुद्बिभ्रते
दैत्यं दारयते बलिं छलयते क्षत्रक्षयं कुर्वते ।
पौलस्त्यं जयते हलं कलयते कारुण्यमातन्वते
म्लेच्छान्मूर्च्छयते दशाकृतिकृते कृष्णाय तुभ्यं नमः ॥ १६ ॥

॥ गुर्जरीरागेण गीयते ॥ गीतम् २ ॥

श्रितकमलाकुचमण्डल धृतकुण्डल ए ।
कलितललितवनमाल जय जयदेव हरे ॥ १७ ॥

दिनमणिमण्डलमण्डन भवखण्डन ए ।
मुनिजनमानसहंस जय जयदेव हरे ॥ १८ ॥

कालियविषधरगञ्जन जनरञ्जन ए ।
यदुकुलनलिनदिनेश जय जयदेव हरे ॥ १९ ॥

मधुमुरनरकविनाशन गरुडासन ए ।
सुरकुलकेलिनिदान जय जयदेव हरे ॥ २० ॥

अमलकमलदललोचन भवमोचन ए ।
त्रिभुवनभवननिधान जय जयदेव हरे ॥ २१ ॥

जनकसुताकृतभूषण जितदूषण ए ।
समरशमितदशकण्ठ जय जयदेव हरे ॥ २२ ॥

अभिनवजलधरसुन्दर धृतमन्दर ए ।
श्रीमुखचन्द्रचकोर जय जयदेव हरे ॥ २३ ॥

श्रीजयदेवकवेरिदं कुरुते मुदम् ए ।
मङ्गलमुज्ज्वलगीतं जय जयदेव हरे ॥ २४ ॥

पद्मापयोधरतटीपरिरम्भलग्न-
काश्मीरमुद्रितमुरो मधुसूदनस्य ।
व्यक्तानुरागमिव खेलदनङ्गखेद-
स्वेदाम्बुपूरमनुपूरयतु प्रियं वः ॥ २५ ॥

वसन्ते वासन्तीकुसुमसुकुमारैरवयवैर्
भ्रमन्तीं कान्तारे बहुविहितकृष्णानुसरणाम् ।
अमन्दं कन्दर्पज्वरजनितचिन्ताकुलतया
वलद्बाधां राधां सरसमिदमूचे सहचरी ॥ २६ ॥

॥ वसन्तरागेण गीयते ॥ गीतम् ३ ॥

ललितलवङ्गलतापरिशीलनकोमलमलयसमीरे ।
मधुकरनिकरकरम्बितकोकिलकूजितकुञ्जकुटीरे ॥
विहरति हरिरिह सरसवसन्ते
नृत्यति युवतिजनेन समं सखि विरहिजनस्य दुरन्ते ॥ ध्रुवम् ॥ २७ ॥

उन्मदमदनमनोरथपथिकवधूजनजनितविलापे ।
अलिकुलसंकुलकुसुमसमूहनिराकुलबकुलकलापे ॥ विह० ॥ २८ ॥

मृगमदसौरभरभसवशंवदनवदलमालतमाले ।
युवजनहृदयविदारणमनसिजनखरुचिकिंशुकजाले ॥ विह० ॥ २९ ॥

मदनमहीपतिकनकदण्डरुचिकेशरकुसुमविकासे ।
मिलितशिलीमुखपाटलिपटलकृतस्मरतूणविलासे ॥ विह० ॥ ३० ॥

विगलितलज्जितजगदवलोकनतरुणकरुणकृतहासे ।
विरहिनिकृन्तनकुन्तमुखाकृतिकेतकदन्तुरिताशे ॥ विह० ॥ ३१ ॥

माधविकापरिमलललिते नवमालिकजातिसुगन्धौ ।
मुनिमनसामपि मोहनकारिणि तरुणाकारणबन्धौ ॥ विह० ॥ ३२ ॥

स्फुरदतिमुक्तलतापरिरम्भणमुकुलितपुलकितचूते ।
वृन्दावनविपिने परिसरपरिगतयमुनाजलपूते ॥ विह० ॥ ३३ ॥

श्रीजयदेवभणितमिदमुदयति हरिचरणस्मृतिसारम् ।
सरसवसन्तसमयवनवर्णनमनुगतमदनविकारम् ॥ विह० ॥ ३४ ॥

दरविदलितमल्लीवल्लिचञ्चत्पराग-
प्रकटितपटवासैर्वासयन् काननानि ।
इह हि दहति चेतः केतकीगन्धबन्धुः
प्रसरदसमबाणप्राणवद्गन्धवाहः ॥ ३५ ॥

उन्मीलन्मधुगन्धलुब्धमधुपव्याधूतचूताङ्कुर-
क्रीडत्कोकिलकाकलीकलकलैरुद्गीर्णकर्णज्वराः ।
नीयन्ते पथिकैः कथंकथमपि ध्यानावधानक्षण-
प्राप्तप्राणसमासमागमरसोल्लासैरमी वासराः ॥ ३६ ॥

अनेकनारीपरिरम्भसम्भ्रम-
स्फुरन्मनोहारिविलासलालसम् ।
मुरारिमारादुपदर्शयन्त्यसौ
सखी समक्षं पुनराह राधिकाम् ॥ ३७ ॥

॥ रामकरीरागेण गीयते ॥ गीतम् ४ ॥

चन्दनचर्चितनीलकलेवरपीतवसनवनमाली ।
केलिचलन्मणिकुण्डलमण्डितगण्डयुगस्मितशाली ॥
हरिरिह मुग्धवधूनिकरे विलासिनि विलसति केलिपरे ॥ ध्रुवम् ॥ ३८ ॥

पीनपयोधरभारभरेण हरिं परिरम्य सरागम् ।
गोपवधूरनुगायति काचिदुदञ्चितपञ्चमरागम् ॥ हरिरिह० ॥ ३९ ॥

कापि विलासविलोलविलोचनखेलनजनितमनोजम् ।
ध्यायति मुग्धवधूरधिकं मधुसूदनवदनसरोजम् ॥ हरिरिह० ॥ ४० ॥

कापि कपोलतले मिलिता लपितुं किमपि श्रुतिमूले ।
चारु चुचुम्ब नितम्बवती दयितं पुलकैरनुकूले ॥ हरिरिह० ॥ ४१ ॥

केलिकलाकुतुकेन च काचिदमुं यमुनाजलकूले ।
मञ्जुलवञ्जुलकुञ्जगतं विचकर्ष करेण दुकूले ॥ हरिरिह० ॥ ४२ ॥

करतलतालतरलवलयावलिकलितकलस्वनवंशे ।
रासरसे सहनृत्यपरा हरिणा युवतिः प्रशशंसे ॥ हरिरिह० ॥ ४३ ॥

श्लिष्यति कामपि चुम्बति कामपि कामपि रमयति रामाम् ।
पश्यति सस्मितचारुपरामपरामनुगच्छति वामाम् ॥ हरिरिह० ॥ ४४ ॥

श्रीजयदेवकवेरिदमद्भुतकेशवकेलिरहस्यम् ।
वृन्दावनविपिने ललितं वितनोतु शुभानि यशस्यम् ॥ हरिरिह ॥ ४५ ॥

विश्वेषामनुरञ्जनेन जनयन्नानन्दमिन्दीवर-
श्रेणीश्यामलकोमलैरुपनयन्नङ्गैरनङ्गोत्सवम् ।
स्वच्छन्दं व्रजसुन्दरीभिरभितः प्रत्यङ्गमालिङ्गितः
शृङ्गारः सखि मूर्तिमानिव मधौ मुग्धो हरिः क्रीडति ॥ ४६ ॥

अद्योत्सङ्गवसद्भुजङ्गकवलक्लेशादिवेशाचलं
प्रालेयप्लवनेच्छयानुसरति श्रीखण्डशैलानिलः ।
किं च स्निग्धरसालमौलिमुकुलान्यालोक्य हर्षोदयाद्
उन्मीलन्ति कुहूः कुहूरिति कलोत्तालाः पिकानां गिरः ॥ ४७ ॥

इति श्रीगीतगोविन्दे सामोददामोदरो नाम प्रथमः सर्गः ॥

॥ द्वितीयः सर्गः ॥

। अक्लेशकेशवः ।

विहरति वने राधा साधारणप्रणये हरौ
विगलितनिजोत्कर्षादीर्ष्यावशेन गतान्यतः ।
क्वचिदपि लताकुञ्जे गुञ्जन्मधुव्रतमण्डली-
मुखरशिखरे लीना दीनाप्युवाच रहः सखीम् ॥ १ ॥

॥ गुर्जरीरागेण गीयते ॥ गीतम् ५ ॥

संचरदधरसुधामधुरध्वनिमुखरितमोहनवंशम् ।
चलितदृगञ्चलचञ्चलमौलिकपोलविलोलवतंसम् ॥
रासे हरिमिह विहितविलासं स्मरति मनो मम कृतपरिहासम् ॥ ध्रुवम् ॥ २ ॥

चन्द्रकचारुमयूरशिखण्डकमण्डलवलयितकेशम् ।
प्रचुरपुरन्दरधनुरनुरञ्जितमेदुरमुदिरसुवेशम् ॥ रासे० ॥ ३ ॥

गोपकदम्बनितम्बवतीमुखचुम्बनलम्भितलोभम् ।
बन्धुजीवमधुराधरपल्लवमुल्लसितस्मितशोभम् ॥ रासे० ॥ ४ ॥

विपुलपुलकभुजपल्लववलयितबल्लवयुवतिसहस्रम् ।
करचरणोरसि मणिगणभूषणकिरणविभिन्नतमिस्रम् ॥ रासे० ॥ ५ ॥

जलदपटलवलदिन्दुविनिन्दकचन्दनतिलकललाटम् ।
पीनघनस्तनमण्डलमर्दननिर्दयहृदयकपाटम् ॥ रासे० ॥ ६ ॥

मणिमयमकरमनोहरकुण्डलमण्डितगण्डमुदारम् ।
पीतवसनमनुगतमुनिमनुजसुरासुरवरपरिवारम् ॥ रासे० ॥ ७ ॥

विशदकदम्बतले मिलितं कलिकलुषभयं शमयन्तम् ।
मामपि किमपि तरङ्गदनङ्गदृशा मनसा रमयन्तम् ॥ रासे० ॥ ८ ॥

श्रीजयदेवभणितमतिसुन्दरमोहनमधुरिपुरूपम् ।
हरिचरणस्मरणं प्रति संप्रति पुण्यवतामनुरूपम् ॥ रासे० ॥ ९ ॥

गणयति गुणग्रामं भामं भ्रमादपि नेहते
वहति च परीतोषं दोषं विमुञ्चति दूरतः ।
युवतिषु वलस्तृष्णे कृष्णे विहारिणि मां विना
पुनरपि मनो वामं कामं करोति करोमि किम् ॥ १० ॥

॥ मालवरागेण गीयते ॥ गीतम् ६ ॥

निभृतनिकुञ्जगृहं गतया निशि रहसि निलीय वसन्तम् ।
चकितविलोकितसकलदिशा रतिरभसरसेन हसन्तम् ॥
सखि हे केशिमथनमुदारं
रमय मया सह मदनमनोरथभावितया सविकारम् ॥ ध्रुवम् ॥ ११ ॥

प्रथमसमागमलज्जितया पटुचाटुशतैरनुकूलम् ।
मृदुमधुरस्मितभाषितया शिथिलीकृतजघनदुकूलम् ॥ सखि० ॥ १२ ॥

किसलयशयननिवेशितया चिरमुरसि ममैव शयानम् ।
कृतपरिरम्भणचुम्बनया परिरभ्य कृताधरपानम् ॥ सखि० ॥ १३ ॥

अलसनिमीलितलोचनया पुलकावलिललितकपोलम् ।
श्रमजलसकलकलेवरया वरमदनमदादतिलोलम् ॥ सखि० ॥ १४ ॥

कोकिलकलरवकूजितया जितमनसिजतन्त्रविचारम् ।
श्लथकुसुमाकुलकुन्तलया नखलिखितघनस्तनभारम् ॥ सखि० ॥ १५ ॥

चरणरणितमणिनूपुरया परिपूरितसुरतवितानम् ।
मुखरविशृङ्खलमेखलया सकचग्रहचुम्बनदानम् ॥ सखि० ॥ १६ ॥

रतिसुखसमयरसालसया दरमुकुलितनयनसरोजम् ।
निःसहनिपतिततनुलतया मधुसूदनमुदितमनोजम् ॥ सखि० ॥ १७ ॥

श्रीजयदेवभणितमिदमतिशयमधुरिपुनिधुवनशीलम् ।
सुखमुत्कण्ठितगोपवधूकथितं वितनोतु सलीलम् ॥ सखि० ॥ १८ ॥

हस्तस्रस्तविलासवंशमनृजुभ्रूवल्लिमद्बल्लवी-
वृन्दोत्सारिदिगन्तवीक्षितमतिस्वेदार्द्रगण्डस्थलम् ।
मामुद्वीक्ष्य विलक्षितं स्मितसुधामुग्धाननं कानने
गोविन्दं व्रजसुन्दरीगणवृतं पश्यामि हृष्यामि च ॥ १९ ॥

दुरालोकस्तोकस्तबकनवकाशोकलतिका-
विकासः कासारोपवनपवनोऽपि व्यथयति ।
अपि भ्राम्यद्भृङ्गीरणितरमणीया न मुकुल-
प्रसूतिश्चूतानां सखि शिखरिणीयं सुखयति ॥ २० ॥

इति श्रीगीतगोविन्दे अक्लेशकेशवो नाम द्वितीयः सर्गः ॥

॥ तृतीयः सर्गः ॥

। मुग्धमधुसूदनः ।

कंसारिरपि संसारवासनाबन्धशृङ्खलाम् ।
राधामाधाय हृदये तत्याज व्रजसुन्दरीः ॥ १ ॥

इतस्ततस्तामनुसृत्य राधिकामनङ्गबाणव्रणखिन्नमानसः ।
कृतानुतापः स कलिन्दनन्दिनीतटान्तकुञ्जे विषसाद माधवः ॥ २ ॥

॥ गुर्जरीरागेण गीयते ॥ गीतम् ७ ॥

मामियं चलिता विलोक्य वृतं वधूनिचयेन ।
सापराधतया मयापि न वारितातिभयेन ॥
हरिहरि हतादरतया गता सा कुपितेव ॥ ध्रुवम् ॥ ३ ॥

किं करिष्यति किं वदिष्यति सा चिरं विरहेण ।
किं धनेन जनेन किं मम जीवितेन गृहेण ॥ हरिहरि० ॥ ४ ॥

चिन्तयामि तदाननं कुटिलभ्रु कोपभरेण ।
शोणपद्ममिवोपरि भ्रमताकुलं भ्रमरेण ॥ हरिहरि० ॥ ५ ॥

तामहं हृदि संगतामनिशं भृशं रमयामि ।
किं वनेऽनुसरामि तामिह किं वृथा विलपामि ॥ हरिहरि० ॥ ६ ॥

तन्वि खिन्नमसूयया हृदयं तवाकलयामि ।
तन्न वेद्मि कुतो गतासि न तेन तेऽनुनयामि ॥ हरिहरि० ॥ ७ ॥

दृश्यसे पुरतो गतागतमेव मे विदधासि ।
किं पुरेव ससंभ्रमं परिरम्भणं न ददासि ॥ हरिहरि० ॥ ८ ॥

क्षम्यतामपरं कदापि तवेदृशं न करोमि ।
देहि सुन्दरि दर्शनं मम मन्मथेन दुनोमि ॥ हरिहरि० ॥ ९ ॥

वर्णितं जयदेवकेन हरेरिदं प्रवणेन ।
किन्दुबिल्वसमुद्रसम्भवरोहिणीरमणेन ॥ हरिहरि० ॥ १० ॥

हृदि बिसलताहारो नायं भुजङ्गमनायकः
कुवलयदलश्रेणी कण्ठे न सा गरलद्युतिः ।
मलयजरजो नेदं भस्म प्रियारहिते मयि
प्रहर न हरभ्रान्त्यानङ्ग क्रुधा किमु धावसि ॥ ११ ॥

पाणौ मा कुरु चूतसायकममुं मा चापमारोपय
क्रीडानिर्जितविश्व मूर्छितजनाघातेन किं पौरुषम् ।
तस्या एव मृगीदृशो मनसिजप्रेङ्खत्कटाक्षाशुग-
श्रेणीजर्जरितं मनागपि मनो नाद्यापि संधुक्षते ॥ १२ ॥

भ्रूचापे निहितः कटाक्षविशिखो निर्मातु मर्मव्यथां
श्यामात्मा कुटिलः करोतु कबरीभारोऽपि मारोद्यमम् ।
मोहं तावदयं च तन्वि तनुतां बिम्बाधरो रागवान्
सद्वृत्तस्तनमण्डलस्तव कथं प्राणैर्मम क्रीडति ॥ ॥ १३ ॥

तानि स्पर्शसुखानि ते च तरलाः स्निग्धा दृशोर्विभ्रमास्
तद्वक्त्राम्बुजसौरभं स च सुधास्यन्दी गिरां वक्रिमा ।
सा बिम्बाधरमाधुरीति विषयासङ्गेऽपि चेन्मानसं
तस्यां लग्नसमाधि हन्त विरहव्याधिः कथं वर्धते ॥ १४ ॥

भ्रूपल्लवं धनुरपाङ्गतरङ्गितानि
बाणा गुणः श्रवणपालिरिति स्मरेण ।
तस्यामनङ्गजयजङ्गमदेवतायाम्
अस्त्राणि निर्जितजगन्ति किमर्पितानि ॥ १५ ॥

इति श्रीगीतगोविन्दे मुग्धमधुसूदनो नाम तृतीयः सर्गः ॥

॥ चतुर्थः सर्गः ॥

। स्निग्धमधुसूदनः ।

यमुनातीरवानीरनिकुञ्जे मन्दमास्थितम् ।
प्राह प्रेमभरोद्भ्रान्तं माधवं राधिकासखी ॥ १ ॥

॥ कर्णाटरागेण गीयते ॥ गीतम् ८ ॥

निन्दति चन्दनमिन्दुकिरणमनु विन्दति खेदमधीरम् ।
व्यालनिलयमिलनेन गरलमिव कलयति मलयसमीरम् ॥
सा विरहे तव दीना
माधव मनसिजविशिखभयादिव भावनया त्वयि लीना ॥ ध्रुवम् ॥ २ ॥

अविरलनिपतितमदनशरादिव भवदवनाय विशालम् ।
स्वहृदयमर्म्मणि वर्म करोति सजलनलिनीदलजालम् ॥ सा वि० ॥ ३ ॥

कुसुमविशिखशरतल्पमनल्पविलासकलाकमनीयम् ।
व्रतमिव तव परिरम्भसुखाय करोति कुसुमशयनीयम् ॥ सा वि० ॥ ४ ॥

वहति च गलितविलोचनजलभरमाननकमलमुदारम् ।
विधुमिव विकटविधुन्तुददन्तदलनगलितामृतधारम् ॥ सा वि० ॥ ५ ॥

विलिखति रहसि कुरङ्गमदेन भवन्तमसमशरभूतम् ।
प्रणमति मकरमधो विनिधाय करे च शरं नवचूतम् ॥ सा वि० ॥ ६ ॥

प्रतिपदमिदमपि निगदति माधव तव चरणे पतिताहम् ।
त्वयि विमुखे मयि सपदि सुधानिधिरपि तनुते तनुदाहम् ॥ सा वि० ॥ ७ ॥

ध्यानलयेन पुरः परिकल्प्य भवन्तमतीव दुरापम् ।
विलपति हसति विषीदति रोदिति चञ्चति मुञ्चति तापम् ॥ सा वि० ॥ ८ ॥

श्रीजयदेवभणितमिदमधिकं यदि मनसा नटनीयम् ।
हरिविरहाकुलबल्लवयुवतिसखीवचनं पठनीयम् ॥ सा वि० ॥ ९ ॥

आवासो विपिनायते प्रियसखीमालापि जालायते
तापोऽपि श्वसितेन दावदहनज्वालाकलापायते ।
सापि त्वद्विरहेण हन्त हरिणीरूपायते हा कथं
कन्दर्पोऽपि यमायते विरचयञ्शार्दूलविक्रीडितम् ॥ १० ॥

॥ देशाख्यरागेण गीयते ॥ गीतम् ९ ॥

स्तनविनिहितमपि हारमुदारम् ।
सा मनुते कृशतनुरतिभारम् ॥
राधिका विरहे तव केशव ॥ ध्रुवम् ॥ ११ ॥

सरसमसृणमपि मलयजपङ्कम् ।
पश्यति विषमिव वपुषि सशङ्कम् ॥ राधिका० ॥ १२ ॥

श्वसितपवनमनुपमपरिणाहम् ।
मदनदहनमिव वहति सदाहम् ॥ राधिका० ॥ १३ ॥

दिशि दिशि किरति सजलकणजालम् ।
नयननलिनमिव विगलितनालम् ॥ राधिका० ॥ १४ ॥

नयनविषयमपि किसलयतल्पम् ।
कलयति विहितहुताशविकल्पम् ॥ राधिका० ॥ १५ ॥

त्यजति न पाणितलेन कपोलम् ।
बालशशिनमिव सायमलोलम् ॥ राधिका० ॥ १६ ॥

हरिरिति हरिरिति जपति सकामम् ।
विरहविहितमरणेव निकामम् ॥ राधिका० ॥ १७ ॥

श्रीजयदेवभणितमिति गीतम् ।
सुखयतु केशवपदमुपनीतम् ॥ राधिका० ॥ १८ ॥

सा रोमाञ्चति सीत्करोति विलपत्युत्कम्पते ताम्यति
ध्यायत्युद्भ्रमति प्रमीलति पतत्युद्याति मूर्च्छत्यपि ।
एतावत्यतनुज्वरे वरतनुर्जीवेन्न किं ते रसात्
स्वर्वैद्यप्रतिम प्रसीदसि यदि त्यक्तोऽन्यथा नान्तकः ॥ १९ ॥

स्मरातुरां दैवतवैद्यहृद्य त्वदङ्गसङ्गामृतमात्रसाध्याम् ।
विमुक्तबाधां कुरुषे न राधामुपेन्द्र वज्रादपि दारुणोऽसि ॥ २० ॥

कन्दर्पज्वरसंज्वरातुरतनोराश्चर्यमस्याश्चिरं
चेतश्चन्दनचन्द्रमःकमलिनीचिन्तासु संताम्यति ।
किंतु क्लान्तिवशेन शीतलतनुं त्वामेकमेव प्रियं
ध्यायन्ती रहसि स्थिता कथमपि क्षीणा क्षणं प्राणिति ॥ २१ ॥

क्षणमपि विरहः पुरा न सेहे
नयननिमीलनखिन्नया यया ते ।
श्वसिति कथमसौ रसालशाखां
चिरविरहेण विलोक्य पुष्पिताग्राम् ॥ २२ ॥

इति श्रीगीतगोविन्दे स्निग्धमाधवो नाम चतुर्थः सर्गः ॥

॥ पञ्चमः सर्गः ॥

। साकांक्षपुण्डरीकाक्षः ।

अहमिह निवसामि याहि राधाम्
अनुनय मद्वचनेन चानयेथाः ।
इति मधुरिपुणा सखी नियुक्ता
स्वयमिदमेत्य पुनर्जगाद राधाम् ॥ १ ॥

॥ देशवराडीरागेण गीयते ॥ गीतम् १० ॥

वहति मलयसमीरे मदनमुपनिधाय ।
स्फुटति कुसुमनिकरे विरहिहृदयदलनाय ॥
तव विरहे वनमाली सखि सीदति ॥ ध्रुवम् ॥ २ ॥

दहति शिशिरमयूखे मरणमनुकरोति ।
पतति मदनविशिखे विलपति विकलतरोऽति ॥ तव वि० ॥ ३ ॥

ध्वनति मधुपसमूहे श्रवणमपिदधाति ।
मनसि वलितविरहे निशि निशि रुजमुपयाति ॥ तव वि० ॥ ४ ॥

वसति विपिनविताने त्यजति ललितधाम ।
लुठति धरणिशयने बहु विलपति तव नाम ॥ तव वि० ॥ ५ ॥

भणति कविजयदेवे विरहिविलसितेन ।
मनसि रभसविभवे हरिरुदयतु सुकृतेन ॥ तव वि० ॥ ६ ॥

पूर्वं यत्र समं त्वया रतिपतेरासादिताः सिद्धयस्
तस्मिन्नेव निकुञ्जमन्मथमहातीर्थे पुनर्माधवः ।
ध्यायंस्त्वामनिशं जपन्नपि तवैवालापमन्त्रावलीं
भूयस्त्वत्कुचकुम्भनिर्भरपरीरम्भामृतं वाञ्छति ॥ ७ ॥

॥ गुर्जरीरागेण गीयते ॥ गीतम् ११ ॥

रतिसुखसारे गतमभिसारे मदनमनोहरवेशम् ।
न कुरु नितम्बिनि गमनविलम्बनमनुसर तं हृदयेशम् ॥
धीरसमीरे यमुनातीरे वसति वने वनमाली ॥ ध्रुवम् ॥ ८ ॥

नामसमेतं कृतसंकेतं वादयते मृदुवेणुम् ।
बहु मनुते ननु ते तनुसंगतपवनचलितमपि रेणुम् ॥ धीर० ॥ ९ ॥

पतति पतत्रे विचलति पत्रे शङ्कितभवदुपयानम् ।
रचयति शयनं सचकितनयनं पश्यति तव पन्थानम् ॥ धीर० ॥ १० ॥

मुखरमधीरं त्यज मञ्जीरं रिपुमिव केलिसुलोलम् ।
चल सखि कुञ्जं सतिमिरपुञ्जं शीलय नीलनिचोलम् ॥ धीर० ॥ ११ ॥

उरसि मुरारेरुपहितहारे घन इव तरलबलाके ।
तडिदिव पीते रतिविपरीते राजसि सुकृतविपाके ॥ धीर० ॥ १२ ॥

विगलितवसनं परिहृतरसनं घटय जघनमपिधानम् ।
किसलयशयने पङ्कजनयने निधिमिव हर्षनिदानम् ॥ धीर० ॥ १३ ॥

हरिरभिमानी रजनिरिदानीमियमपि याति विरामम् ।
कुरु मम वचनं सत्वररचनं पूरय मधुरिपुकामम् ॥ धीर० ॥ १४ ॥

श्रीजयदेवे कृतहरिसेवे भणति परमरमणीयम् ।
प्रमुदितहृदयं हरिमतिसदयं नमत सुकृतकमनीयम् ॥ धीर० ॥ १५ ॥

विकिरति मुहुः श्वासानाशाः पुरो मुहुरीक्षते
प्रविशति मुहुः कुञ्जं गुञ्जन्मुहुर्बहु ताम्यति ।
रचयति मुहुः शय्यां पर्याकुलं मुहुरीक्षते
मदनकदनक्लान्तः कान्ते प्रियस्तव वर्तते ॥ १६ ॥

त्वद्वाम्येन समं समग्रमधुना तिग्मांशुरस्तं गतो
गोविन्दस्य मनोरथेन च समं प्राप्तं तमः सान्द्रताम् ।
कोकानां करुणस्वनेन सदृशी दीर्घा मदभ्यर्थना
तन्मुग्धे विफलं विलम्बनमसौ रम्योऽभिसारक्षणः ॥ १७ ॥

आश्लेषादनु चुम्बनादनु नखोल्लेखादनु स्वान्तज-
प्रोद्बोधादनु संभ्रमादनु रतारम्भादनु प्रीतयोः ।
अन्यार्थं गतयोर्भ्रमान्मिलितयोः संभाषणैर्जानतोर्
दम्पत्योरिह को न को न तमसि व्रीडाविमिश्रो रसः ॥ १८ ॥

सभयचकितं विन्यस्यन्तीं दृशं तिमिरे पथि
प्रतितरु मुहुः स्थित्वा मन्दं पदानि वितन्वतीम् ।
कथमपि रहः प्राप्तामङ्गैरनङ्गतरङ्गिभिः
सुमुखि सुभगः पश्यन्स त्वामुपैतु कृतार्थताम् ॥ १९ ॥

इति श्रीगीतगोविन्देऽभिसारिकावर्णने साकाङ्क्षपुण्डरीकाक्षो नाम पञ्चमः सर्गः ॥

॥ षष्ठः सर्गः ॥

। कुण्ठवैकुण्ठः ।

अथ तां गन्तुमशक्तां चिरमनुरक्तां लतागृहे दृष्ट्वा ।
तच्चरितं गोविन्दे मनसिजमन्दे सखी प्राह ॥ १ ॥

॥ नटरागेण गीयते ॥ गीतम् १२ ॥

पश्यति दिशि दिशि रहसि भवन्तम् ।
तदधरमधुरमधूनि पिबन्तम् ॥
नाथ हरे सीदति राधा वासगृहे ॥ ध्रुवम् ॥ २ ॥

त्वदभिसरणरभसेन वलन्ती ।
पतति पदानि कियन्ति चलन्ती ॥ नाथ हरे० ॥ ३ ॥

विहितविशदबिसकिसलयवलया ।
जीवति परमिह तव रतिकलया ॥ नाथ हरे० ॥ ४ ॥

मुहुरवलोकितमण्डनलीला ।
मधुरिपुरहमिति भावनशीला ॥ नाथ हरे० ॥ ५ ॥

त्वरितमुपैति न कथमभिसारम् ।
हरिरिति वदति सखीमनुवारम् ॥ नाथ हरे० ॥ ६ ॥

श्लिष्यति चुम्बति जलधरकल्पम् ।
हरिरुपगत इति तिमिरमनल्पम् ॥ नाथ हरे० ॥ ७ ॥

भवति विलम्बिनि विगलितलज्जा ।
विलपति रोदिति वासकसज्जा ॥ नाथ हरे० ॥ ८ ॥

श्रीजयदेवकवेरिदमुदितम् ।
रसिकजनं तनुतामतिमुदितम् ॥ नाथ हरे० ॥ ९ ॥

विपुलपुलकपालिः स्फीतसीत्कारमन्त-
र्जनितजडिमकाकुव्याकुलं व्याहरन्ती ।
तव कितव विधायामन्दकन्दर्पचिन्तां
रसजलधिनिमग्ना ध्यानलग्ना मृगाक्षी ॥ १० ॥

अङ्गेष्वाभरणं करोति बहुशः पत्रेऽपि संचारिणि
प्राप्तं त्वां परिशङ्कते वितनुते शय्यां चिरं ध्यायति ।
इत्याकल्पविकल्पतल्परचनासंकल्पलीलाशत-
व्यासक्तापि विना त्वया वरतनुर्नैषा निशां नेष्यति ॥ ११ ॥

इति श्रीगीतगोविन्दे वासकसज्जावर्णने कुण्ठवैकुण्ठो नाम षष्ठः सर्गः ॥

॥ सप्तमः सर्गः ॥

। नागरनारायणः ।

अत्रान्तरे च कुलटाकुलवर्त्मपात-
संजातपातक इव स्फुटलाञ्छनश्रीः ।
वृन्दावनान्तरमदीपयदंशुजालैर्
दिक्सुन्दरीवदनचन्दनबिन्दुरिन्दुः ॥ १ ॥

प्रसरति शशधरबिम्बे विहितविलम्बे च माधवे विधुरा ।
विरचितविविधविलापं सा परितापं चकारोच्चैः ॥ २ ॥

॥ मालवरागेण गीयते ॥ गीतम् १३ ॥

कथितसमयेऽपि हरिरहह न ययौ वनम् ।
मम विफलमिदममलरूपमपि यौवनम् ॥
यामि हे कमिह शरणं सखीजनवचनवञ्चिता ॥ ध्रुवम् ॥ ३ ॥

यदनुगमनाय निशि गहनमपि शीलितम् ।
तेन मम हृदयमिदमसमशरकीलितम् ॥ यामि हे० ॥ ४ ॥

मम मरणमेव वरमतिवितथकेतना ।
किमिह विषहामि विरहानलमचेतना ॥ यामि हे० ॥ ५ ॥

मामहह विधुरयति मधुरमधुयामिनी ।
कापि हरिमनुभवति कृतसुकृतकामिनी ॥ यामि हे० ॥ ६ ॥

अहह कलयामि वलयादिमणिभूषणम् ।
हरिविरहदहनवहनेन बहुदूषणम् ॥ यामि हे० ॥ ७ ॥

कुसुमसुकुमारतनुमतनुशरलीलया ।
स्रगपि हृदि हन्ति मामतिविषमशीलया ॥ यामि हे० ॥ ८ ॥

अहमिह निवसामि नगणितवनवेतसा ।
स्मरति मधुसूदनो मामपि न चेतसा ॥ यामि हे० ॥ ९ ॥

हरिचरणशरणजयदेवकविभारती ।
वसतु हृदि युवतिरिव कोमलकलावती ॥ यामि हे० ॥ १० ॥

तत्किं कामपि कामिनीमभिसृतः किं वा कलाकेलिभिर्
बद्धो बन्धुभिरन्धकारिणि वनोपान्ते किमु भ्राम्यति ।
कान्तः क्लान्तमना मनागपि पथि प्रस्थातुमेवाक्षमः
संकेतीकृतमञ्जुवञ्जुललताकुञ्जेऽपि यन्नागतः ॥ ११ ॥

अथागतां माधवमन्तरेण सखीमियं वीक्ष्य विषादमूकाम् ।
विशङ्कमाना रमितं कयापि जनार्दनं दृष्टवदेतदाह ॥ १२ ॥

॥ वसन्तरागेण गीयते ॥ गीतम् १४ ॥

स्मरसमरोचितविरचितवेशा ।
गलितकुसुमदरविलुलितकेशा ॥
कापि मधुरिपुणा विलसति युवतिरधिकगुणा ॥ ध्रुवम् ॥ १३ ॥

हरिपरिरम्भणवलितविकारा ।
कुचकलशोपरि तरलितहारा ॥ कापि० ॥ १४ ॥

विचलदलकललिताननचन्द्रा ।
तदधरपानरभसकृततन्द्रा ॥ कापि० ॥ १५ ॥

चञ्चलकुण्डलदलितकपोला ।
मुखरितरसनजघनगतिलोला ॥ कापि० ॥ १६ ॥

दयितविलोकितलज्जितहसिता ।
बहुविधकूजितरतिरसरसिता ॥ कापि० ॥ १७ ॥

विपुलपुलकपृथुवेपथुभङ्गा ।
श्वसितनिमीलितविकसदनङ्गा ॥ कापि० ॥ १८ ॥

श्रमजलकणभरसुभगशरीरा ।
परिपतितोरसि रतिरणधीरा ॥ कापि० ॥ १९ ॥

श्रीजयदेवभणितहरिरमितम् ।
कलिकलुषं जनयतु परिशमितम् ॥ कापि० ॥ २० ॥

विरहपाण्डुमुरारिमुखाम्बुजद्युतिरियं तिरयन्नपि चेतनाम् ।
विधुरतीव तनोति मनोभुवः सुहृदये हृदये मदनव्यथाम् ॥ २१ ॥

॥ गुर्जरीरागेण गीयते ॥ गीतम् १५ ॥

समुदितमदने रमणीवदने चुम्बनवलिताधरे ।
मृगमदतिलकं लिखति सपुलकं मृगमिव रजनीकरे ॥
रमते यमुनापुलिनवने विजयी मुरारिरधुना ॥ ध्रुवम् ॥ २२ ॥

घनचयरुचिरे रचयति चिकुरे तरलिततरुणानने ।
कुरबककुसुमं चपलासुषमं रतिपतिमृगकानने ॥ रमते० ॥ २३ ॥

घटयति सुघने कुचयुगगगने मृगमदरुचिरूषिते ।
मणिसरममलं तारकपटलं नखपदशशिभूषिते ॥ रमते० ॥ २४ ॥

जितबिसशकले मृदुभुजयुगले करतलनलिनीदले ।
मरकतवलयं मधुकरनिचयं वितरति हिमशीतले ॥ रमते० ॥ २५ ॥

रतिगृहजघने विपुलापघने मनसिजकनकासने ।
मणिमयरसनं तोरणहसनं विकिरति कृतवासने ॥ रमते० ॥ २६ ॥

चरणकिसलये कमलानिलये नखमणिगणपूजिते ।
बहिरपवरणं यावकभरणं जनयति हृदि योजिते ॥ रमते० ॥ २७ ॥

रमयति सुदृशं कामपि सुभृशं खलहलधरसोदरे ।
किमफलमवसं चिरमिह विरसं वद सखि विटपोदरे ॥ रमते० ॥ २८ ॥

इह रसभणने कृतहरिगुणने मधुरिपुपदसेवके ।
कलियुगचरितं न वसतु दुरितं कविनृपजयदेवके ॥ रमते० ॥ २९ ॥

नायातः सखि निर्दयो यदि शठस्त्वं दूति किं दूयसे
स्वच्छन्दं बहुवल्लभः स रमते किं तत्र ते दूषणम् ।
पश्याद्य प्रियसंगमाय दयितस्याकृष्यमाणं गुणैर्
उत्कण्ठार्तिभरादिव स्फुटदिदं चेतः स्वयं यास्यति ॥ ३० ॥

॥ देशाख्यरागेण गीयते ॥ गीतम् १६ ॥

अनिलतरलकुवलयनयनेन ।
तपति न सा किसलयशयनेन ॥
सखि या रमिता वनमालिना ॥ ध्रुवम् ॥ ३१ ॥

विकसितसरसिजललितमुखेन ।
स्फुटति न सा मनसिजविशिखेन ॥ सखि या० ॥ ३२ ॥

अमृतमधुरमृदुतरवचनेन ।
ज्वलति न सा मलयजपवनेन ॥ सखि या० ॥ ३३ ॥

स्थलजलरुहरुचिकरचरणेन ।
लुठति न सा हिमकरकिरणेन ॥ सखि या० ॥ ३४ ॥

सजलजलदसमुदयरुचिरेण ।
दलति न सा हृदि चिरविरहेण ॥ सखि या० ॥ ३५ ॥

कनकनिकषरुचिशुचिवसनेन ।
श्वसिति न सा परिजनहसनेन ॥ सखि या० ॥ ३६ ॥

सकलभुवनजनवरतरुणेन ।
वहति न सा रुजमतिकरुणेन ॥ सखि या० ॥ ३७ ॥

श्रीजयदेवभणितवचनेन ।
प्रविशतु हरिरपि हृदयमनेन ॥ सखि या० ॥ ३८ ॥

मनोभवानन्दन चन्दनानिल प्रसीद रे दक्षिण मुञ्च वामताम् ।
क्षणं जगत्प्राण विधाय माधवं पुरो मम प्राणहरो भविष्यसि ॥ ३९ ॥

रिपुरिव सखीसंवासोऽयं शिखीव हिमानिलो
विषमिव सुधारश्मिर्यस्मिन्दुनोति मनोगते ।
हृदयमदये तस्मिन्नेवं पुनर्वलते बलात्
कुवलयदृशां वामः कामो निकामनिरङ्कुशः ॥ ४० ॥

बाधां विधेहि मलयानिल पञ्चबाण
प्राणान्गृहाण न गृहं पुनराश्रयिष्ये ।
किं ते कृतान्तभगिनि क्षमया तरङ्गैर्
अङ्गानि सिञ्च मम शाम्यतु देहदाहः ॥ ४१ ॥

इति श्रीगीतगोविन्दे विप्रलब्धावर्णने नागरनारायणो नाम सप्तमः सर्गः ॥

॥ अष्टमः सर्गः ॥

। विलक्ष्यलक्ष्मीपतिः ।

अथ कथमपि यामिनीं विनीय स्मरशरजर्जरितापि सा प्रभाते ।
अनुनयवचनं वदन्तमग्रे प्रणतमपि प्रियमाह साभ्यसूयम् ॥ १ ॥

॥ भैरवीरागेण गीयते ॥ गीतम् १७ ॥

रजनिजनितगुरुजागररागकषायितमलसनिवेशम् ।
वहति नयनमनुरागमिव स्फुटमुदितरसाभिनिवेशम् ॥
हरिहरि याहि माधव याहि केशव मा वद कैतववादं
तामनुसर सरसीरुहलोचन या तव हरति विषादम् ॥ ध्रुवम् ॥ २ ॥

कज्जलमलिनविलोचनचुम्बनविरचितनीलिमरूपम् ।
दशनवसनमरुणं तव कृष्ण तनोति तनोरनुरूपम् ॥ हरिहरि० ॥ ३ ॥

वपुरनुहरति तव स्मरसङ्गरखरनखरक्षतरेखम् ।
मरकतशकलकलितकलधौतलिपेरिव रतिजयलेखम् ॥ हरिहरि० ॥ ४ ॥

चरणकमलगलदलक्तकसिक्तमिदं तव हृदयमुदारम् ।
दर्शयतीव बहिर्मदनद्रुमनवकिसलयपरिवारम् ॥ हरिहरि० ॥ ५ ॥

दशनपदं भवदधरगतं मम जनयति चेतसि खेदम् ।
कथयति कथमधुनापि मया सह तव वपुरेतदभेदम् ॥ हरिहरि० ॥ ६ ॥

बहिरिव मलिनतरं तव कृष्ण मनोऽपि भविष्यति नूनम् ।
कथमथ वञ्चयसे जनमनुगतमसमशरज्वरदूनम् ॥ हरिहरि० ॥ ७ ॥

भ्रमति भवानबलाकवलाय वनेषु किमत्र विचित्रम् ।
प्रथयति पूतनिकैव वधूवधनिर्दयबालचरित्रम् ॥ हरिहरि० ॥ ८ ॥

श्रीजयदेवभणितरतिवञ्चितखण्डितयुवतिविलापम् ।
शृणुत सुधामधुरं विबुधा विबुधालयतोऽपि दुरापम् ॥ हरिहरि० ॥ ९ ॥

तवेदं पश्यन्त्याः प्रसरदनुरागं बहिरिव
प्रियापादालक्तच्छुरितमरुणच्छायहृदयम् ।
ममाद्य प्रख्यातप्रणयभरभङ्गेन कितव
त्वदालोकः शोकादपि किमपि लज्जां जनयति ॥ १० ॥

इति श्रीगीतगोविन्दे खण्डितावर्णने विलक्ष्यलक्ष्मीपतिर्नाम अष्टमः सर्गः ॥

।। नवमः सर्गः ।।

। मन्दमुकुन्दः ।

तामथ मन्मथखिन्नां रतिरसभिन्नां विषादसम्पन्नाम् ।
अनुचिन्तितहरिचरितां कलहान्तरितामुवाच सखी ।। १ ।।

गुर्जरीरागेण गीयते ।। गीतम् १८ ।।

हरिरभिसरति वहति मधुपवने ।
किमपरमधिकसुखं सखि भुवने ।।
माधवे मा कुरु मानिनि मानमये ।। ध्रुवम् ।। २ ।।

तालफलादपि गुरुमतिसरसम् ।
किं विफलीकुरुषे कुचकलशम् ।। माध० ।। ३ ।।

कति न कथितमिदमनुपदमचिरम् ।
मा परिहर हरिमतिशयरुचिरम् ।। माध० ।। ४ ।।

किमिति विषीदसि रोदिषि विकला ।
विहसति युवतिसभा तव सकला ।। माध० ।। ५ ।।

सजलनलिनीदलशीतलशयने ।
हरिमवलोकय सफलय नयने ।। माध० ।। ६ ।।

जनयसि मनसि किमिति गुरुखेदम् ।
शृणु मम वचनमनीहितभेदम् ।। माध० ।। ७ ।।

हरिरुपयातु वदतु बहुमधुरम् ।
किमिति करोषि हृदयमतिविधुरम् ।। माध० ।। ८ ।।

श्रीजयदेवभणितमतिललितम् ।
सुखयतु रसिकजनं हरिचरितम् ।। माध० ।। ९ ।।

स्निग्धे यत्परुषासि यत्प्रणमति स्तब्धासि यद्रागिणि
द्वेषस्थासि यदुन्मुखे विमुखतां यातासि तस्मिन्प्रिये ।
युक्तं तद्विपरीतकारिणि तव श्रीखण्डचर्चा विषं
शीतांशुस्तपनो हिमं हुतवहः क्रीडामुदो यातनाः ॥ १० ॥

इति श्रीगीतगोविन्दे कलहान्तरितावर्णने मन्दमुकुन्दो नाम नवमः सर्गः ॥

॥ दशमः सर्गः ॥

। चतुरचतुर्भुजः ।

अत्रान्तरे मसृणरोषवशामसीम-
निःश्वासनिःसहमुखीं सुमुखीमुपेत्य ।
सव्रीडमीक्षितसखीवदनां दिनान्ते
सानन्दगद्गदपदं हरिरित्युवाच ॥ १ ॥

॥ देशवराडीरागेण गीयते ॥ गीतम् १९ ॥

वदसि यदि किंचिदपि दन्तरुचिकौमुदी हरति दरतिमिरमतिघोरम् ।
स्फुरदधरसीधवे तव वदनचन्द्रमा रोचयतु लोचनचकोरम् ॥
प्रिये चारुशीले मुञ्च मयि मानमनिदानं
सपदि मदनानलो दहति मम मानसं देहि मुखकमलमधुपानम् ॥ ध्रुवम् ॥ २ ॥

सत्यमेवासि यदि सुदति मयि कोपिनी देहि खरनखरशरघातम् ।
घटय भुजबन्धनं जनय रदखण्डनं येन वा भवति सुखजातम् ॥ प्रिये० ॥ ३ ॥

त्वमसि मम भूषणं त्वमसि मम जीवनं त्वमसि मम भवजलधिरत्नम् ।
भवतु भवतीह मयि सततमनुरोधिनी तत्र मम हृदयमतियत्नम् ॥ प्रिये० ॥ ४ ॥

नीलनलिनाभमपि तन्वि तव लोचनं धारयति कोकनदरूपम् ।
कुसुमशरबाणभावेन यदि रञ्जयसि कृष्णमिदमेतदनुरूपम् ॥ प्रिये० ॥ ५ ॥

स्फुरतु कुचकुम्भयोरुपरि मणिमञ्जरी रञ्जयतु तव हृदयदेशम् ।
रसतु रशनापि तव घनजघनमण्डले घोषयतु मन्मथनिदेशम् ॥ प्रिये० ॥ ६ ॥

स्थलकमलगञ्जनं मम हृदयरञ्जनं जनितरतिरङ्गपरभागम् ।
भण मसृणवाणि करवाणि पदपङ्कजं सरसलसदलक्तकरागम् ॥ प्रिये० ॥ ७ ॥

स्मरगरलखण्डनं मम शिरसि मण्डनं देहि पदपल्लवमुदारम् ।
ज्वलति मयि दारुणो मदनकदनारुणो हरतु तदुपाहितविकारम् ॥ प्रिये० ॥ ८ ॥

इति चटुलचाटुपटुचारु मुरवैरिणो राधिकामधि वचनजातम् ।
जयति पद्मावतीरमणजयदेवकविभारतीभणितमतिशातम् ॥ प्रिये० ॥ ९ ॥

परिहर कृतातङ्के शङ्कां त्वया सततं घन-
स्तनजघनयाक्रान्ते स्वान्ते परानवकाशिनि ।
विशति वितनोरन्यो धन्यो न कोऽपि ममान्तरं
स्तनभरपरीरम्भारम्भे विधेहि विधेयताम् ॥ १० ॥

मुग्धे विधेहि मयि निर्दयदन्तदंश-
दोर्वल्लिबन्धनिबिडस्तनपीडनानि ।
चण्डि त्वमेव मुदमञ्च न पञ्चबाण-
चण्डालकाण्डदलनादसवः प्रयान्तु ॥ ११ ॥

व्यथयति वृथा मौनं तन्वि प्रपञ्चय पञ्चमं
तरुणि मधुरालापैस्तापं विनोदय दृष्टिभिः ।
सुमुखि विमुखीभावं तावद्विमुञ्च न मुञ्च मां
स्वयमतिशयस्निग्धो मुग्धे प्रियोऽहमुपस्थितः ॥ १२ ॥

बन्धूकद्युतिबान्धवोऽयमधरः स्निग्धो मधूकच्छविर्
गण्डश्चण्डि चकास्ति नीलनलिनश्रीमोचनं लोचनम् ।
नासाभ्येति तिलप्रसूनपदवीं कुन्दाभदन्ति प्रिये
प्रायस्त्वन्मुखसेवया विजयते विश्वं स पुष्पायुधः ॥ १३ ॥

दृशौ तव मदालसे वदनमिन्दुसंदीपकं
गतिर्जनमनोरमा विधुतरम्भमूरुद्वयम् ।
रतिस्तव कलावती रुचिरचित्रलेखे भ्रुवाव्
अहो विबुधयौवतं वहसि तन्वि पृथ्वीगता ॥ १४ ॥

इति श्रीगीतगोविन्दे मानिनीवर्णने चतुरचतुर्भुजो नाम दशमः सर्गः ॥

॥ एकादशः सर्गः ॥

। सानन्ददामोदरः ।

सुचिरमनुनयेन प्रीणयित्वा मृगाक्षीं
गतवति कृतवेशे केशवे कुञ्जशय्याम् ।
रचितरुचिरभूषां दृष्टिमोषे प्रदोषे
स्फुरति निरवसादां कापि राधां जगाद ॥ १ ॥

॥ वसन्तरागेण गीयते ॥ गीतम् २० ॥

विरचितचाटुवचनरचनं चरणे रचितप्रणिपातम् ।
संप्रति मञ्जुलवञ्जुलसीमनि केलिशयनमनुयातम् ॥
मुग्धे मधुमथनमनुगतमनुसर राधिके ॥ ध्रुवम् ॥ २ ॥

घनजघनस्तनभारभरे दरमन्थरचरणविहारम् ।
मुखरितमणिमञ्जीरमुपैहि विधेहि मरालविकारम् ॥ मुग्धे० ॥ ३ ॥

शृणु रमणीयतरं तरुणीजनमोहनमधुपविरावम् ।
कुसुमशरासनशासनबन्दिनि पिकनिकरे भज भावम् ॥ मुग्धे० ॥ ४ ॥

अनिलतरलकिसलयनिकरेण करेण लतानिकुरम्बम् ।
प्रेरणमिव करभोरु करोति गतिं प्रतिमुञ्च विलम्बम् ॥ मुग्धे० ॥ ५ ॥

स्फुरितमनङ्गतरङ्गवशादिव सूचितहरिपरिरम्भम् ।
पृच्छ मनोहरहारविमलजलधारममुं कुचकुम्भम् ॥ मुग्धे० ॥ ६ ॥

अधिगतमखिलसखीभिरिदं तव वपुरपि रतिरणसज्जम् ।
चण्डि रसितरशनारवडिण्डिममभिसर सरसमलज्जम् ॥ मुग्धे० ॥ ७ ॥

स्मरशरसुभगनखेन करेण सखीमवलम्ब्य सलीलम् ।
चल वलयक्वणितैरवबोधय हरिमपि निजगतिशीलम् ॥ मुग्धे० ॥ ८ ॥

श्रीजयदेवभणितमधरीकृतहारमुदासितवामम् ।
हरिविनिहितमनसामधितिष्ठतु कण्ठतटीमविरामम् ॥ मुग्धे० ॥ ९ ॥

सा मां द्रक्ष्यति वक्ष्यति स्मरकथां प्रत्यङ्गमालिङ्गनैः
प्रीतिं यास्यति रंस्यते सखि समागत्येति चिन्ताकुलः ।
स त्वां पश्यति वेपते पुलकयत्यानन्दति स्विद्यति
प्रत्युद्गच्छति मूर्च्छति स्थिरतमःपुञ्जे निकुञ्जे प्रियः ॥ १० ॥

अक्ष्णोर्निक्षिपदञ्जनं श्रवणयोस्तापिच्छगुच्छावलीं
मूर्ध्नि श्यामसरोजदाम कुचयोः कस्तूरिकापत्रकम् ।
धूर्तानामभिसारसत्वरहृदां विष्वङ्निकुञ्जे सखि
ध्वान्तं नीलनिचोलचारु सुदृशां प्रत्यङ्गमालिङ्गति ॥ ११ ॥

काश्मीरगौरवपुषामभिसारिकाणाम्
आबद्धरेखमभितो रुचिमञ्जरीभिः ।
एतत्तमालदलनीलतमं तमिस्रं
तत्प्रेमहेमनिकषोपलतां तनोति ॥ १२ ॥

हारावलीतरलकाञ्चनकाञ्चिदाम-
केयूरकङ्कणमणिद्युतिदीपितस्य ।
द्वारे निकुञ्जनिलयस्य हरिं निरीक्ष्य
व्रीडावतीमथ सखी निजगाद राधाम् ॥ १३ ॥

॥ वराडीरागेण गीयते ॥ गीतम् २१ ॥

मञ्जुतरकुञ्जतलकेलिसदने ।
विलस रतिरभसहसितवदने ॥
प्रविश राधे माधवसमीपमिह ॥ ध्रुवम् ॥ १४ ॥

नवभवदशोकदलशयनसारे ।
विलस कुचकलशतरलहारे ॥ प्रविश० ॥ १५ ॥

कुसुमचयरचितशुचिवासगेहे ।
विलस कुसुमसुकुमारदेहे ॥ प्रविश० ॥ १६ ॥

चलमलयवनपवनसुरभिशीते ।
विलस रसवलितललितगीते ॥ प्रविश० ॥ १७ ॥

मधुमुदितमधुपकुलकलितरावे ।
विलस मदनरससरसभावे ॥ प्रविश० ॥ १८ ॥

मधुरतरपिकनिकरनिनदमुखरे ।
विलस दशनरुचिरुचिरशिखरे ॥ प्रविश० ॥ १९ ॥

विततबहुवल्लिनवपल्लवघने ।
विलस चिरमलसपीनजघने ॥ प्रविश० ॥ २० ॥

विहितपद्मावतीसुखसमाजे ।
कुरु मुरारे मङ्गलशतानि
भणति जयदेवकविराजे ॥ प्रविश० ॥ २१ ॥

त्वां चित्तेन चिरं वहन्नयमतिश्रान्तो भृशं तापितः
कन्दर्पेण तु पातुमिच्छति सुधासंबाधबिम्बाधरम् ।
अस्याङ्कं तदलंकुरु क्षणमिह भ्रूक्षेपलक्ष्मीलव-
क्रीते दास इवोपसेवितपदाम्भोजे कुतः सम्भ्रमः ॥ २२ ॥

सा ससाध्वससानन्दं गोविन्दे लोललोचना ।
सिञ्जानमञ्जुमञ्जीरं प्रविवेश निवेशनम् ॥ २३ ॥

॥ वराडीरागेण गीयते ॥ गीतम् २२ ॥

राधावदनविलोकनविकसितविविधविकारविभङ्गम् ।
जलनिधिमिव विधुमण्डलदर्शनतरलिततुङ्गतरङ्गम् ॥
हरिमेकरसं चिरमभिलषितविलासं
सा ददर्श गुरुहर्षवशंवदवदनमनङ्गनिवासम् ॥ ध्रुवम् ॥ २४ ॥

हारममलतरतारमुरसि दधतं परिरभ्य विदूरम् ।
स्फुटतरफेनकदम्बकरम्बितमिव यमुनाजलपूरम् ॥ हरि० ॥ २५ ॥

श्यामलमृदुलकलेवरमण्डलमधिगतगौरदुकूलम् ।
नीलनलिनमिव पीतपरागपटलभरवलयितमूलम् ॥ हरि० ॥ २६ ॥

तरलदृगञ्चलचलनमनोहरवदनजनितरतिरागम् ।
स्फुटकमलोदरखेलितखञ्जनयुगमिव शरदि तडागम् ॥ हरि० ॥ २७ ॥

वदनकमलपरिशीलनमिलितमिहिरसमकुण्डलशोभम् ।
स्मितरुचिरुचिरसमुल्लसिताधरपल्लवकृतरतिलोभम् ॥ हरि० ॥ २८ ॥

शशिकिरणच्छुरितोदरजलधरसुन्दरसकुसुमकेशम् ।
तिमिरोदितविधुमण्डलनिर्मलमलयजतिलकनिवेशम् ॥ हरि० ॥ २९ ॥

विपुलपुलकभरदन्तुरितं रतिकेलिकलाभिरधीरम् ।
मणिगणकिरणसमूहसमुज्ज्वलभूषणसुभगशरीरम् ॥ हरि० ॥ ३० ॥

श्रीजयदेवभणितविभवद्विगुणीकृतभूषणभारम् ।
प्रणमत हृदि सुचिरं विनिधाय हरिं सुकृतोदयसारम् ॥ हरि० ॥ ३१ ॥

अतिक्रम्यापाङ्गं श्रवणपथपर्यन्तगमन-
प्रयासेनेवाक्ष्णोस्तरलतरतारं पतितयोः ।
इदानीं राधायाः प्रियतमसमालोकसमये
पपात स्वेदाम्बुप्रसर इव हर्षाश्रुनिकरः ॥ ३२ ॥

भजन्त्यास्तल्पान्तं कृतकपटकण्डूतिपिहित-
स्मितं याते गेहाद्बहिरवहितालीपरिजने ।
प्रियास्यं पश्यन्त्याः स्मरशरसमाकूलसुभगं
सलज्जा लज्जापि व्यगमदिव दूरं मृगदृशः ॥ २३ ॥

इति श्रीगीतगोविन्दे राधिकामिलने सानन्ददामोदरो नामैकादशः सर्गः ॥

॥ द्वादशः सर्गः ॥

। सुप्रीतपीताम्बरः ।

गतवति सखीवृन्देऽमन्दत्रपाभरनिर्भर-
स्मरपरवशाकूतस्फीतस्मितस्नपिताधराम् ।
सरसमनसं दृष्ट्वा राधां मुहुर्नवपल्लव-
प्रसवशयने निक्षिप्ताक्षीमुवाच हरिः प्रियाम् ॥ १ ॥

॥ विभासरागेण गीयते ॥ गीतम् २३ ॥

किसलयशयनतले कुरु कामिनि चरणनलिनविनिवेशम् ।
तव पदपल्लववैरिपराभवमिदमनुभवतु सुवेशम् ॥
क्षणमधुना नारायणमनुगतमनुसर राधिके ॥ ध्रुवम् ॥ २ ॥

करकमलेन करोमि चरणमहमागमितासि विदूरम् ।
क्षणमुपकुरु शयनोपरि मामिव नूपुरमनुगतिशूरम् ॥ क्षण० ॥ ३ ॥

वदनसुधानिधिगलितममृतमिव रचय वचनमनुकूलम् ।
विरहमिवापनयामि पयोधररोधकमुरसि दुकूलम् ॥ क्षण० ॥ ४ ॥

प्रियपरिरम्भणरभसवलितमिव पुलकितमतिदुरवापम् ।
मदुरसि कुचकलशं विनिवेशय शोषय मनसिजतापम् ॥ क्षण० ॥ ५ ॥

अधरसुधारसमुपनय भाविनि जीवय मृतमिव दासम् ।
त्वयि विनिहितमनसं विरहानलदग्धवपुषमविलासम् ॥ क्षण० ॥ ६ ॥

शशिमुखि मुखरय मणिरशनागुणमनुगुणकण्ठनिनादम् ।
श्रुतियुगले पिकरुतविकले मम शमय चिरादवसादम् ॥ क्षण० ॥ ७ ॥

मामतिविफलरुषा विकलीकृतमवलोकितुमधुनेदम् ।
मीलितलज्जितमिव नयनं तव विरम विसृज रतिखेदम् ॥ क्षण० ॥ ८ ॥

श्रीजयदेवभणितमिदमनुपदनिगदितमधुरिपुमोदम् ।
जनयतु रसिकजनेषु मनोरमरतिरसभाववविनोदम् ॥ क्षण० ॥ ९ ॥

मारङ्के रतिकेलिसंकुलरणारम्भे तया साहस-
प्रायं कान्तजयाय किञ्चिदुपरि प्रारम्भि यत्सम्भ्रमात् ।
निष्पन्दा जघनस्थली शिथिलिता दोर्वल्लिरुत्कम्पितं
वक्षो मीलितमक्षि पौरुषरसः स्त्रीणां कुतः सिध्यति ॥ १० ॥

अथ कान्तं रतिक्लान्तमपि मण्डनवाञ्छया ।
निजगाद निराबाधा राधा स्वाधीनभर्तृका ॥ ११ ॥

॥ रामकरीरागेण गीयते ॥ गीतम् २४ ॥

कुरु यदुनन्दन चन्दनशिशिरतरेण करेण पयोधरे ।
मृगमदपत्रकमत्र मनोभवमङ्गलकलशसहोदरे ॥
निजगाद सा यदुनन्दने क्रीडति हृदयानन्दने ॥ ध्रुवम् ॥ १२ ॥

अलिकुलगञ्जनमञ्जनकं रतिनायकसायकमोचने ।
त्वदधरचुम्बनलम्बितकज्जलमुज्ज्वलय प्रिय लोचने ॥ निज० ॥ १३ ॥

नयनकुरङ्गतरङ्गविकासनिरासकरे श्रुतिमण्डले ।
मनसिजपाशविलासधरे शुभवेश निवेशय कुण्डले ॥ निज० ॥ १४ ॥

भ्रमरचयं रचयन्तमुपरि रुचिरं सुचिरं मम संमुखे ।
जितकमले विमले परिकर्मय नर्मजनकमलकं मुखे ॥ निज० ॥ १५ ॥

मृगमदरसवलितं ललितं कुरु तिलकमलिकरजनीकरे ।
विहितकलङ्ककलं कमलानन विश्रमितश्रमशीकरे ॥ निज० ॥ १६ ॥

मम रुचिरे चिकुरे कुरु मानद मानसजध्वजचामरे ।
रतिगलिते ललिते कुसुमानि शिखण्डिशिखण्डकडामरे ॥ निज० ॥ १७ ॥

सरसघने जघने मम शम्बरदारणवारणकन्दरे ।
मणिरशनावसनाभरणानि शुभाशय वासय सुन्दरे ॥ निज० ॥ १८ ॥

श्रीजयदेववचसि रुचिरे हृदयं सदयं कुरु मण्डने ।
हरिचरणस्मरणामृतकृतकलिकलुषभवज्वरखण्डने ॥ निज० ॥ १९ ॥

रचय कुचयोः पत्रं चित्रं कुरुष्व कपोलयोर्
घटय जघने काञ्चीमञ्च स्रजा कबरीभरम् ।
कलय वलयश्रेणीं पाणौ पदे कुरु नूपुराव्
इति निगदितः प्रीतः पीताम्बरोऽपि तथाकरोत् ॥ २० ॥

यद्गान्धर्वकलासु कौशलमनुध्यानं च यद्वैष्णवं
यच्छृङ्गारविवेकतत्त्वमपि यत्काव्येषु लीलायितम् ।
तत्सर्वं जयदेवपण्डितकवेः कृष्णैकतानात्मनः
सानन्दाः परिशोधयन्तु सुधियः श्रीगीतगोविन्दतः ॥ २१ ॥

श्रीभोजदेवप्रभवस्य रामादेवीसुतश्रीजयदेवकस्य ।
पराशरादिप्रियवर्गकण्ठे श्रीगीतगोविन्दकवित्वमस्तु ॥ २२ ॥

इति श्रीजयदेवकृतौ श्रीगीतगोविन्दे सुप्रीतपीताम्बरो नाम द्वादशः सर्गः ॥

॥ इति गीतगोविन्दं समाप्तम् ॥

गीतगोविन्दस्थपद्यानां सूची

Textual Criticism of the *Gītagovinda*

1 Collection of the Textual Evidence

My early work toward a verse translation of the *Gītagovinda* convinced me that the poem's complexity demanded a detailed study of its form and content in terms of the various esthetic and religious traditions in which it is embedded. Several published commentaries on the poem revealed variations in the text that demanded textual analysis. I began collecting manuscript and printed materials relating to the *Gītagovinda* in 1971, with the aid of listings in the *New Catalogus Catalogoram,* edited by K. Kunjunni Raja (Madras: University of Madras, 1971), vol. VI, pp. 26–37. The role of the *Gītagovinda* as a sacred work and its wide dissemination in the centuries following its composition encouraged me to search for early dated manuscripts in every region of the Indian subcontinent. It became clear in the initial stages of my study that textual variants do not follow the usual pattern of geographically located types.

Manuscripts and printed editions of the *Gītagovinda* readily divide into two groups, which I call the Longer Recension and the Shorter Recension. They are distinguished by the inclusion or exclusion of about fifteen *kāvya* verses, most of which are *maṅgala*-type verses occurring at the close of each of the twelve sections of the poem. Aside from this obvious divergence, the text of the *kāvya* verses and the songs has been preserved without major variations. Regional variation occurs mainly in the designation of *rāga* names. The absence of *tāla* designations in two of the earliest manuscripts is significant in relation to the randomness of *tāla* names in other manuscripts.

The Longer Recension of the text (LR) is prominently associated with the commentaries entitled *Rasikapriyā, Rasakadambakallolinī,* and *Bālabodhinī.* It is the most widely copied and printed form of the text, based on the critical excellence of Kumbhakarṇa's *Rasikapriyā* and on the importance of Caitanyadāsa's *Bālabodhinī* in Bengali Vaishnavism.

The Shorter Recension (SR) is found associated with several lesser-known commentaries, including Mānāṅka's untitled *ṭippaṇikā,* as well as *Sarvāṅgasundarī, Śrutirañjanī,* and *Rasamañjarī.* It is not widely printed, but it is represented in manuscripts from every region of the subcontinent. It is significantly represented in the earliest known manuscripts of the *Gītagovinda.* These include two palm-leaf manuscripts in the Bir Library collection of the National Archives, Kathmandu. They are in variant forms of Newari script and bear dates in the Nepali era (567 and 616) that are reasonably approximated by A.D. 1447 and 1496. A paper manuscript in Devanagari script in the library of the University of Bombay, dated *saṁvat* 1573 (ca. A.D. 1515), also has the text of the SR. A paper manuscript in Devanagari script in the Lalbhai Dalpatbhai Institute of Indology, Ahmedabad, dated *saṁvat* 1569, *śāka* 1434 (ca. A.D. 1512) is accompanied by the *ṭippaṇikā* of Mānāṅka, as is an undated paper manuscript from the collection of Pandit Bālā Shankar Bhattajī of Gujarat, which is illustrated by paintings in the Gujarati style of the fifteenth century. The readings of the four dated manuscripts form the basis of the present critical edition. They are corroborated by readings from a paper manuscript in Devanagari script of an anonymous commentary, in the collection of the Bhandarkar Oriental Research Institute, Poona, dated *saṁvat* 1557, *śāka* 1422 (ca. A.D. 1500).

More than fifty manuscripts located and examined in the Orissa State Museum in Bhubaneswar, in the Raghunandan Library in Puri, in the Bhandarkar Oriental Research Institute in Poona, in the Adyar Library in Madras, and in the Oriental Research Institute in Mysore confirm the wide distribution and integrity of SR. This primary evidence has been corroborated by microfilms and descriptive reports from the major libraries in Baroda, Varanasi, Calcutta, Tanjore, Tirupati, and Trivandrum. The earliest dated manuscripts of LR known to me belong to the sixteenth century and are associated with the commentary *Rasikapriyā*, or commentaries derived from it.

2 *Dated Manuscripts of the Fifteenth and Early Sixteenth Centuries: Basic Evidence of the Shorter Recension*

BIR. Bir Library, National Archives, Kathmandu, Nepal. Two manuscripts, in variant forms of Newari script, were chosen for study from among more than forty-five manuscripts of the *Gītagovinda* in the collection of the Bir Library on the basis of their dated colophons and old appearance. The manuscripts are listed in *Saṁkṣiptasucīpatram*, compiled by Buddhisāgara Parājuli (Kathmandu, 1963), pp. 35–36. They are briefly described in the four-volume handwritten catalog of the Bir Library.

BIR.1 No. 45 of vol. IV (complete). Examined in the National Archives and collated from a microfilm prepared at the library. The manuscript consists of 39 palm leaves, each having five lines per side. The script is called "Bhujiṁmola" in *Prācina Lipi Varṇamālā* by Pandit Śaṅkaramāna Rājavaṁśī (Kathmandu, *vikrama saṁvat* 2017, A.D. 1960), pp. 15–19. In *Indian Paleography* (English trans. of 1896 German edition, Calcutta: K. L. Mukhopadhyay, 1962), plate VI, p. 95, Georg Bühler describes this script as "Nepalese hooked characters." Bühler cites the evidence of Bendall's *Catalogue of Sanskrit Buddhist Manuscripts from Nepal* (Cambridge, 1883) that the hooked characters came to Nepal from Bengal in the twelfth century and ceased to be used after the fifteenth. It is the opinion of Theodore Riccardi, Jr., that this evidence has not been contradicted by recent research in Nepalese epigraphy. The manuscript is dated ca. A.D. 1447.

Text begins: *auṁ namo harihārāya,* followed by *GG* I.1. Text ends with a colophon: *śreyo 'stu. saṁvat 567 aśvini-kṛṣṇa-pañcamyāṁ tithau, mṛgaśira-nakṣatre, variyāna-yoge, śukra-vāsare, thva-dina-konhu, gītagovinda-saṁpūrṇa-juro. śrī-yaṁgala-deśe śrī-kailāsakūṭa-vaja-mahāpātra-śrī-udayasiṁhadevasyārthena śrī-mānīgalaka-viccha-vijayarāmena likhitam iti. śubham astu sarvadā.*

This manuscript was examined and compared with Lassen's edition by Valentini De Rigo; his notes were published in an article, "Un antico inedito del *Gītagovinda,*" *Revista degli Studi Orientali,* 18 (1940), fasc. 1, pp. 59–90. There are many mistakes and misunderstandings evident in his reading of the manuscript, which was based on photographs brought to Italy from Nepal by S. E. Formichi. Because of the similarity of the no. 5 in Bhujiṁmolla with the no. 2 in Devanagari, De Rigo reads the date as 267 and is forced into an elaborate attempt to relate the date to *Lakṣmaṇa saṁvat.*

The date in the Bir Library catalogue is given as *nepalī saṁvat* 467 (ca. A.D. 1347); however, this is not consistent with the form of the numbers in this script as they are used throughout the manuscript. The catalog error is reflected in the version of this colophon published by Luciano Petech in Appendix III of his *Medieval History of Nepal* (Rome: Instituto Italiano per il Medio ed Estremo Oriente, 1958), pp. 199–200. Petech compares this colophon with another, whose date he reads as 473, which also has the identifying phrase *śrī-yaṁgala-deśe śrī-kailāsakuṭa-vaja-mahāpātra-śrī-*

udayasiṁhadeva. He takes the problematic word *vaja* to be an abbreviation of *vaṁśaja* and translates the identification as follows: "Udayasiṁhadeva, the nobleman (*mahāpātra*) descended from the dynasty of Kailāsakūṭa in the district of Patan (Yaṁgala)." His misreading of the date makes him miss the possible connection between the *mahāpātra* for whom these *Gītagovinda* and *Navagrahadaśavicāra* manuscripts were written and the *mahāpātra* Udayasiṁhadeva, who was powerful during the reign of Jayayakṣamalla (1428–80; see Petech, pp. 160–69; cf. D. R. Regmi, *Medieval Nepal,* Calcutta: K. L. Mukhopadhyay, 1965, pt. I, pp. 425–51, pt. III, pp. 54–85).

The analysis of this colophon was done with the help of Theodore Riccardi. It was he who provided the readings of the Old Newari phrase *thva-dina-kohnu,* "on this day," and the word *juro,* "was." Both are common in colophons of Sanskrit manuscripts written in Nepal. On this basis, he suggests that the unresolved words *vaja* and *viccha* may also be Newari forms. I have tentatively accepted Petech's interpretation of *vaja* and speculate that *viccha* may be a *tadbhava* form of the Sanskrit title *vidvat,* which belongs to the copyist Vijayarāma. The manuscript is generally legible, though sibilants are notably confused; the only major omission is song 16 (VII.31–38). *Tāla* names are not given for the songs, except in a few cases, where they are written in the margins in handwriting differing from that of the original copyist. Other emendations are written in the margins in various places.

BIR.2 No. 468 of vol. I, p. 70. Examined in the National Archives and collated from a microfilm copy, obtained through the kind offices of Albrecht Wezler, from the collection of the "Nepal-German Manuscript Preservation Project," which is kept at the Library of the German Oriental Society in Marburg. This manuscript is described by Haraprasad Shastri in his *Catalogue of Palm-leaf and Selected Paper Manuscripts belonging to the Durbar Library, Nepal* (Calcutta: Baptist Mission Press, 1905), vol. I, p. 16, no. 468. The manuscript consists of 22 palm leaves, each having seven lines per side. The script is standard Newari, described in *Prācina Lipi Varṇamālā,* pp. 1–7. The manuscript is dated ca. A.D. 1496.

Text begins: *auṁ namo bhagavate vāsudevāya,* followed by *GG* I.1. The text of the *Gitagovinda* is randomly interspersed with bits of commentary which are strikingly similar to parallel passages in the *ṭippaṇikā* of Mānāṅka, suggesting that a manuscript with that commentary was the source of this copy. The readings corroborate this. *GG* XII.21 is followed in the manuscript by a song in eight verses to be sung in *lalitarāga;* it is the same as the *Gaṅgastavaprabandha* that is printed as an appendix to the Telang and Panshikar edition (Bombay: Nirṇayasāgara Press, 1899), pp. 175–76. This is followed by *GG* XII.22 and a long colophon whose significant portions read: *nepāle rasa-candra-ṣaṇmukhe* (= 616) *saṁvatsare prālikhat, chandaḥśāstrayugaṁ vidagdhakam api śrīgītagovindakam. . . . rājye śrī-jayarāyamalla-nṛpateś cintāmaneḥ prārthināṁ śrīśaure ratikelisundarakathām autsukyataḥ prālikhat. . . . śubham astu.*

Jayarāyamalla is identified by Regmi (*Medieval Nepal,* vol. I, pp. 452 ff.) as a son of Jayayakṣamalla, who is noted in the discussion of Bir.1.

BOM Bombay University Library. One manuscript was chosen for study from several manuscripts of the *Gītagovinda* in the library's collections because of its early date and the apparent independence of its readings. It was examined in the library and collated from a microfilm provided by the library. It is no. 4163 in the library listing. It is described by H. D. Velankar in *A Descriptive Catalogue of Sanskrit Manuscripts in the "Itcharan Suryaram Desai Collection" in the Library of the University of Bombay* (Bombay: University of Bombay, 1953), p. 120, no. 599. The manuscript consists of 12 folios of paper numbered 16–25, 27–28, each having seven lines per side. The script is Devanagari. The manuscript is dated ca. A.D. 1515. The *Gītagovinda* text begins following: *namo bhagavate vāsudevāya.* The text ends with a brief colophon: *śubham astu. saṁvat 1573 samaye marge śudi 9 bhaume. rāmarāmarāmarāmarāmarāmarāma.*

With the exception of song 2, whose *tāla* is designated as *māṭhatāla, tāla* names are not given for the songs. The missing folio contains the portion of the text from XI.24–33.

AHM Lalbhai Dalpatbhai Institute of Indology, Ahmedabad, Muniśrī Puṇyavijayajī Collection, no. 1428. The manuscript is incomplete, with only fragments of commentary in *sarga* 12. Collated from a microfilm provided by the institute, in conjunction with the critical edition of Mānāṅka's *ṭippaṇikā* by V. M. Kulkarni (Ahmedabad: L. D. Bharatiya Sanskriti Vidyamandira, 1965), which is based on this manuscript, designated P in Kulkarni's critical appatatus. The manuscript consists of 50 folios of paper, each having about six lines per side. The script is Devanagari. The manuscript is dated ca. A.D. 1512. Text begins: *aum namo śrīvāsudevāya.* Text ends with a brief colophon: *srīkṛṣṇārpaṇam astu. saṁ 1569 varṣe śāke 1434 pravartamāne likhitā.*

The manuscript that R. K. Majumdar describes in "A 15th Century Gītagovinda Ms. with Gujarātī Paintings," *Journal of the University of Bombay,* 6, pt. 7 (1937), could not be located through Majumdar's information that the manuscript "comes from the collection of my friend Pandit Bālā Shankar Bhattajī Agnihotri, who is a descendant from an old learned family, and who is the hereditary priest of the Kālikā Mātā temple, on Pāvāgadh Hill, to the east of Gujarat." But Majumdar's description of the manuscript and his quotes from the *ṭippaṇikā* of Mānāṅka that accompanies the text establish the relation between this manuscript and others that have the *ṭippaṇikā.*

BORI Bhandarkar Oriental Research Institute, Poona. One manuscript was chosen for study from among about thirty-five manuscripts of the *Gītagovinda* in the collection because of its early date and the apparent independence of the commentary. It was studied from a microfilm provided by the Bhandarkar Institute through the offices of Dr. H. S. Biligiri. It is no. 208 in vol. XIII, pt. I of *A Descriptive Catalogue of the Government Collections of Manuscripts Deposited at the Bhandarkar Oriental Research Institute* by P. K. Gode (Poona, 1940), p. 256. The manuscript is incomplete; it consists of 32 folios of paper, numbered 1–30, 36, 37 (folios 31–35 are missing), each having about fifteen lines per side. The script is Devanagari, with *pṛṣṭhamātras.* The manuscript is dated ca. A.D. 1500. The first leaf is worn; the legible bit of commentary begins: . . . *kadācit grāmāt. sutena saha . . . . sthānaṁ gataḥ. sa nandagopaḥ rādhikā . . . . kāraṇāt. he rādhe imaṁ kṛṣṇaṁ tvam etagṛham prāpaya.* The text ends with a colophon: *śrī. saṁvat pañcadaśa ākhāḍhādi 1557 varṣe śāke 1422 pravarttamāne. dakṣiṇāyane. śaradattau. bhādrā . . . māse. kṛṣṇpakṣe. dvitīyāṁ tithau rabudhavāsare. gau(?)rī āgrāmavāstavya. bhaṭṭadevadāsa-paṭhanārtha unnatpuragrāmavāstavya rājarāmā paramāratasya sutarāṇā. granthasaṁkhyā 1700 gītagovindaṭikā li . . . śrī. cha. śrī. cha.*

Leaf no. 30 contains commentary on *GG* X.9, and leaf no. 37 contains commentary on XI.33. There is no commentary on *sarga* 12, which suggests a close relation between this and Ahm. The commentary is a simple *ṭikā* similar in type to Mānāṅka's *ṭippaṇikā,* but its glosses and explanations are different from those of Mānāṅka. Throughout the manuscript, songs and verses are cited for reference but are not quoted in full; readings are taken from the commentary.

3 Selected Commentaries on the *Gītagovinda*

Commentaries Based on the Shorter Recension (SR)

MĀNĀṄKA The untitled *ṭippaṇikā* of Mānāṅka, who refers to himself as *mahībhuj* in the second of three verses that introduce the commentary:

kavīnaṁ matim ālokya satāṁ ca sukhabuddhaye |
kṛtā ṭippaṇikā mukhyā mānāṅkena mahībhujā ||

He does not further identify himself in the commentary, nor is there any other work clearly attributable to him. The limiting date of the commentary is fixed by the manuscript Bir.2 (ca. A.D. 1496), which contains bits of this commentary, and by the manuscript Ahm (ca. A.D. 1512). The author of the *ṭippaṇikā* is clearly different from the Mānāṅka who composed the *Vṛndāvana-yamaka-kāvya,* which is referred to by Bhoja in his *Śṛṅgāra Prakāśa* (V. Raghavan, *Bhoja's Śṛṅgāra Prakāśa,* Madras: Punarvasu, 1963, pp. 808–9).

The *ṭippaṇikā* is a simple commentary that consists mainly of glosses on individual words and analyses of compounds. The author does not identify meters or figures of speech. He does not interpret the verses and songs in terms of any discernible sectarian viewpoint. He occasionally cites lexical works like *Amarakoṣa* and *Anekārthakoṣa,* the grammatical *sūtras* called *Kātantra,* and various other works.

Mānāṅka's commentary on the controversial opening verse of the *Gītagovinda* is notable for its simple presentation of alternative interpretations:

rādhāmādhavayoḥ rahaḥkelayaḥ nirjanasthānakrīḍāḥ jayanti
sarvotkarṣeṇa vartante | rādhā kāpi gopāṅganā mukhyā |
mādhavaḥ kṛṣṇarūpī nārāyaṇaḥ | sā ca sa ca tau tayoḥ |
vyabhicarati ceti vaśāt arcitapadasya pūrvanipātaḥ |
yathā naranārāyaṇau umāmaheśvarau kākamayūrāv ityādi |
yamunā nadī | tasyāḥ kūlaṁ taṭaṁ tasmin | ādhāro saptamī |
kiṁbhūtayoḥ pratyadhvakuñjadrumaṁ calitayoḥ gatayoḥ |

adhvani adhvani prati kuñje kuñje prati drume drume prati |
vīpsāyām avyayībhāvaḥ | adhvakuñjadrumaṁ kāmukānāṁ ramaṇīyaṁ
saṅketasthānam | kasmād gatayoḥ nandanideśataḥ | nando gopaḥ
sarvābhīramukhyo yamunātaṭavṛndāvanagoṣṭhasthitaḥ san
bālakabhayahetum ākalaya dadhyādikrayavikrayādinā 'harniśaṁ
bhayahīnāṁ rādhām ādideśa | katham | ittham | itthaṁ katham |
he rādhe tat tasmād dhetor imaṁ bālakaṁ gṛhaṁ prāpaya | nītvā
gṛhaṁ gaccha | svamanovāñchitaṁ goptur kāmāntargatābhiprāyeṇa
yadi evaṁ rādhā vadati | tataḥ kasmāt | yato naktaṁ rātrāv
ayaṁ bhīruḥ bālyabhāvad atiśayena bhīta iti punaḥ
rādhāyāḥ svagatam evam | aho āścaryam etat | dinamaṇau vidyamāne 'pi
kathaṁ naktalakṣaṇam | tadāha | meghair jaladharair ambaram
ākāśaṁ meduraṁ vyāptaṁ channaṁ netrabhīṣaṇam | tamāladrumais
tāpicchatarubhir gāḍāñjanasaṁnibhair vanabhuvo 'raṇyabhūmayaḥ
śyāmā nibiḍāndhkāratulyāḥ | anena hetunā naktalakṣaṇaṁ
vināpi bālako 'jñānatvād vane bibheti | vidyamāne bhayahetau
punaḥ kim | ato mātur antikaṁ nayety arthaḥ ||

Readings are taken from the edition of V. M. Kulkarni, cited for the manuscript Ahm above. This manuscript and a Devanagari manuscript of the text and commentary in the Adyar Library (DC #1038, XXXV.C.148) were also consulted. A manuscript of the *Gītagovinda* with the commentary of Mānāṅka is codex C in Lassen's edition. Manuscripts A and B in Kulkarni's edition are cited in the variant readings from Kulkarni's notes.

NĀRĀYAṆADĀSA The *Sarvāṅgasundarī* of Nārāyaṇadāsa, who is identified as a court poet of the fourteenth-century Kalinga king Narasiṁhadeva II by K. N. Mahapatra in *A Descriptive Catalogue of Sanskrit Manuscripts of Orissa* (Bhubaneswar: Orissa Sahitya Akademi, 1960), vol. II, pp. lxx–lxxii, and in an article entitled "Sarvāṅgasundarī Ṭīkā on the Gītagovinda," *The Orissa Historical Research Journal,* 13, no. 3 (1965), 26–41. Mahapatra bases his argument on two references to a Nārāyaṇa who was the grandfather of Viśvanātha, the author of *Sāhityadarpaṇa;* see P. V. Kane, *The Sāhityadarpaṇa* (reprint, Delhi: Motilal Banarsidass, 1965), pp. iii–viii. The evidence seems inconclusive, but the author of the commentary does demonstrate a broad knowledge of Sanskrit poetry and poetics in his quotations from works like *Kumārasaṁbhava, Kāvyadarśa, Kāvyaprakāśa,* and *Sarasvatīkaṇṭhābharaṇa.* The commentary offers analyses of words and verses that do not show obvious influence from any of the other early commentaries I have examined, but the author does refer to a Dhṛtidāsa, whom Mahapatra identifies as an earlier commentator on the *Gītagovinda*. The interpretations of the word *padmāvatī,* as it occurs in the text, are quoted from Mahapatra's article, as examples of Nārāyaṇadāsa's commentary:

I.2—*atra vāgdevatetvanena kaveḥ pāṇḍityaṁ padmāvatī caraṇacāraṇetvanena lakṣmyābhaktyātiśayena dāridryāpagamaḥ* |
avaśyam kavinā dāridryopaśamāya yatanīyaṁ |
X.9—*padmāvatīramaṇañcāsau jayadevakaviścetivigrahaḥ* |
etenānyāṅganāvaimukhyaṁ jayadevakavinātmanaḥ pratipāditam |
XI.21—*vihitaḥ padmāvatyāḥ nijapreyasyāḥ sukhasamājaḥ sukhacayo yeneti vigrahaḥ* ||

A single palm-leaf manuscript of this commentary in Oriya script (L.129a) was examined in the Manuscripts Library of the Orissa State Museum in Bhubaneswar, with the help of K. N. Mahapatra. Neither a microfilm copy nor a transcription could be obtained. Another palm-leaf manuscript in Oriya script, with seventeenth-century paintings, was examined in the private collection of Kalicharan Patnaik in Cuttack. Both manuscripts begin: *śrī kṛṣṇāya namaḥ.*

sarvāṅgasundarī rādhā kṛṣṇaḥ sarvāṅgasundaraḥ |
tayor ānandajananī ṭīkā sarvāṅgasundarī ||
natvā śrī haricaraṇaṁ kurute sarvāṅgasundarī ṭīkām |
śrī nārāyaṇadāsakavirājo 'yaṁ gītagovinde ||

Two manuscripts in Bengali script (G.3522, 58 folios; G.10813, 10 folios —inc.) were located in the Asiatic Society, Calcutta, but these were not examined.

LAKṢMĪDHARA The *Śrutirañjanī-vyākhyā* of Lakṣmīdhara, also called Lakṣmaṇasūri, associated with the court of Tirumala I of the Aravidu dynasty of Vijayanagara (ca. A.D. 1567–75). In some of the many manuscripts of this commentary that are found throughout South India, the authorship of the commentary is attributed to Tirmalarāja. From an account given by Lakṣmīdhara of his own family in the introductory verses of the *Ṣaḍbhāṣacandrikā* (edited by K. P. Trivedi, Bombay Sanskrit Series, no. 71; Bombay: Government Central Press, 1916), vv. 6–13, we learn that he belonged to a family of Cerukūri in the region of the Krishna river in Andhra country. Lord Veṅkaṭa was the family deity and he was a worshipper of Śiva Dakṣiṇāmūrti. This information is corroborated by similar references in the introductory verses and colophon that are found in many manuscripts of the *Gītagovinda* commentary. For further discussion of Lakṣmīdhara and his works, see V. Raghavan "Literary Notes," *Annals of the Bhandarkar Oriental Research Institute,* 18 (1937), 198–201.

The analyses of words and verses in this commentary focus on the literary aspects of the *Gītagovinda*. Following several introductory verses, the commentary begins:

atha khalu tatra bhavān jayadevanāmā mahākaviḥ saṅgītasāhityasārasya pāradṛśvā gītaprabandhanirmāṇāpadeśena sakalapurūsārthasampādana-mandarāyamānāṁ gopikāmanoharavarṇanāṁ manasi nidhāya cikīrṣitasya śrīgītagovindādhyasya prabandhasya pracayam āśāsānaḥ

> *kāvyaṁ yaśase 'rthakṛte vyavahāravide śivetarakṣataye |*
> *sadyaḥ paranirvṛtaye kāntāsammitatayopadeśayuje ||*

ity ālaṁkārikavacanaprāmāṇyāt kāvyasyānekaśreyaḥ sādhanatāṁ kāvyā-lāpāṁś ca varjayed ity asyāsatkāvyaviṣayatāṁ ca paśyan āśīrnamaskriyā vastunirdeśo vāpi tanmukham ity āryaparivādanam anusaran kātyāya-nīsamārādhanāya kālindītaṭaṁ pratigatasya nandagopasyoktivyājena prāp-taṁ rādhāmādhavayor vihārarūpaṁ vastu kāvyabījatvena nirdiśati—meghair ityādi|

Readings are taken from a microfilm copy of a Nandinagari palm-leaf manuscript in the Mysore Oriental Research Institute, no. S1767, listed in the *Catalogue of Sanskrit Manuscripts in the Government Oriental Library, Mysore* (Mysore: Government Branch Press, 1922), p. 245. The original was compared at the Mysore Institute with a paper manuscript in Kannada script, no. C335, with the help of H. V. Nagaraja Rao, and an incomplete paper manuscript in Devanagari, no. C2188. I was informed in 1974 that a critical edition of the *Gītagovinda* with the *Śrutirañjanī* had been prepared by Dr. K. S. Ramamurti of Śrī Veṅkateśwara University Oriental Research Institute in Tirupati, but I have not been able to obtain a copy of this publication.

ŚAṄKARAMIŚRA The *Rasamañjarī* of Śaṅkaramiśra, printed with Kumbha's *Rasikapriyā* in the edition of Telang and Panshikar (Bombay: Nirṇayasāgara Press, 1899), from which readings are taken. Manuscripts of the commentary are found throughout northern India; see *New Catalogus,* vol. VI, p. 36.

Commentaries Based on the Longer Recension (LR)

KUMBHAKARṆA (KUM) The *Rasikapriyā* of Kumbhakarṇa, who is identified as a king of Mewar in the introductory verses of the commentary. Mahārāṇā Kumbhakarṇa, whose rule is dated ca. A.D. 1433–68, is also known as the author of the *Saṅgītarāja,* an encyclopedic work on the theory of music, dance, and esthetic production. The first volume of the *Saṅgītarāja* has been edited by Premalata Sharma (Varanasi: Banaras Hindu University Press, 1963). In her introduction (pp. 29–61) she critically analyzes the question of Kumbha's authorship of both works.

In the introductory verses to the commentary, especially 15–20, the author says that his purposes are to indicate the appropriate music for each song, to analyze the erotic mood (*śṛṅgārarasa*) of the work, and to illuminate the meaning of the text. There are many quotations from the *Saṅgītarāja,* mainly in reference to the musical characteristics of songs (*prabandhalakṣaṇa*). The commentary also identifies figures of speech (*alaṁkāra*), forms of the hero (*nāyaka*) or heroine (*nāyikā*) depicted, and the names of the meters. The *rāga*s and *tāla*s indicated for the songs in the commentary generally differ from those found in other versions of the text. They are part of Kumbha's effort to restructure and fix the musical performance of the *Gītagovinda.* The same effort may account for the *maṅgalaśloka* verses that are found at the end of each *sarga* in Kumbha's version of the text. These verses make small claim to composition by Jayadeva, but they may have been part of the work's performance in some version and were incorporated into the text by Kumbha.

Kumbha's elaborate analysis of the opening verse of the *Gītagovinda* includes an attack on the interpretations of other unnamed critics, a fanciful etymology of *mādhava* (from *mā,* or *lakṣmī,* and *dhava,* "husband"; see Bhaṭṭa Kṣīrasvāmin's commentary on *Amarakoṣa* I.18; Poona: Oriental Book Agency, 1941), and an abstract discussion of *ayam* as the key to the verse. Kumbha considers the first half of the verse to be the lover's speech of Krishna, not Nanda's speech about the child Krishna, which would violate poetic taste. He interprets *tad imam,* Krishna's reference to himself in the third person instead of the first person, as a sign of his lost consciousness of his own body. He glosses *nandanideśataḥ* with *nandasamīpāt,* "from the vicinity of Nanda," in contrast with the more obvious interpretations of the compound to mean "on account of Nanda's order." Kumbha glosses *padmāvatīcaraṇacāraṇacakravartī* in *GG* I.2 with *lakṣmīcaraṇasevāgraṇīḥ;* he begins his explanation: *atha padmāvatī aṣṭākṣaramantrādhidaivataṁ tasyāś caraṇacāraṇena paricaryāviśeṣeṇa cakravartī, kavirāja ity arthaḥ.* Readings are taken from the edition of Telang and Panshikar (Bombay: Nirṇayasāgara Press 1899; reprinted 1917, 1949). A microfilm copy of a few folios of a Devanagari manuscript of the commentary, dated *saṁvat* 1619, in the library of Harvard University (no. 1577) was cursorily compared with the printed text and no major variants were noted. Manuscripts of the commentary are found throughout northern India.

BHAGAVADDĀSA The *Rasakadambakalollinī* of Bhagavaddāsa, whose work is dated the latter half of the sixteenth century by P. K. Gode in *Studies in Indian Literary History* (Bombay: Bharatiya Vidya Bhavan, 1953), vol. II, pp. 146–53. References to Kumbhakarṇa in the commentary establish its basic dependence on Kumbha's text; e.g., Bhagavaddāsa, commenting on *GG* I.1, says: *tvayaivāyaṁ gṛhiṇīmāna syāt iti sakhyāguḍhaṁ parisitam iti kumbhakarṇokteḥ* (leaf 5, line 2). The reading is identical with the contents of two manuscripts in the Bhandarkar Oriental Research Institute noted by Gode, p. 150. Besides quoting Kumbha, Bhagavaddāsa analyses the poetic and devotional aspects of the poem with reference to works like *Kṛṇṣakarṇāmṛta, Bhāgavatapurāṇa, Bhagavadgītā, Nāṭyaśāstra, Daśarūpaka, Śṛṅgāratilaka, Saṅgītaratnākara, Rasāmṛtasindhu, Kāvyaprakāśa.*

Readings are taken from a photocopy of a manuscript (no. 1579) in the Harvard University Library. This has been compared in places with a microfilm copy of the Devanagari manuscript in the Oriental Institute, Baroda, serial no. 205, dated *saṁvat* 1839, listed by R. Nambiyar in *An Alphabetical List of Manuscripts in the Oriental Institute, Baroda* (Baroda: Central Library, 1950), vol. II, pp. 990–91. None of the four manuscripts of the *Rasakadambakalollinī* in the Bhandarkar Institute was available in the library on several occasions when I inquired about them.

CAITANYADĀSA (CAIT) The *Bālabodhinī* of Caitanyadāsa, also known as Pūjarī Goswāmin, who was a Bengali Vaishnava scholar living in Vṛndāvana in the latter half of the sixteenth and early seventeenth centuries. He also wrote the *Subodhinī* on the *Kṛṣṇakarṇāmṛta.* Caitanyadāsa's Sanskrit commentary follows the text of Kumbha, but the emphasis of the commentary is on the interpretation of the erotic relationship of Rādhā and Krishna as an allegory of the spiritual relationship between the human soul and the loving god Krishna. It places the *Gītagovinda* within the Vaishnava tradition of the *Bhāgavata Purāṇa,* but it recognizes Rādhā as

Krishna's consort, called *Devī* and *Kṛṣṇamayī*. The importance of Rādhā's friend in terms of the concept of *sakhībhāva* is evident throughout the commentary; e.g., the speech of the opening verse is attributed to the *sakhī*.

Readings are taken from the edition of Harekrishna Mukhopādhyāya, entitled *Kavijayadeva o śrīgītagovinda* (Calcutta: Gurudas Mukhopādhyāy, 1957, B.S. 1362); they closely follow those of Kumbha's text.

In addition to these seven outstanding commentaries on the *Gītagovinda,* note should be made of three others edited by A. Sharma, K. Deshpande, and V. Sundara Sharma (Hyderabad: Osmania University Sanskrit Academy, 1969). All follow the text of LR. The *Padadyotanikā* of Nārayaṇa Paṇḍita and the *Jayantī* of Ammaṇṇa's son, the physician, are both simple and undistinguished. The *Sañjīvanī* of Vanamālibhaṭṭa focuses on the erotic esthetics of the poem. The entire poem is interpreted in terms of the technical details of erotic literature. Even the heroic mood of each of the ten incarnations in the *daśāvatārastuti* is seen in the context of postures and gestures of lovemaking. For example, the forms of the Boar and the Man-lion (I.7, 8) are related to erotic conventions of biting and scratching; see pp. 22–25 in the Osmania edition.

4 *Previous Editions of the Gītagovinda*

Aside from the editions of the *Gītagovinda* made on the basis of the commentaries cited above, the only previous critical edition of the text is that of Cristianus Lassen, published with Latin notes and translation in Bonn in 1836. The edition is entitled *Gita Govinda Jayadevae poetae indici drama lyricum*. It is based on five manuscript codices, described on pp. xi–xiii of the Prolegomena:

A. Bengali manuscript with Caitanyadāsa's *Bālabodhinī*.
B. Devanagari manuscript, without commentary.
C. Devanagari manuscript, with Mānāṅka's commentary; read *dṛpyaṇikā* for *ṭippaṇikā*.
D. Devanagari manuscript, with Nārāyaṇa Paṇḍita's *Pādadyōtanikā*.
E. Bengali manuscript, without commentary.

Lassen bases his text on the text of Caitanyadāsa; codices D and E generally agree with it, and B and C often vary in ways that agree with the readings of the present edition.

None of the many editions I have gathered from various regions of India are critical. They are mainly reprints of the Telang and Panshikar text, with notable variation only in *rāga* and *tāla* names. In his Oriya script edition of the *Gītagovinda,* accompanied by an Oriya verse translation (Cuttack: Das, 1970), Kalicharan Patnaik uncritically conflates the text of the manuscript containing Nārāyaṇadāsa's commentary with readings from some version of LR.

5 *Secondary Evidence*

The occurrence of verses from the *Gītagovinda* in Śrīdharadāsa's anthology, the *Saduktikarṇāmṛta,* compiled in Bengal in A.D. 1205, is used to set the limiting date of the poem's composition. Among the thirty verses attributed to Jayadeva in the critical edition of S. C. Banerji (Calcutta: K. L. Mukhopadhyay, 1965), two are in all versions of SR and are in the present edition of the *Gītagovinda* (*Skm.* 659 = *GG* VI.11; *Skm.* 1144 = *GG* XII.10). Three others are also found in texts of LR and are included in the present edition as variants (*Skm.* 294 = *GG* XI.33†; *Skm.* 1134 = *GG* XII.23† [A]; *Skm.* 1160 = *GG* XII.23† [C]). Their inclusion in Kumbhakarṇa's "edited" text of the *Gītagovinda* must have been based on their attribution to the poet and some association with the *Gītagovinda* at an early date. Since none of the manuscripts Banerji used for his edition antedates the seventeenth century, the occurrence of verses in the anthology cannot be used to establish the "authenticity" of verses or readings. As noted above in footnote 5 to section 1 of the introduction, many of the remaining verses attributed to Jayadeva in the *Saduktikarṇāmṛta* show thematic and stylistic similarities to *Gītagovinda* verses.

A stone-inscription of Mahārāja Sāraṅgadeva Vāghelā of Aṇahillapattan, dated A.D. 1291 (*vikrama saṁvat* 1348), opens with Jayadeva's invocation to Krishna in his ten incarnate forms (*GG* I.16). The text is given by R. K. Majumdar in "A 15th Century Gītagovinda Ms." It varies little from the standard version of this verse. *Pada* (c) reads: *setuṁ bandhayate halim kalayate kārunyam ātanvate.* This reading is not found in any of the manuscripts of the *Gītagovinda* I examined.

One verse (*GG* III.11) is cited in the tenth *pariccheda* of Viśvanātha's *Sāhityadarpaṇa,* which is dated the fourteenth century. See P. V. Kane's edition (Delhi: Motilal Banarsidass, 1965), X. 39. This verse is found in both recensions of the *Gītagovinda,* without variation.

6 The Significance of the Critical Edition

It has already been stated that the early dated manuscripts of SR, two of which are associated with the *ṭippaṇikā* of Mānāṅka, are taken as the basis of the present edition. The independence of readings and the wide geographical distribution of manuscripts of SR by the fifteenth century suggest that this recension of the text was based on an established oral or written tradition. Minor variations in the texts of manuscripts of SR occur, both in the *kāvya* verses and in the songs. In determining problematic readings, I have generally chosen what is common to the conservative Newari manuscript Bir.1, and at least one of the other early manuscripts of SR. Where this has not been possible, I have tried to choose a meaningful reading that could best explain the variants. For details of this method and a bibliography of Indian textual criticism, see my *Phantasies of a Love-Thief: The Caurapañcāśikā Attributed to Bilhaṇa* (New York: Columbia University Press, 1971), pp. 96–175.

On the basis of available manuscript evidence of LR, it seems reasonable to assert that the fifteenth-century critic and music theorist Kumbhakarṇa "edited" the version of the *Gītagovinda* on which he based his commentary, the *Rasikapriyā.* This version was then followed by other commentaries, most notably that of Caitanyadāsa, through whose commentary the poem was "popularized" in Bengali Vaishnava circles. This accounts for the predominance of LR in Bengali manuscripts after the sixteenth century. Unfortunately, no earlier dated Bengali manuscripts have been found to test this theory, but the location of manuscripts in Oriya and Bengali script of the commentary *Sarvāṅgasundarī,* which is based on SR, suggests that a tradition of SR existed in the region.

The broad difference between the two recensions involves the inclusion or exclusion of twelve *manglaśloka* verses. The same twelve are included in all versions of LR. They are absent in versions of SR, with the exception of the *maṅgalaśloka* at the end of the first *sarga,* which is included in the manuscripts Bir.2 and Bom and in some manuscripts of the Mānāṅka *ṭippaṇikā*. Since the recension that excludes the *maṅgalaśloka* verses is the basis of the present edition, these verses are given as "variant verses" after the variant readings of each *sarga*.

I speculate that the *maṅgalaśloka* verse at the end of the first *sarga* came to be associated with the performance of the *Gītagovinda* at some time before or during the fifteenth century and that the remaining *maṅgalaśloka* verses were added by Kumbhakarṇa, or someone else, for the sake of structural symmetry. The presence or absence of the *maṅgalaśloka* verses affects the tone and movement of the entire *Gītagovinda*. The repeated invocations to Krishna, in terms that recall the standard literature of devotional Vaishnavism, seem inappropriate to Jayadeva's delineation of the relationship between Rādhā and Krishna. Although Rādhā is named in more than half of them (I.47†; III.15†; V.19†; VI.11†; VII.41†; X.14†; XI.33†), the conventional style and orthodox Vaishnava content of the verses tend to dull the intensity of her relationship with Krishna, which is central to every other aspect of Jayadeva's lyrical structure. Thus, the case for their authenticity in Jayadeva's text of the *Gītagovinda* seems weak in terms of literary analysis, as well as in terms of textual history.

A complex and critically important portion of the text involves six verses that are found in the text of Kumbhakarṇa's commentary, and other versions of LR, following song 23 in the twelfth *sarga*. These occur in versions of SR in a pattern that sets the manuscript Bir.1 apart from the others and suggests that Kumbhakarṇa was aware of different versions of SR when he "edited" his text of the *Gītagovinda*. Among the verses, one verse in Āryā meter occurs in two forms, each of which clearly belongs to one recension or the other. The form of SR is included in the critical edition (*GG* XII.11). Of the remaining verses, three (variant verses XII.10† [A], [B], [C]) are in LR and in all versions of SR except the version represented by the manuscript Bir.1. This manuscript has two different verses in the same place (variant verses XII.10† [D], [E]), which are also in LR. The fact that the oldest dated manuscripts of Mānāṅka's *ṭippaṇikā* are defective in this portion of the text adds to the difficulty of determining the authenticity of one set of verses as compared with the other. However, the close relationship of the text of Mānāṅka with the texts of Bir.2, Bom, and the *Sarvaṅgasundarī* of Nārāyaṇadāsa suggests that a defective manuscript may be at the basis of these variations, this set being an attempt to fill the gap in the text. The verses in Bir.1 may represent the "authentic" version, but the evidence does not seem clear enough to include them in the critical text. Neither set adds significantly to the literary quality of the text. A seventh verse in this portion of the text is found in all versions of both recensions, as well as in the *Saduktikarṇāmṛta* (*Skm.* 1144). It is included in the critical edition (*GG* XII.10).

7 Variant Readings

Variants are noted for the following versions:

SR: Bir.1, Bir.2, Bom, Ahm

LR: Kumbhakarṇa (abbrev. "Kum"), Caitanyadāsa (abbrev. "Cait")

Other versions of SR and LR do not offer the independent testimony of these sources; their variants are of minimal importance and are not cited. As elsewhere in this volume, text citations are to the critical edition printed here. Roman numerals I–XII refer to the *sargas;* arabic numerals refer consecutively to verses and stanzas within each *sarga.* General reference to a *gīta* (abbrev. *g*) is designated by the number of the song, e.g., I.*g*1. Variant verses are designated by daggers (†) after the numbers of the verses they follow.

Sarga I

I.2–4	Bir.1 has verses in the order 3, 4, 2; LR reverses the order of 3 and 4.
I.*g*1	Bir.1, Bir.2 *gauḍamālavarāga.*
I.11	(c) Bir.2, Ahm *raghupatirūpa.*
I.16	(b) Kum *daityān.*
I.19	(b) Bir.1 *yadukulapadmanideśa*
I.21	(b) Kum °*nidāna.*
I.23	Following this verse, LR adds a stanza:

tava caraṇe praṇatā vayam iti bhāvaya e |
kuru kuśalaṁ praṇateṣu jaya jayadeva hare ||

We worship at your feet. Quicken us!
Favor your worshippers! Triumph, God of Triumph, Hari!

I.31 (b) Bir.2, Bom *ketaki.*

I.32 (a) Kum °*mālatijāti*°.

I.35–36 Bir.1 reverses the order of 35 and 36; Bom, Cait have I.47 following I.36.

I.43–44 Bir.1 reverses the order of 43 and 44.

I.44 (b) Kum °*cārutarām.*

I.45 (a) Bom, Ahm *śrījayadevabhaṇitam idam.*

I.47 (a) Kum *nityotsaṅga* (*udyotsaṅga* is given as a variant, which is confirmed by other versions of LR).

I.47† Bir.2, Bom, LR (also included in Kulkarni manuscripts A and B of Mānāṅka; readings of manuscript B are often those of Bir.2, suggesting some direct relationship between them):

rāsollāsabhareṇa vibhramabhṛtām ābhīravāmabhruvām
abhyarṇaṁ pariramya nirbharam uraḥ premāndhayā
rādhāyā |
sādhu tvad vacanaṁ sudhāmayam iti vyāhṛtya gītastuti—
vyājād utkaṭacumbitaḥ smitamanohārī hariḥ pātu vaḥ ||

Rādhā, blinded by her ardent love,
Came into the midst of beautiful cowherds' wives
Who were still shaking with rapture
From dancing in Krishna's rite of love.
Pretending to praise his song,
She ardently embraced his chest,
Mumbled about his mouth's potent nectar,
And deeply kissed her smiling seducer.
Let Hari protect you!

Sarga II

II.6 (b) Bir.2, Bom, LR (also Mānāṅka, Kulkarni manuscripts A and B) *pīnapayodharaparisaramardana*°.

II.10 (a) Bir.2, Bom *bhrāmaṁ.*

II.11 (b) Bir.1 *ratirabhasavaśena.*

II.g6 Bir.1 *vasantarāga;* Bir.2, Bom *gauḍamālavarāga.*

II.19 (c) Bom, Kum *vilajjitaṁ.*

II.20† LR:

bhrūvallīkamalīkadarśitabhujāmūlordhvahastastanam |
sākūtasmitam ākulākulagaladdhammillam ullāsita-

gopīnāṁ nibhṛtaṁ nirīkṣya gamitākāṅkṣaś ciraṁ cintayan
antarmugdhamanoharaṁ haratu vaḥ kleśaṁ navaḥ
keśavaḥ ||

Secretly watching lascivious smiles of cowherds wives
And disheveled braids
As they lift their hands to creeper brows
To show him their breasts,
His desire for them leaves—
He turns at last to brood on the sensitive heart he took.
Krishna is changed! Let him calm your anguish!

Sarga III

III.4 (b) Bir.2 *kiṁ mama sukhena gṛheṇa;* Bom *kiṁ mama kiṁ sukhena gṛhena;* Kum (var.) *mama kiṁ gṛheṇa sukhena.*

III.6–8 Bir.1 verse sequence 8, 6, 7; Bom verse sequence, 6, 8, 7.

III.10 (a) Bir.1, Bir.2 *praṇaterna.*
(b) Bir.1 *kindubilli;* Bir.2 *kindubilla;* Ahn *tindubilva.*

III.13–15 LR verse sequence 15, 13, 14.

III.15† LR:

tiryakkaṇṭhavilolamaulitaralottaṁsasya vaṁśoccatad-
dīptasthānakṛtāvadhānalalanālakṣair na saṁlakṣitāḥ |
saṁmugdhe madhusūdanasya madhure rādhāmukhendau sudhā-
sāre kandalitāś ciraṁ dadhatu vaḥ kṣemaṁ kaṭākṣormayaḥ ||

The crown of demon Madhu's foe trembles, earrings dance
Against his tilting neck
As myriad adoring women fix their attention
On the brilliance of his bamboo flute's high notes
And fail to note the waves of glances falling
Like blossoms in the rainy season
On Rādhā's bewildered nectar-sweet moon face.
Let the demon foe's glances secure long peace for you!

Sarga IV

IV.g8 Kum reverses lines of the *dhruvapada: mādhava . . . sā virahe. . . .*

IV.5 (a) Bir.2 *vilolavilocana°;* Bom, Cait *valitavilocana°;* Kum *calitavilocana°.*

IV.10 (b) Bir.1, Bir.2 *karālāyate.*

IV.11 (b) Bom, LR *ivabhāram.*

IV.15–16 Kum reverses the order of verses 15 and 16.

IV.15 (b) Bir.1, Bir.2 (also Mānāṅka, Kulkarni manuscripts A and B) *hūtāśanakalpam.*

IV.g9 Bir.1, Bir.2 *vibhāsarāga;* Bom *deśīvarārīrāga;* Cait *deśāgarāga.*

IV.19 Ahm omits verse (Mānāṅka, Kulkarni manuscript B has verse without commentary).
(c) Bir.1, Bir.2 *etāddṛśyat.*
(d) LR *hastakaḥ.*

IV.20 (a) Bir.2, Ahm *°vaidyakṛtya.*
(c) Kum *nivṛttabādhāṁ.*

IV.21 (c) Cait *śītalataraṁ.*

IV.22† LR (also Mānāṅka, Kulkarni manuscript A; manuscript B has no variants):

vṛṣṭivyākulagokulāvanarasād uddhṛtya govardhanaṁ
bibhradvallavavallabhābhir adhikānandāc ciraṁ cumbitaḥ |
darpeṇeva tadarpitādharataṭīsindūràmudrāṅkito
bāhur gopatanos tanotu bhavatāṁ śreyāṁsi kaṁsadviṣaḥ ||

When he lifted Mt. Govardhana to save the cowherds' woods
From a flood of torrential rain,
Cowherds' wives high on blissful emotion
Kissed him long into the night
And his arm was branded with pride
By vermilion marks from their open lips.
Let demon Kaṁsa's foe, incarnate in a cowherd's body,
Bring joy to you who hear!

Bom, LR title *sarga* IV *snigdhamadhusūdanaḥ.*

Sarga V

V.4 (b) Kum *kalitavirahe.*

V.6 (a) Bir.2, Bom, Kum *viraha°.*

V.g11 LR adds a second line to the *dhruvapada:*
gopīpīnapayodharamardanacañcalakarayujaśālī ||

With restless hands that squeeze full breasts of cowherdesses.

V.8 (b) Bir.2 °*vilambinim.*

V.9 (b) Bir.2, Bom, Kum *tanu te.*

V.17 (a) Bom, Ahm *tvadvākyena.*

V.18 (c) Ahm *gatayoḥ kramān.*

V.19 Bom omits verse.

(d) Bir.1, Bir.2 *tvāṁ upaiti.*

V.19† LR:

rādhāmugdhamukhāravindamadhupas trailokyamaulisthalī-
nepathyocitanīlaratnam avanībhārāvatārāntakaḥ |
svacchandaṁ vrajasundarījanamanastoṣapradoṣodayaḥ
kaṁsadhvaṁsanadhūmaketur avatu tvāṁ devakīnandanaḥ ||

He drinks honey like a bee from Rādhā's tender lotus mouth.
He crowns the crest of the universe like a dark sapphire jewel.
He incarnates as death for demons who burden earth.
He spreads a veil of dusk to please the hearts of cowherd girls.
He destroys demon Kaṁsa like a fiery meteor.
May Devakī's son Krishna favor you.

Sarga VI

VI.g12 Bir.2 *dhanaśīrāga;* Bom *gauḍīkarṇādarāga;* Ahm *guṇakarīrāga* (Mānāṅka, Kulkarni manuscript B has *naṭarāga,* as Bir.1); LR *goṇḍakarīrāga* (var. *guṇakarī*).

VI.3 (a) Bir.1 *vasantī*

(b) Bir.2 *hasantī*

VI.11† LR:

kiṁ viśrāmyasi kṛṣṇabhogibhavane bhāṇḍīrabhūmīruhi
bhrātaryāsi na dṛṣṭigocaram itaḥ sānandanandāspadam |
rādhāyā vacanaṁ tadadhvagamukhān nandāntike gopato
govindasya jayanti sāyam atithiprāśastyagarbhā giraḥ ||

"Why do you rest under the fig tree?
It is as full of black snakes as Krishna's love-nest.
Why don't you go to Nanda's joyful house, brother?
It is visible from here."
Rādhā's words are repeated by a cowherd pilgrim
Near Nanda's home
And Krishna's songs offering sanctuary to the guest
Triumphantly fill the twilight.

Bir.2, Cait title *sarga* VI *dhṛṣṭavaikuṇṭhaḥ;* Bom *utkaṇṭha°;* Ahm *sotkaṇṭha°;* Kum *dhanyavaikuṇṭhaḥ.*

Sarga VII

VII.1 (c) Ahm *aṁśudīpair.*

VII.g13 Bir.1, Bom *gauḍamālavarāga;* Bir.2 *deśīrāga.*

VII.3 (b) Bir.1 *amalam api rūpaṁ;* Bir.2 *etad anurūpam api.*

VII.4 (b) Bir.1, Bir.2 *°śarapīḍitam.*

VII.5 (a) Kum *varam iti* (also Mānāṅka, Kulkarni manuscripts A, B).
(b) Ahm, Kum *kim iti.*

VII.6–7 Bir.1, Bir.2 reverse the order of verses 6 and 7.

VII.9 (a) The high degree of variation among manuscript readings here may be explained by a metrical flaw in the text of some early version and various attempts to adjust it; or, the confusions may be mainly orthographic. Bir.1 *nivigalitavanavetasā;* Bir.2 *na vigalitavinavetasā;* Bom *nagalitavanavetasā;* Ahm *na vigalitabalacetasā* (Mānāṅka cites the variant that is close to the reading: *anugaṇitavanavetaseti pāṭhe*).

VII.11 (b) LR *vanābhyarṇe kim udbhrāmyati.*

VII.g14 Bir.1, Bir.2 add the vocative *sakhi* at the end of the *dhruvapada.*

VII.15 Ahm *vikacajalajalitā°.*

VII.21 (a) Bom, LR *vedanām.*

VII.g15 .Bir.1 *rāmakarīrāga.*

VII.23 (b) Kum *kurabakakusumaṁ.*

VII.24 (b) Bir.1 *maṇimaya°;* Bir.2, Bom *maṇirasa°.*

VII.26 (b) Bir.1, Bir.2 *maṇirasa°.*

VII.28 (a) Bir.1, Bir.2, Ahm *khalu.*

VII.29 (a) Kum *°racitaṁ.*

VII.g16 Bir.1 omits the entire song; Bir.2 *varalīrāga;* LR *deśavarāḍīrāga.*

VII.31 (b) Bir.2, Bom *patati.*

VII.36 (a) Bir.2, Bom, Ahm *kanakanicaya* (though this reading deserves precedence in terms of its occurrence in SR, the meaning of the phrase *kanakanikaṣa°* seems preferable in the context of the compound).

VII.38 Bir.2, Ahm reverse order of lines in the stanza.

VII.41† (A) Bir.2 (also Mānāṅka, Kulkarni manuscript B), cited as a variant in Kum, included in text of LR at IX.10†):

sāndrānandapurandarādidiviṣadvṛndair amandādarād
ānamrair mukuṭendranīlamaṇibhiḥ saṁdarśitendindiram |
svacchandaṁ makarandasundaramilanmandākinīmeduraṁ
śrīgovindapadāravindam aśubhaskandāya vandāmahe ||

Like a blue lotus, reflecting beelike sapphires on divine crowns
As swarms of intensely blissful gods led by Indra eagerly bow,
Free as flower nectar flowing spontaneously in Ganges water
Is Govinda's lotus foot; we praise it for destroying misfortune.

(B) LR:

prātar nīlanicolam acyutam uraḥ saṁvītapītāmbaraṁ
rādhāyāś cakitaṁ vilokya hasati svairaṁ sakhīmaṇḍale |
vrīḍācañcalam añcalaṁ nayanayor ādhāya rādhānena
śrīgovindapadāravindam aśubhaskandāya vandāmahe ||

In the morning, seeing her dark scarf on himself,
His yellow cloth on her quivering chest, and Rādhā's alarm,
He laughs freely within the circle of her friends;
As he pulls from her eyes the cloth quivering with shame
On Rādhā's face, his mouth sweetly smiles.
Let Nanda's son be bliss for the world!

Sarga VIII

VIII.1 (b) Bir.1, Bir.2 *anunayavinayaṁ.*

VIII.4 (a) Bir.1, Bir.2 *anuvahati.*

VIII.5† Bir.1 adds a stanza not found elsewhere:

candanarucirakucadvayasaṅgamasaṅgatababhrucaṇḍabimbam |
hṛdayam idam tava tulayati mādhava navaghanagataśaśi-
bimbam ||

VIII.9 (a) Bir.1 *harivañcita.*

(b) Bir.1, Bir.2 *vibudhālayo 'pi sukhaṁ durāpam.*

VIII.10 (b) Kum °*dhyotihṛdayam.*

VIII.10† LR:

antarmohanamaulighūrṇanacalanmandāravibhraṁśana-
stambhākarṣaṇadṛṣṭiharṣaṇamahāmantraḥ kuraṅgīdṛśām |

dṛpyaddānavadūyamānadiviṣaddurvāraduḥkhāpadāṁ
bhraṁśaḥ kaṁsaripor vipolayatu vaḥ śreyāṁsi vaṁśīravaḥ ||

It is like a great spell seducing doe-eyed women,
Swaying their garlanded heads, loosening mandāra flowers,
Subduing their feelings, delighting their minds' eyes.
It deflects the distress gods feel from the unbearable pain
Of arrogant demons' oppression.
Let the sound of Kaṁsa's foe Krishna's flute bring good to you!

Sarga IX

IX.1 (b) Bom, Cait *rahaḥ sakhī;* Kum *rahasi sakhī* (both are metrically faulty in terms of the scheme of the basic Āryā pattern, in which the second half should consist of 27 beats).

IX.2 (b) LR *bhavane.*

IX.3 The rhyming of °*sarasam* and °*kalaśam* is notable; it is found in both recensions.

IX.6 (a) Kum °*nalina*°.

IX.10 (c) Bir.2, Bom, LR *tadyuktaṁ.*

IX.10† See VII.41†
Ahm, LR title *sarga* IX *mugdhamukundaḥ.*

Sarga X

X.1 (a) Ahm °*śeṣavaśādasīma-;* Kum °*roṣavaśāmapāra-.*
(b) Bir.1 *samupetya rādhām.*

X.g19 Bir.1 *deśīrāga;* Bir.2 *deśavarīrāga;* Ahm *deśīyavarāḍī.*

X.7 (b) Ahm, LR *caraṇadvayaṁ;* Bir.1 *sarasagalad*°.

X.8 (a) Kum *dhehi.*

X.9 (a) Bir.1 *madhuvairiṇo.*
(b) Ahm *jayatu jayadevakavibhāratībhūṣitaṁ māninījanajanitaśatam;* Kum *jayati,* etc., as Ahm.

X.10 (b) Kum °*kāśinī.*
(d) LR *praṇayini parīrambhārambhe.*

X.11 Bir.1 uncertain; Bom omits verse.
(c) Bir.2, Kum *mudam udvaha;* Ahm *mudam āpnuhi.*

X.11† LR (meter is Ardhasamacatuṣpadī: a = c [12]; b = d [13]):
śaśimukhi tava bhāti bhaṅgurabhrūr
yuvajanamohakarālakālasarpī |

taduditabhayabhañjanāya yunāṁ
tvadadharasīdhusudhaiva siddhamantraḥ ||

Moon-faced Rādhā, your curving brow
Is a dreadful black serpent
Beguiling youthful lovers,
But the elixir of your lips
Is a magical spell
For dispelling the fears
That young men suffer from it.

X.12 Bir.1 omits verse.
(c) Kum *vañca na.*

X.14 (a) Bir.1 *indumatyāsthitaṁ;* Ahm *indusaṁkāśakaṁ.*
(b) Bir.1, Bir.2 *vidhṛta;* LR *vijita.*

X.14† LR:

sa prītiṁ tanutāṁ hariḥ kuvalayāpīḍena sārdhaṁ raṇe
rādhāpīnapayodharasmaraṇakṛtkumbhena saṁbhedavān |
yatra svidyati mīlati kṣaṇam api kṣipraṁ tadālokana-
vyāmohena jitaṁ jitaṁ jitam abhūt kaṁsasya kolāhalaḥ ||

Let Hari spread joy—
When he made contact with Kaṁsa's mount in lusty battle
The elephant's swollen temples
Made him recall Rādhā's full breasts,
So he broke into sweat and shut his eyes for just a second—
Immediately, in the confusion of seeing him thus,
Kaṁsa's roar sounded, "It is won!" "It is won!" "It is won!"

Sarga XI

XI.3 (b) LR °*nikāram.*

XI.5 (a) Bir.2, Bom, Ahm °*nikurumbam.*

XI.10 (b) Bir.1 *cintānvitaḥ.*
(c) Bir.1, Ahm *sa dūraṁ.*

XI.11 (c) Ahm, Kum *abhisārasaṁbhramajuṣāṁ.*

XI.13 (b) Bir.2, Cait *mañjīrakaṅkaṇa*°.
(d) LR *sakhīm iyam ity uvāca.*

XI.g21 Bir.2, Bom have the *dhruvapada* placed between the two halves of the stanza.

XI.15 Bir.1 omits stanza.

XI.17 (a) Ahm, Kum *mṛducalamalayapavana*°.
(b) Bom, Cait *rativalita*°; Ahm, Kum *madanaśaranikarabhīte*.

XI.18–20 LR verse sequence 20, 18, 19.

XI.18 (b) Bir.2 *madanaśararabhasa*°; Kum *kusumaśarasarasa*°.

XI.19 (a) Bir.2, Ahm *madhutarala*°.

XI.20 (a) Ahm °*sughane*.

XI.21 (c) LR °*kavirājarāje* (the additional syllables seem to be an attempt to conform with the metrical pattern of the *dhruvapada*).

XI.22 (b) Bom, Ahm, LR *ca*.
(c) Ahm, LR *asyāṅkaṁ*.

XI.23 (d) Kum *praviveśābhiveśanam*.

XI.g22 Bom missing leaf no. 26, XI.24–33; Bir.1, Bir.2 (*dhruvapada*) *anaṅgavikāsam*.

XI.25 (a) Bir.2 *parilambya*.

XI.28 (b) Bir.1 *smitarucikusuma*.

XI.29 (a) Bir.1 *cañcalaghanodarasundaravimalakusumavarakeśam*.

XI.31 LR *hariṁ suciraṁ*.

XI.30–31 These stanzas appear differently in Bir.1:

vipulapulakabharadarśitamadanaśarabaṇanikaravikāram |
bhūṣaṇamaṇigaṇakiraṇavibhāvitavirahadahanaparivāram || 30 ||
śrījayadevabhaṇitam atiśobhanavibhavavibhūṣaṇabhāram |
praṇamata manasi nidhāya hariṁ bhavajaladhitāraśubhasāram || 31 ||

XI.32 Bir.1 omits.
(b) Kum *amalataratāram gamitayoḥ*.
(c) Kum °*samāyātasamaye*.

XI.33 (c) Kum °*vaśākūta*°.

XI.33† LR (*Saduktikarṇāmṛta* 294):

jayaśrīvinyastair mahita iva mandārakusumaiḥ
svayaṁ sindūreṇa dviparaṇamudā mudrita iva |
bhujāpīḍakrīḍāhatakuvalayāpīḍakariṇaḥ
prakīrṇāsṛgbindur jayati bhujadaṇḍo murajitaḥ ||

It seems worshipped with mandāra flowers scattered by Triumph,

Self-marked with sindhur as a sign of joy in battling the elephant—
Playfully slaying demon Kaṁsa's mount with an embrace of arms,
Dripping with splattered blood, the stern arm of Mura's foe triumphs.

Kum has two additional verses that are not found in other versions of LR.
Bom, Cait title *sarga* XI *sānandagovindaḥ;* Kum *sāmodadāmodaraḥ.*

Sarga XII

XII.1 (c) Bir.2, Bom, Ahm *sarasam alasaṁ.*
XII.g23 Bir.1, Bir.2 *rāmakarīrāga.*
(*dhruvapada*) Kum *anubhaga māṁ;* Cait *anubhaga rādhike.*
XII.6 (a) LR *bhāmini.*
XII.8 (b) Kum *lajjitam iva nayanaṁ tava viramati sṛjasi vṛthā ratikhedam.*
XII.10 (a) Kum *vāmāṅke.*
XII.10† (A) Bir.2, Bom, LR:

pratyūhaḥ pulakāṅkureṇa nibiḍāśleṣe nimeṣeṇa ca
krīḍākūtavilokite 'dharasudhāpāne kathānarmabhiḥ |
ānandādhigamena manmathakalāyuddhe 'pi yasminn abhūd
udbhūtaḥ sa tayor babhūva suratārambhaḥ priyaṁbhāvukaḥ ||

Bristling body hairs interrupted their close embrace,
Blinking stopped their watching for signs of love-play,
Banter hindered their drinking nectar from each other's lips,
Boundless bliss interrupted the battle of love's subtle art—
What became explicit as passion took over was love's stimulant.

(B) Bir.2, Bom, LR:

dorbhyāṁ saṁyamitaḥ payodharabhareṇāpīḍitaḥ pāṇijair
āviddho daśanaiḥ kṣatādharapuṭaḥ śroṇītaṭenāhataḥ |
hastenānamitaḥ kace 'dharamadhusayandena saṁmohitaḥ
kāntaḥ kām api tṛptim āpa tad aho kāmasya vāmā gatiḥ ||

Her arms bound him,
Her heavy breasts oppressed him,
Her nails scratched him,
Her teeth broke his lips' soft hollows,
Her sloping hips struck him,
Her hand on his hair made him bend,
A stream of her lips' honey confounded him,
Yet her lover attained ineffable pleasure—
This paradox is the way of love.

(C) Bir.2, Bom, LR:
tasyāḥ pāṭalapāṇijāṅkitaṁ uro nidrākaṣāye dṛśau
nirdhauto 'dharaśoṇimā vilulitasrastasrajo murdhajāḥ |
kāñcīdāma daraślathāñcalam iti prātar nikhātair dṛśor
ebhiḥ kāmaśarais tadadbhutam abhūt patyur manaḥ kīlitam ||

Her chest was branded with red nailmarks,
Her eyes were bloodshot from lack of sleep,
The crimson hue was drained from her lips,
Wilted garlands lay disheveled in her hair,
Her girdle cords lay a little slack—
At dawn the arrows of love buried in his eyes
Impaled the wondrous heart of her consort.

(D) Bir.1, LR:
vyālolaḥ keśapāśas taralitam alakaiḥ svedalolau kapolau
kliṣṭā daṣṭādharaśrīḥ kucakalaśarucā hāritā hārayaṣṭiḥ |
kāñcī kāñcid gatāśāṁ stanajaghanapadaṁ pāṇinācchādya sadyaḥ
paśyantī satrapaṁ sā tadapi vilulitaśragdhareyaṁ dhinoti ||

Her braid is a dangling mass of curling locks,
Her two cheeks are full of sweat,
The glow of her bitten lip is dulled,
Her pearl necklace is paled by the gleam of full breasts,
The hope that glowed from her girdle is gone
As she covers her bare breasts and loins at once with each hand,
Looking at him with bashfulness—
Even this girl in her disheveled garlands satisfies him.

Kum (a) *vyākośaḥ, svedamokṣau;* (b) *bimbādhara°;* (c) *kāñcī-kāntir hatāśā;* (d) *satrapā, mugdhakāntir 'dhinoti.*

(E) Bir.1, LR:

īṣanmīlitadṛṣṭi mugdhahasitaṁ sītkāradhārāvaśād
avyaktākulakelikākuvikasaddantāṁśudhautādharam |
śvāsonnaddhapayodharopari pariṣvaṅgāt kuraṅgīdṛśo
harṣotkarṣavimuktiniḥsahatanor dhanyo dhayatyānanaṁ ||

As her body lies powerless after expressions of high joy
From his forcefully embracing her breast
As it heaved with sighing,
The graceful Lord drinks the doe-eyed girl's face—
Her eyes are slightly opened
Her lips are polished by the gleam of her teeth,
Opened by indistinct, confused love sounds
From the force of her sucking air in bewildered laughter.

Kum (a) *mugdhavilasat°;* (c) *śāntastabdhapayodharaṁ bhṛśapari°.*

XII.11 Bom omits; LR has a variant verse in Āryā meter:

atha sahasā suprītā suratānte sā nitāntakhinnāṅgī |
rādhā jagāda sādaram idam ānandena govindam ||

Cait (a) *iti manasā nigadantaṁ.*

XII.g24 Bir.1 adds a line to the *dhruvapada:*

smaraśaraviṣasaṁprasaradkuvalayadyutilocane ||

XII.14 (a) Bir.1 *°nivāsakare.*

XII.17 (a) Kum *manasija°.*

XII.19 (a) Bir.2, Bom *jayade* (for *rucire*).

XII.20 (b) Kum *mugdhasrajā.*

(c) Kum *maṇinūpurā.*

XII.20† Cait (also Bhagavaddāsa):

paryaṅkīkṛtanāganāyakaphaṇāśreṇīmaṇīnāṁ gaṇe
saṁkrāntapratibimbasaṁvalanayā bibhradvibhuprakriyām |
pādāmbhoruhadhārivāridhisutām akṣṇāṁ didṛkṣuḥ śataiḥ
kāvyavyūham ivācarann upacitībhūto hariḥ pātu vaḥ ||

He undertook the work of divine power
By projecting reflected images
Into gems massed on the hood of the serpent-king
Who served as his couch.
He seemed to expand himself.
Undertaking a multitude of manifest forms,

Eager to see, with hundreds of eyes,
The ocean's daughter offer water for bathing his feet.
May Hari protect you!

XII.21 (b) Kum °*tattvaracanākāvyeṣu.*

XII.22 Bom, Ahm omit verse.

XII.22† LR (*Bhagavaddāsa* agrees with Cait; cf. Kum variants):

sādhvī mādhvīka cintā na bhavati bhavataḥ śarkare karkarāsi
drākṣe drakṣyanti ke tvām amṛta mṛtam asi kṣīra nīraṁ rasaste |
mākanda kranda kāntādhara dharaṇītalaṁ gaccha yacchanti yāvad
bhāvaṁ śṛṅgārasārasvataṁ iha jayadevasya viṣvagvacāṁsi ||

Liquor, the thought of you becomes improper.
Sugar, you become unsweet.
Grape, who will look at you?
Nectar, you become mortal.
Milk, you taste like water.
Mango, lament! Lover's lips, fall to the ground!—
So long as Jayadeva's pervasive words
Sustain emotion that holds the essence of erotic mood.

Kum (c) *dhara na tulāṁ gaccha yacchantı bhāvaṁ;* (d) *yāvac chṛṅgārasāraṁ śubham iva jayadevasya vaidagdhavācaḥ.* Kum has an additional verse that is not found in other versions of LR.

A Glossary of Sanskrit Words

The Sanskrit text and English translation of the *Gītagovinda* have been established with the aid of a complete word index to the work. However, for the sake of *vṛkṣarakṣaṇa,* only those words that are used with frequency and characteristic meaning within the context of the poem are cited here. Words that are used frequently but without special significance in the poem are not cited. The following, for example, are omitted: standard words for the body and its parts (*akṣa, aṅga, adhara, ānana, uraḥ,* etc.), words for aspects of nature (*anila, indu, kamala, kisalaya, kusuma, candra, candana,* etc.), and conventional adjectives descriptive of physical or mental states (*alasa, komala, klānta, kheda, ghana, calana, cumbana,* etc.). The many words for various kinds of ornaments and for ornaments in general (*ābharaṇa, kuṇḍala, nūpura, mañjīra, maṇḍana,* etc.) are also omitted, despite their evocative importance in the text. The words themselves are too standard to need definition, but the stress that Jayadeva lays on the appropriately ornamented body, culminating in the final song, is important. The epithets of Krishna are to be found above in section 4 to the introduction.

The vocabulary of the poem is highly concentrated. The glossary seems a reasonable alternative to repetitive textual notes, especially since many words are rich in implied meanings and overtones. Since the contexts of separate occurrences affect my English renderings in the translation, glossary meanings do not always cover all the English variants. However, the meanings cited should clarify the rendering in any given context. Meanings of words in the *Gītagovinda* have been established mainly on the basis of interpretations given in the commentaries of Mānāṅka, Kumbhakarṇa, Śaṅkaramiśra, and Caitanyadāsa; others have been consulted where these interpretations are conflicting or inconclusive.

Frequent reference has also been made to relevant portions of the *Nāṭyaśāstra,* the *Subhāṣitaratnakoṣa,* and the literature of Bengali Vaishnavism. The *Nāṭyaśāstra* is the basic practical text of Indian esthetics. The *Subhāṣitaratnakoṣa* is a representative anthology of Sanskrit poetry, including a large selection of love poetry; its contents were collected in eastern India in the century preceding Jayadeva's period of literary activity there. The excellent edition by Gokhale and Kosambi and the superbly annotated translation by Ingalls make it a good source of comparison for assessing Jayadeva's word usage. Ingalls's discussions of words have been cited repeatedly with the purpose of referring both Sanskrit and English readers to wider contexts of interpretation. The literature of Bengali Vaishnavism has been referred to in order to give some sense of how particular words and concepts were treated by the later tradition for which the *Gītagovinda* was a basic text of inspiration. This literature is cited mainly through references in the studies of De and Dimock.

What is clear from these comparative notes is that the *Gītagovinda* is an esthetic vision based on the background of *kāvya* literature and classical *rasa* theory. The vocabulary of religious speculation so characteristic of the *Bhagavadgītā* and the *Bhāgavata Purāṇa* is notably absent. Words such as *dharma*, *karma*, and *bhakti* are not found. There is a clearly tantric attitude in the poet's concentration on detailed vocabulary of the sexual act, but the sexual act is not isolated from the emotional context of love in the *Gītagovinda*, as it is in technical tantric literature. Jayadeva's message is that the emotions of love, expressed in the rich vocabulary and intense esthetic means of lyrical poetry, are to be experienced by a *rasika* in order for Krishna's saving grace to be felt.

Rich verbal environments are created by the almost onomatopoeic piling together of words that subtly reveal states of mind and stages of love. Word compounds, which are an important feature of Sanskrit language, are exexploited in the songs. The alliterative patterns that abound here are most often contained in long *bahuvrīhi* compounds. These are generally translatable into strings of adjectives and adjective phrases in English, with the final member serving as a base for the modifiers preceding it. Each compound taken as a whole functions epithetically to delineate some characteristic of its subject. Few attempts have been made in the glossary to explain words in their various compound occurrences. Only where the translated combination acquires a secondary technical meaning is commentary offered; e.g., *ekarasa* is discussed under *rasa* and *rahaḥkeli* under *rahas*.

Text citations are to the critical edition printed in this volume. Roman numerals I–XII designate the twelve *sargas* into which the *Gītagovinda* is divided in all manuscripts. Arabic numerals refer consecutively to verses within each *sarga*; no distinction is made between *śloka* verses and *gīta* verses. The *dhruvapada* citations are distinguished by an asterisk placed after the number of the first *pada* in each song, so that I.27* is the *dhruvapada* of the third *gīta* in the first *sarga*.

Declinable words are listed in stem form. Finite verbs are given in root form after the stem. Adverbs are not usually distinguished as such because of their frequent ambiguity in the text. Words are generally grouped around basic stems for the purpose of controlling and emphasizing repetitive units of meaning.

ABBREVIATIONS USED IN THE GLOSSARY

Abbreviated references to Sanskrit texts and selected studies in the glossary are listed here in English alphabetical order.

Sanskrit Texts

Agni P — *Agni Purāṇa,* Ānandāśrama Sanskrit Series, no. 41 (Poona, 1900).

Amar — *Amarakoṣa or Nāmaliṅgānuśāsana,* edited with the commentary *Rāmaśramī* by H. Sastri (Varanasi: Chowkhamba Sanskrit Series Office, 1970).

BG — *Bhagavadgītā = Mbh* VI.23–40; translated by Franklin Edgerton, part 2, Harvard Oriental Series, vol. 39 (Cambridge, Mass.: Harvard University Press, 1952).

Bhart — *Bhartrihari: Poems,* text with translation by Barbara Stoler Miller (New York: Columbia University Press, 1967).

Bh P — *Bhāgavata Purāṇa,* Gita Press edition (Gorakhpur, 1962).

Dhv — *Dhvanyāloka* of Ānandavardhana, critical edition, edited by K. Krishnamoorthy (Dharwar: Karnatak University, 1974).

DR — *Daśarūpa* by Dhanaṁjaya, edited and translated by G. C. O Haas (1912; reprint, Delhi: Motilal Banarsidass, 1962).

GG — *Gītagovinda;* all references are to this edition.

Kāmasūt — *Kāmasūtra* of Vātsyāyana, edited with the commentary *Jayamaṅgala* of Yashodhar[a], Kashi Sanskrit Series, no. 29 (Varanasi: Chowkhamba Sanskrit Series Office, 1929).

KD — *Kāvyadarśa* of Daṇḍin, edited and translated by V. N. Ayer (Madras: Ramaswamy Sastrulu, 1964).

KS — *Kumārasaṁbhava* of Kālidāsa, critical edition, edited by Suryakanta (New Delhi: Sahitya Akademi, 1962).

Mālav — *Mālavikāgnimitra* of Kālidāsa, edited and translated by C .R. Devadhar (Delhi: Motilal Banarsidass, 1966).

Mbh — *Mahābhārata.* Critical edition, edited by V. S. Sukthankar, et al. (Poona: Bhandarkar Oriental Research Institute, 1933–66); translated by J. A. B. van Buitenen (Chicago: University of Chicago Press, 1973–), vols. 1 and 2.

NŚ — *Nāṭyaśāstra* ascribed to Bharatamuni, edited and translated by M. Ghosh, 4 vols. (Calcutta: Granthalaya, 1956–67).

Ragh — *Raghuvaṁśa* of Kālidāsa, edited with Mallinātha's *Sañjīvinī* by H. D. Velankar (Bombay: Nirṇayasāgara Press, 1948).

Rām *Rāmāyaṇa* of Vālmīki, critical edition, edited by G. H. Bhatt, et al. 6 vols. (Baroda: Oriental Institute, 1960–71).

SKB *Sarasvatīkaṇṭhābharaṇa* of Bhoja, edited, with the commentary of Rāmasiṁha on I–III and of Jagaddhara on IV, by W. L. S. Pansikar, Kāvyamālā, no. 94 (Bombay: Nirṇayasāgara Press, 1934).

SR *Saṅgītaratnākara,* edited by V. C. Apte, Ānandāśrama Sanskrit Series, no. 35, 2 vols. (Poona: Ānandāśrama Press, 1942).

SRK *Subhāṣitaratnakoṣa* compiled by Vidyākara, edited by D. D. Kosambi and V. V. Gokhale, Harvard Oriental Series, vol. 42 (Cambridge, Mass.: Harvard University Press, 1957).

Ujjv *Ujjvalanīlamaṇi* of Rupa Goswāmin, edited by R. Vidyaratna (Berhampur: Rādhāraman Press, 1935).

VV *Vasanta Vilāsa,* critical edition, edited and translated from Old Gujaratī, Sanskrit, and Prākrit by W. Norman Brown (New Haven: American Oriental Society, 1962).

Selected Studies

De, *VFM* S. K. De, *Vaiṣṇava Faith and Movement in Bengal* (Calcutta: K. L. Mukhopadhyay, 1961).

Dimock, *Krishna* Edward C. Dimock, Jr., and Denise Levertov, *In Praise of Krishna: Songs from the Bengali* (New York: Anchor Books, 1967).

Dimock, *PHM* Edward C. Dimock, Jr., *The Place of the Hidden Moon: Erotic Mysticism in the Vaiṣṇava-Sahajiyā Cult of Bengal* (Chicago: University of Chicago Press, 1966).

Fiske, "Notes on Rasa" Adele M. Fiske, "Notes on *Rasa* in Vedic and Buddhist Texts," *Mahfil,* 8, nos. 3 and 4 (1971), 215–228.

Gerow, *Glossary* Edwin Gerow, *A Glossary of Indian Figures of Speech* (The Hague: Mouton, 1971).

Ingalls, "Beauty" Daniel H. H. Ingalls, "Words for Beauty in Classical Sanskrit Poetry," *Indological Studies in Honor of W. Norman Brown* (New Haven: American Oriental Society, 1962), pp. 87–107.

Ingalls, *SCP* Daniel H. H. Ingalls, trans., *An Anthology of Sanskrit Court Poetry,* Harvard Oriental Series, vol. 44 (Cambridge, Mass.: Harvard University Press, 1965).

Konow, "Anaṅga" Sten Konow, "Anaṅga, the Bodiless Cupid," in *Antidupon: Festschrift Jacob Wackernagel* (Göttingen: Vanenhoeck, 1923), pp. 1–8.

Masson/Patwardhan, *Rapture* J. L. Masson and M. V. Patwardhan, *Aesthetic Rapture: The Rasādhyāya of the Nāṭyaśāstra,* 2 vols. (Poona: Deccan College, 1970).

Raghavan, *Bhoja* V. Raghavan, *Bhoja's Śṛṅgāra Prakāśa* (Madras: Punarvasu, 1963).

Schmidt, *Beiträge* Richard Schmidt, *Beiträge zur indischen Erotik* (Leipzig: Lotus Verlag, 1902).

adbhuta. Marvelous, wondrous (I.8, 9, 45); see *Mbh* VI.33.20 (*BG* 11.20); VI.40.74, 76, 77 (*BG* 18.74, 76, 77). In the *daśavidharūpastuti* (I.8, 9) reference to *adbhutarasa,* the esthetic mood of wonder, is implied; it identifies the mood of the song, which is in contrast with the dominant mood of *śṛṅgāra* in the poem; see *NŚ.* VI.39–41; prose 75–76. Also, the *alaṁkāra* called *adbhutopamā,* a simile involving some marvel, is used in stanza I.8 to intensify the marvel of the Man-lion form: normally lotuses are opened by bees, but the marvel here is that a lotus hand opens a bee, which is the demon's black body; see *KD,* II.24; Gerow, *Glossary,* p. 148; see *rasa, śṛṅgāra,* also the epithet *Daśavidharūpa.*

anaṅga. Love, the bodiless god, referring to his body's destruction by Śiva when he tried to arouse desire for Pārvatī in the great ascetic; like *kandarpa, kāma, madana, manasija, manoja, manmatha, smara,* etc., this epithet of the god of love is also used to denote the concept "love," the line between the personification and the concept being blurred (I.25, 46; II.8; III.2, 15; V.19; VII.18; XI.6, 24*); also *atanu* (IV.19; VII.8). Other common epithets of Love refer to his role as the bowman of flower arrows: *asamabāṇa* (I.35); *asamaśara* (IV.6; VII.4; VIII.7); *kusumaviśikha* (IV.4); *kusumaśara* (X.5; XI.4); *cūtasāyaka* (III.12); *pañcabāṇa* (VII.41; X.11); *puṣpāyudha* (X.13). See Ingalls, *SCP,* intr. 14, pp. 149–150; Konow, "Anaṅga."

anugata. Lit., "followed by," or "following"; of lovers' relations it means "faithful" (I.34; II.7; VIII.7; XI.2*, XII.2*); also *anu* √*gam* (I.44); *anugamana* (VII.4). See *anukūla* in the classification of the *nāyaka* (*DR,* II.11): *anukūlas tv ekanāyikaḥ.* In *GG, anukūla* is not used in this technical meaning (I.41; II.12; XII.4), but the commentator Kumbhakarṇa refers to Krishna as *anukulo nāyakaḥ* at X.8; XII.8, etc.

anusaraṇa. Lit., "following"; used of lovers seeking to meet (I.26); also *anu* √*sṛ* (I.47; III.6; V.8; VIII.2*; XI.2*; XII.2*); *anusṛtya* (III.2).

abhisāra. Lovers' meeting (V.8, 17; VI.6; XI.11); also *abhisaraṇa* (VI.3); *abhi* √ *sṛ* (IX.2; XI.7); *abhisṛta* (VII.11). The *abhisārikā* state of the *nāyikā* is described in *GG sarga* XI, culminating in Rādhā's abandoned modesty (see *lajjā*); see *NŚ* XXIV.219:

> *hitvā lajjāṁ tu yā śliṣṭā madena madanena vā|*
> *abhisārayate kāntaṁ sā bhaved abhisārikā||*

amṛta. Elixir, nectar of immortality (IV.20; V.7; VII.33; XII.4, 19); °*dhāra,* the moon (IV.5); see *sudhā.*

asūyā. Envy (III.7). A *vyabhicāribhāva* associated with pride and anger; see *NŚ* VII.36.

ānanda. Bliss (I.46); *sānanda,* blissful (X.1; XI.23; XII.21); also *ā* √*nand* (XI.10); *ānandana* (VII.39; XII.12*); see *mud, sukha, harṣa.*

īrṣyā. Envy (II.1); see *asūyā,* with which *īrṣyā* is synonymous.

utkaṇṭha. Longing (VII.30); *utkaṇṭhitagopavadhū* (II.18), referring to *virahotkaṇṭhitā,* one of the states of the *nāyikā;* see *NS* XXIV.213:

> *anekakāryavyāsaṅgād yasyā nāgacchati priyaḥ|*
> *anāgamanaduḥkhārtā virahotkaṇṭhitā tu sā||*

udāra. Sublime, exquisite; of Jayadeva's speech (I.15; see *Rām,* I.2.41: *udāravṛttārthapadair manoramais tadāsya rāmasya cakāra kīrtiman*); of Krishna and Rādhā (II.7, 11*; IV.5, 11; VIII.5; X.8).

kandarpa. Love (I.26; IV.10, 21; VI.10; XI.22); see *anaṅga.*

kalahāntaritā. Lit., "separated by a quarrel," a female so separated from her lover (IX.1). One of the states of a *nāyikā; NŚ* XXIV.215 (cf. *Kāmasūt* 2.10.40–49):

> *īrṣyākalahavikrānto yasyā nāgacchati prihaḥ|*
> *amarṣavaśasaṁtaptā kalahāntaritā bhavet||*

kalā. Art, esp. the art or arts of love; *keli*° (I.42); °*keli* (VII.11); *gāndharva*° (XII.21); *rati*° (VI.4); *ratikeli*° (XI.30); *vilāsa*° (I.4; IV.4); also *kalāvatī,* an artful girl, the name of an *apsaras* (VII.10; X.14).

kali. The dark age, last and worst of the four cyclical ages of cosmic time; °*kaluṣa,* the foulness of the dark age (II.8; VII.20; XII.19); °*yuga* (VII.29).

kānta. Loved, lovely, °*padāvalī* (I.4); *kānta* (m.), lover, Krishna (VII.11; XII.10, 11); cf. Ingalls, "Beauty," p. 93. Technically used of a lover who shows no signs of infidelity (*NŚ,* XXIV.301):

> *anyanārīsamudbhūtaṁ cihnaṁ yasya na dṛṣyate|*
> *adhare vā śarīre vā sa kānta iti bhaṇyate||*

kāntā. mistress, Rādhā (V.16); see *dayita, priya.*

kāma. Love, the god of love (V.14; VII.40); see *anaṅga.* Also *kāmam* √*kṛ,* desire (II.10); *nikāma* (IV.17; VII.40); *sakāmam* (IV.17); *kamanīya,* desirable (I.11; IV.4; V.15); *kāminī,* a loving woman (VII.6, 11; XII.2). *Kāma* is not contrasted with *preman* in *GG* as it is in later Vaishnava works; see *preman.*

kuñja. Thicket, esp. a secret place for love in the forest (I.1, 27, 42; II.1; III.2; V.11, 16; VII.11; XI.1, 14); also *nikuñja* (II.11; V.7; XI.10, 11, 13).

kutūhala. Curiosity, desire (I.4); cf. *KS,* VIII.3; also *kutuka* (I.42).

kupitā. An angry woman (III.3*); also *kopinī* (X.3); *kopa* (III.5). Cf. *bhāma,* anger, Krishna's (II.10).

keli. Play, esp. sensual play, sexual pleasure (I.1, 20, 38, 38*, 42, 45; V.11; VII.11; XI.2, 14); *rati*° (I.2; XI.30; XII.10).

krīḍā. Play, esp. sensual play (III.12; IX.10); also √*krīḍ* (I.46; III.13); *krīḍat* (I.36; XII.12*); *śārdūlavikrīḍita,* a pun on the name of the meter (IV.10).

khaṇḍita. Lit., "broken"; jealous, referring to lovers; °*yuvati* (VIII.9) refers to the state of the *nāyikā* technically called *khaṇḍitā* (NŚ, XXIV.216):

> *vyāsaṅgād ucite yasyāḥ vāsake nāgataḥ priyaḥ|*
> *tadanāgamanārtā tu khaṇḍitety abhidhīyate||*

Cf. *khaṇḍana,* destroying (I.18; X.3, 8; XII.19).

khelana. Play (I.40); also *khelat* (I.25); *khelita* (XI.27).

gīta. Song, singing (I.24; IV.18; XI.17); °*govinda* (XII.21, 22).

caraṇa. Foot; an object of worship and erotic delight, with the distinction between these often ambiguous (I.2, 34; II.5, 9, 16; IV.7; VII.10, 27, 34; VIII.5; XI.2, 3; XII.2, 3, 19). Worship of Krishna's feet is efficacious in calming the chaos of the Kali Yuga; see *pada.*

carita. Conduct, rhythm of movement, story (I.2; VI.1; IX.1, 9).

cāraṇa. Minstrel; Jayadeva calls himself *cāraṇacakravartī* (I.2); cf. *Rām,* V.1.1, 176.

cāru. Cherished, intimately lovely (I.41 [adv.], 44; II.3; X.2*, 9; XI.11); see Ingalls, "Beauty," p. 44.

cintā. Anxious thought, brooding (I.26; IV.21; VI.10; XI.10). A *vyabhicāribhāva* associated with frustrated desire, *NŚ* VII.50, 51.

cetas. Mind, heart, the seat of rational thought, imagination, and emotion (I.35; IV.21; VII.9, 30; VIII.6); also *cetanā* (VII.5, 21); see *manas, hṛd.*

jaya. Triumph, may be personified; whatever insures triumph (III.15; VIII.4). *Jayadeva,* god of triumph, an epithet of Krishna (I.17*) that parallels *Jagadīśa* in the refrain of the first song; it is the poet's signature throughout *GG;* see references in section 4 of the introduction. Also √*ji* (I.5*, 16, 17*); *jita* (I.22; XII.15); *nirjita* (III.12, 15); *vi* √*ji* (X.13); *vijayin* (VII.22*); see Ingalls, "Beauty," p. 100.

tamāla. A large dark-barked shade tree (I.1, 29; XI.12); usually glossed with *tāpiccha* in commentaries. See *Amar,* II.4.68: *kālaskandhas tamālaḥ syāt tāpicchaḥ; Ragh,* VI.64; *SRK,* 216; *Agni P.* 202.2; among flowers used for *pūjā, tamāla* flowers grant enjoyment and salvation. In Kannada, it is named *honge* and its shade is proverbially said to give as much comfort as a mother's womb.

dayita. Lover (I.41; VII.17, 30); also *adaya* (VII.40); *nirdaya* (II.6; VII.30; VIII.8; X.11); *sadaya* (I.13; V.15). See *kānta, priya.*

dāsa. Slave, used of Krishna (XI.22; XII.6); see *KS,* V.86.

dukūla. Fine silk cloth, worn by Krishna and Rādhā (I.42, II.12; XI.26; XII.4).

dūtī. Female messenger (VII.30); see *sakhī, sahacarī;* see Ingalls, *SCP,* intr. 18.3; 25.

dhyāna. Meditation (I.36; IV.8; VI.10); also √*dhyai* (I.40; IV.19; VI.11); *dhyāyat* (IV.21; V.7); *anudhyāna* (XII.21).

nideśa. Command, order; *nanda*° (I.1); *manmatha*° (X.6).

pañcama. The fifth degree of the scale of a *rāga;* a particular *rāga* characterized by erotic mood (I.39; X.12); see Ingalls, *SCP,* Intr. 8.2. The commentator Kumbhakarṇa relates its sound to the sound of cuckoos in spring.

pada. Foot; like *caraṇa* (q.v.), an object of worship and erotic delight (VII.29; X.7, 8, 13; XI.22; XII.2, 20); also *pāda* (VIII.10). *Pada* also means "foot" or "measured unit" of poetry (I.4; X.1).

pauruṣa. Virility (III.12); °*rasa* (XII.10).

prabandha. A literary composition (I.2); see *Mālav,* I.1 (prose): *prathitayaśasāṁ bhāsakavisaumillakaviputrādīnāṁ prabandhān atikramya.* In the technical vocabulary of Indian classical music, *prabandha* refers to a composition containing songs. The strict metrical patterns of *GG* songs belong to a style called *chandaḥprabandha;* see *SR,* IV (*Prabandhādhyāya*); *NŚ* XXXII (*Dhruvāvidhāna*).

praṇaya. Expressed love (II.1; VIII.10).

priya. Lit., "loved," or "loving" (IV.10); *priya* (m.), lover, the distinction between adjective and noun remaining blurred (IV.21; V.16;

VII.30; VIII.1; X.12; XI.32, 33; XII.5, 13); see *NŚ* XXIV.298; *priya* (n.), pleasure (I.25); *priyā*, mistress (III.11; VIII.10; X.2*, 13; XII.1); see *kāntā, dayita*. Also *prīta*, loved, delighted (V.18; XII.20); *prīti*, pleasure, delight (XI.10); *prīṇayitvā* (XI.1).

preman. Ardent love (IV.1; XI.12); used in *GG* as in *kāvya* literature (e.g., *Bhart*, 107, 115, 124; *SKB*, V.97, 98, notes twelve types of *preman*); the contrast of *preman* with *kāma* characteristic of later Vaishnava literature is absent; see Dimock *PHM*, 161–164, 211 f.

bhaṇita. Lit., "spoken," (n.) speech, translated "sung" or "song" as it occurs in the so-called *bhaṇita* stanzas of most songs (I.34; II.9, 18; IV.9, 18; VII.20, 38; VIII.9; IX.9; X.9; XI.9, 31; XII.9); cf. *bhaṇat* (V.6, 15; XI.21); *bhaṇana* (VII.29); see *bharatī, vacana*. These signature stanzas are related to the signature lines known as *bhanitā*, which are the conventional endings of later Bengali Vaishnava songs; cf. Dimock, *Krishna*, pp. xix–xx.

bhaya. Fear (II.8; III.3; IV.2*; V.19); also *bhīti* (I.12); *bhīru* (I.1); see *śaṅkā, sādhvasa*.

bhāratī. Speech, personified as the goddess of speech (VII.10; X.9); see *NŚ*, XXIII.25, where *bhāratī* is defined as elegant style of speech in drama; see *bhaṇita, vacas, sarasvatī*.

bhāva. Emotion, technically referring to the various aspects of esthetic emotion which lead to the production of *rasa*, q.v. (X.5, 12); *sarasa°* (XI.18); *rasa°* (XII.9); see *NŚ*, VII, summarized in *DR*, IV. *Bhāva* also means "feelings," an *alaṁkāra* of the *nāyikā* (XI.4); see *NŚ*, XXXIV.4–8. Rādhā is addressed as *bhāvinī* (XII.6).

bhāvanā. Imaginative thought, fantasy (IV.2*; VI.5); also *bhāvita*, obsessed by such thought (II.11*).

bhrama. Wandering about, physical or mental confusion, quick movements characteristic of seductive behavior (II.10; V.18); also √*bhram* (VII.11; VIII.8); *bhramat* (I.26; III.5); *bhrānti* (III.11); *bhrāmyat* (II.20); *ud* √*bhram* (IV.19); *udbhrānta* (IV.1); *vibhrama* (III.14); *saṁbhrama* (I.37; III.8; V.18; XI.22; XII.10); *bhramara*, bee (III.5; XII.15; cf. Ingalls, *SCP*, intr. 33.14).

maṅgala. Anything auspicious (I.24); *°śata* (XI.21) *°kalaśasahodhara* (XII.12). This last reference suggests that *kalaśa* (VII.14; IX.3; XII.5, 12) and *kumbha* (V.7; X.6; XI.6), compounded with *kuca* in each case, may refer to the ritual function of Rādhā's "breast pots" in the context of the poem, despite the conventionality of the image; see Ingalls, *SCP*, p. 489, note on v. 269.

maṇḍala. Lit., "circle"; applied to anything circular (I.17, 18; II.3; III.13;

X.6; XI.24, 26; XII.14); also *maṇḍalin* (II.1); although the word is conventionally used to indicate the round quality of breasts, buttocks, ears, the moon, or the sun, reference to their tantric function as "magic circles" may be suggested in the context of the poem.

mada. Intoxication, any intoxicating liquid (II.14, X.14); cf. *unmada* (I.28). *Mada* also means "musk," *kuraṅga*° (IV.6); *mṛga*° (I.29; VII.22, 24; XII.12, 16).

madana. Love (I.28, 30, 34; II.11*, 14; IV.13; V.2, 3, 8, 16; VII.21, 22; VIII.5; X.2*, 8; XI.18); see *anaṅga.*

madhu. Honey, anything sweet (I.36; VI.2; VII.6; X.2*; XI.18); see *sudhā. Madhu* also means "springtime" (I.46); see *vasanta.* It is the name of a demon whom Krishna defeats (I.20); see Krishna's epithets *Mādhava, Madhusūdana, Madhumathana, Madhuripu.* Also note the conventional sexual image of the bee acting like a lover in his activities as the drinker and producer of *madhu: madhukara* (I.27; VII.25); *madhupa* (I.36; V.4; XI.4, 18); and *madhuvrata* (II.1); cf. *bhramara* (see *brahma*). Also *madhūka,* a honey-colored spring flower that blooms at night (X.13).

madhura. Honeyed, sweet (II.2, 4, 12; VI.2; VII.6, 33; VIII.9; IX.8; X.12; XI.19); also *mādhurī,* sweetness (III.14). *Madhura* technically refers to an esthetic quality of sweetness, associated with *śṛṅgāra-rasa* (I.4); cf. *KD* I.51; *Dhv.* II.7. (The abstract term *mādhurya* is more commonly used outside *GG,* e.g. *NŚ* XVII.100; *Dhv.* II.7–8. In later Vaishnava literature of Bengal *mādhurya* is the focal *sthāyibhāva;* see Dimock, *PHM,* pp. 23–24.) *Madhura* also refers to a type of *anuprāsa;* see Gerow, *Glossary,* p. 105.

manas. Mind, heart, the seat of rational thought and emotion (I.4, 32; II.2*, 8, 10; III.12; IV.9; V.4, 6; VII.11, 40; VIII.7; IX.7; XI.9; XII.1, 6; also *mānasa* (III.14; X.2*); see *cetas, hṛd.* Some derivative compounds are *manoratha,* desire (I.28; II.11*; V.17); *manorama,* delightful (X.14; XII.9); *manohara,* enticing (II.7; V.8; XI.6, 27); *manohārin* (I.37).

manasija. Love, the "mind-born" god (I.29; II.15; III.12; IV.2*; VI.1; VII.32; XII.5, 14); also *manoja* (I.40; II.17); *manobhava* (VII.39; XII.12); *manobhū* (VII.21); *manmatha* (III.9; IX.1; X.6); *mānasaja* (XII.17); see *anaṅga.*

maraṇa. Death (IV.17; V.3; VII.5). A *vyabhicāribhāva,* see *NŚ,* VII.86; also *māra,* both death (III.13) and the passion of love personified (XII.10); *mṛta* (XII.6); cf. *antaka* (IV.19).

marman. Mortal spot, point of vulnerability (III.13; IV.3).

māna. Pride, esp. the wounded pride of a neglected *nāyikā* (IX.2*; X.2*); see *DR,* IV.65–67. Rādhā is addressed as *māninī,* a woman who harbors wounded pride (IX.2*); see Ingalls, *SCP,* intr. 21; Krishna is called *abhimānin,* proud (V.14).

mugdha. Originally "confused," coming to mean "foolish," "young," "charmingly innocent"; no single word encompasses all the senses; see Ingalls "Beauty," p. 95 (I.38*, 46 [*mugdho hariḥ* of Krishna]; II.19 [°*ānana,* Krishna's young face]; V.17; X.11, 12; XI.2*). Technically the *mugdhā* is an inexperienced *nāyikā* (*DR,* II.25, 26): *mugdhā navavayaḥkāmā ratau vāmā mṛduḥ krudhi;* see Ingalls, *SCP,* intr. 24.3.

mud. Joy (IX.10, X.11); also *mudita* (II.17; VII.22; XI.18); *atimudita* (VI.9); *pramudita* (V.15); *moda* (XII.9); see *ānanda, sukha, harṣa.*

moha. Delusion, delirium (III.13); also *mohana,* deluding, enticing (I.32; II.2, 9; XI.4).

raṇa. Lit., "delight"; battle, as object of delight (I.11); *rati*° VII.19; XI.7); *ratikelisaṁkula*° (XII.10); (*raṇita* is unrelated, from √*raṇ,* to "sound"; II.16, 20).

rati. Pleasure, sensual passion (I.2; II.11, 17; V.8, 12; VI.4; VII.17, 19, 26; VIII.4, 9; X.7, 14; XI.7, 14, 27, 28, 30; XII.8, 10, 11, 17). Personified as the wife of Love; some of Love's epithets express the relationship: °*pati* (V.7; VII.23); °*nāyaka* (XII.13); as with Love, the line between the personification and the concept is often blurred; see *anaṅga.* Technically, *rati* is the *sthāyibhāva* underlying *śṛṅgārarasa* in esthetic experience; °*rasabhāva* (XII.9); see *NŚ,* VI.45 prose; even where it is not primary, the technical meaning remains important in *GG.* Also *rata,* sensual passion, (V.18); *surata* (II.16); see *Kāmasūt* 2.1.65. Also √*ram* (I.44; II.11*; III.6; VII.22*, 28, 30; XI.10); *rama, mano*° (X.14; XII.9); *ramaṇa* (X.9); *ramaṇī* (VII.22); *ramaṇīya* (I.11; II.20; V.15; XI.4); *ramayat* (II.8); *ramita* (VII.20, 31*); *vi* √*ram* (XII.8); *virāma* (V.14); *avirāma* (XI.9).

raśanā. Girdle (X.6; XI.7; XII.7, 18); often *rasanā* in manuscripts and printed editions, confused with the neuter variant form *rasana* found in compounds (V.13; VII.16, 26); see *Amar,* II.6, 108; *strīkaṭyāṁ mekhala kāñcī saptakī raśanā tathā; klībe sārasanaṁ ca.*

rasa. Basically, "sap," "juice" (XII.6, 16); essence, flavor, taste, any object of taste. Technically, *rasa* is esthetic mood based on *bhāva;* it is the term for the essence of esthetic experience, generally translated "mood" or "emotional mood," but the distinction between basic and technical meanings is intentionally blurred by Jayadeva (I.36, 43; II.11, 17; IV.19; V.18; VI.10; VII.17, 29; VIII.2; XI.17, 18, 24*; XII.9, 10); also *sarasa,* rich in flavor or esthetic mood (I.4, 26, 27*; IV.12; IX.3; X.7; XI.7, 18; XII.1, 18); *virasa,* tasteless (VII.28). The commentators on *GG* gloss *rasa* most consistently with *śṛṅgārarasa,* but also with *amṛta, rāga, anurāga, sukha;* however, there is little agreement with reference to its meaning in particular verses. As an adverb *sarasam* is often glossed with *sarāgam. Rasa* is frequently used in its various senses in *kāvya* literature (e.g. *Bhart,* 30, 98, 102, 105, 107, 122, 137, 172, 183, 184), but in *GG* its technical esthetic sense is especially prominent; cf. Ingalls, "Beauty," p. 98; *NŚ,* VI (*Rasavikalpādhyāya*); Masson/Patawardhan, *Rapture. Ekarasa* (XI.24*), used to describe Hari, suggests that in his *abhilaṣita* state, he both experiences and embodies the essence of the esthetic mood of love; see *śṛṅgāra,* esp. *śṛṅgāraḥ mūrtiman* (I.46); see *KS,* V.82; *Ragh,* VIII.65, IX.43, X.17; Dimock, *PHM,* p. 138. In Buddhist Sanskrit texts *ekarasa* is used of *nirvāṇa;* see Fiske, "Notes on *Rasa.*"

rasika. A sympathetic person with taste for the presentation of esthetic emotion; one who can experience *rasa* (VI.9; IX.9; XII.9); see Raghavan, *Bhoja,* pp. 466 ff. *NS* XXIV.49–70. Cait glosses *rasika* with *bhakta,* "devotee."

rahas. Secrecy, loneliness, a secret, secretly; the distinction between noun and adverb is ambiguous because of the form and syntax of *rahas* (I.1; II.1; V.19). The compound form *rahaḥkeli,* with its conventional (*rūḍha*) sense of "sexual play," seems most appropriate to the context of I.1, but the adverbial interpretation of *rahas* is also cited by commentators. *Rahasi* is more clearly adverbial (IV.6; VI.2). Also, *rahasya,* a secret, a secret doctrine or mystery (I.45); cf. *rahita,* lonely, neglected (III.11); see *viraha.*

rāga. Lit., color, esp. red color; passion, esp. sensual passion; the two meanings form the basis of puns (III.13; VIII.2; X.7; XI.27); also *sarāga* (I.39); *rāgin* (IX.10). In the classical system of Indian music, *rāga* means a melodic pattern (I.39); see *pañcama.* Also √*rañj* (X.5, 6); *rañjana* (I.19, X.7); *anurakta* (VI.1); *anurañjana* (I.46); *anurañjita* (II.3); *anurāga* (I.25; VIII.2, 10); see Ingalls *SCR,* intr. 17; Dimock *PHM,* pp. 186–95.

ruci. Shining beauty, color; appetite, desire; the two aspects of meaning intentionally blurred (I.29, 30; VII.24; X.2; XI.12, 19, 28); also √*ruc* (X.2); *rucira,* shining, pleasing (VII.23, 35; IX.4; X.14; XI.1, 19, 28; XII.15, 17).

roṣa. Anger (X.1); also *ruṣ* (XII.8); *rūṣita* (VII.24); see *kupitā.*

lajjā. Modesty, shame (VI.8; VIII.10; XI.33); also *lajjita* (I.31; II.12; VII.17; XII.8); *alajja* (XI.7); *salajja* (XI.33).

lalita. Sensuous, sensual movement (I.17, 27, 32, 45; II.14; V.5; VII.15, 32; IX.9; XI.17; XII.16, 17). A *sattvabhāva* in both *nāyaka* and *nāyikā;* see *NŚ,* XXIV.22, 37; Ingalls, "Beauty," p. 102; see *līlā, vilāsa.*

līlā. Graceful play (VI.5, 11; VII.8); *līlāyita* (XII.21); *salīlā* (II.18; XI.8); see Ingalls, "Beauty," p. 105; commentators often gloss *līlā* with *svābhāvya,* spontaneity. Like *lalita, vibhrama, vilāsa, līlā* is a *svabhāvaja* quality of the *nāyikā;* cf. *NŚ,* XXIV.12 ff. The etymology and meaning of *līlā* in various contexts remains controversial. In Vaishnava literature *līlā* refers to the graceful pattern of divine activity, symbolized in Krishna's sensual play among the *gopīs* and, on another level, his relation to Rādhā; cf. De, *VFM,* pp. 228 ff.; Dimock, *PHM,* pp. 138–39.

lobha. Greed, lust (II.4; XI.28); also *lubdha* (I.36).

vacana. Speech, esp. the advice of Rādhā's friend and Krishna's speech to Rādhā (IV.9; V.1, 14; VII.3*, 33, 38; XI.2; XII.4); also √*vac* (XII.1). *Vacana* (VII.38) and *vacas* (XII.19) also refer to Jayadeva's speech personified as *vāgdevatā* (I.2); cf. *bhāratī* (see *bhaṇita*), *sarasvatī* (q.v.); *vāc* (I.3) also refers to poetic speech.

vañcita. Deceived, cheated, referring to Rādhā in one of the states of a *nāyikā,* deceived by her friends and by her lover (VII.3*; VIII.9); also √*vañc* (VIII.7). *Vañcita* is glossed in several commentaries with *vipralabdha; vipralabdhā-nāyikā* (*NŚ,* XXIV.217) is the more usual name for this state:

> *tasmād bhūtāṁ priyaḥ prāpya datvā saṅketam eva vā* |
> *nāgataḥ kāraṇeneha vipralabdhā tu sā matā* ||

vana. Forest, specifically Vṛndāvana, where adolescent Krishna loves many cowherd girls; in its springtime transformation it is the *uddīpanavibhāva* for sensual passion in *GG* (I.1, 34, 45; II.1, 20; III.6; V.8*; VII.3, 9, 11, 22*; VIII.8, XI.17). Krishna's epithet *vanamālī* (I.38; V.2*, 8*; VII.31*) refers to his forest adventures; also *vanamāla* (I.17). Cf. *kānana,* forest (I.35; II.19, VII.23); *kāntāra,* wilderness (I.26); see *kuñja.*

vasanta. Springtime (I.26, 27*, 34); see *madhu;* cf. *VV;* Ingalls, *SCP,* intr. 8.

vāma. Perverse, paradoxical (II.10; VII.40; XI.9); also *vāmā,* a coy woman (I.44); *vāmatā,* paradox (VII.39); *vāmya,* spitefulness (V.17); cf. Ingalls, "Beauty," p. 93.

vāsakasajjā. A woman who waits, dressed and ready for her lover (VI.8). One of the states of a *nāyikā* (*NŚ,* XXIV.212):

> *ucite vāsake yā tu ratisambhogalālasā |*
> *maṇḍanaṁ kurute hṛṣṭā sā vai vāsakasajjikā ||*

vikāra. A change of sentiment or behavior (I.34; II.11*; VII.14; X.8; XI.24); glossed by the commentator Kumbhakarṇa with *sāttvikabhāva;* see *NŚ,* VII 91 ff.; *Bhart,* 128 (*mānmatho vikāraḥ*), 187 (*manmathajā vikārāḥ*).

vidhura. Lonely and miserable (VII.2, 6; IX.8).

viparīta. Lit., "inverted"; °*kārin,* acting perversely (IX.10); *rati*°, taking the inverted position in intercourse (V.12); see *Kāmasūt* 2.8.

viraha. Desertion or desolation in love (III.4, 14; IV.2*, 9, 10, 11*, 17, 22; V.2*; VII.5, 7, 21, 35; XII.4, 6); also *virahin* (I.27*, 31; V.2, 6). *Viraha* is the state of love which is dominant *GG;* it corresponds to the aspect of *śṛṅgārarasa* technically known as *vipralambha,* which involves separation and deception in love, in contrast to *saṁbhoga,* which is fulfillment and enjoyment in love; see *NŚ,* VI.44 ff.; neither of these terms is used in *GG;* see Schmidt, *Beiträge,* pp. 124–32, 287–310. *Viraha* is technically used in Bengali Vaishnava theology to designate the intense state of desolation in frustrated love that is the necessary prelude to experiencing *preman* (q.v.); thus *viraha* is a way of salvation; see Dimock, *PHM,* pp. 17, 211. In *GG viraha* is used to describe the suffering of both lovers, Rādhā and Krishna; see Ingalls, *SCP,* intr. 22, 23. The usual translation of *viraha* as "separation" seems inappropriate in the context of *GG.* Although the vocabulary that characterizes *viraha* in *GG* is the conventional Sanskrit vocabulary of wounds from Love's weapons and of heat, pain, exhaustion, and futility, the constant repetition of this imagery is striking here: e.g., *ātaṅka* (X.10); *ātura* (IV.20, 21); *ārti* (VII.30); *klānta* (V.16; VII.11; XII.11); *klānti* (IV.21); *khinna* (III.7; IV.22; IX.1); *kheda* (I.25; IV.2; VIII.6; IX.7; XII.8); *jaḍiman* (VI.10); *jvara* (I.26, 36; IV.19, 21; VIII.7); *tāpa* (IV.8, 10; VII.2; X.12; XII.5); *tāpita* (XI.22); *dahana* (IV.10, 13; VII.7; also √*dah,* I.35; V.3; X.2*; *dagdha,* XII.6); *dāha* (IV.7, 13; VII.41); *dīna* (II.1) *bādha* (I.26; IV.20; VII.41; also *nirābādha,* XII.11; *saṁbādha,* XI.22); *viphala* (V.17; VII.3; XII.8); *viphalin* (IX.3); *vyādhi* (III.14); *vyathā*

(III.13; VII.21; also √*vyath,* II.20; X.12); *śoka* (VIII.10); see *cintā, bhaya, maraṇa, vidhura, viṣāda, śaṅkā.*

vilāsa. Seductive behavior, passion, seduction (I.4, 30, 37, 40; II.2*, 19; IV.4; XII.14); also *vilāsin,* seductive (I.38*); *avilāsa* (XII.6); *vi* √*las* (I.38*; VII.13*; XI.14, repeated 15–20) *vilasita* (V. 6); *lasad* (X.7); *ullasita* (II.4; XI.28); *ullāsa* (I.36). *Vilāsa* is a *sattvabhāva* in both *nāyaka* and *nāyikā;* see *NŚ* XXIV.15, 33; Ingalls, "Beauty," p. 103–4; see *lalita, līlā. Vilāsa* is frequently used for the *līlā* of Rādhā and Krishna in Sahajiyā literature; Dimock *PHM,* pp. 242–43*n*74.

viṣāda. Despair, lassitude (VII.12; VIII.2*; IX.1). A *vyabhicāribhāva;* see *NŚ,* VII.68. Also *vi* √*sad* (III.2; IV.8; IX.5); *pra* √*sad* (IV.19); √*sad* (V.2*; VI.2*).

vihāra. Delight, wandering for pleasure (XI.3); also *vihārin* (II.10); *vi* √*hṛ* (I.27*; II.1).

veśa. Dress, ornament, disguise (II.3; V.8; VII.13; XI.1). Often *veṣa* in manuscripts and printed editions, a form that does not strictly provide the required rhyme where it occurs. As with other variants of rhymed sibilants (e.g. *rasanā/raśanā, kisalaya/kiśalaya*) there is the suggestion of eastern regional pronunciation in which the distinction is absent. See *Amar,* II.6.99: *ākalpaveṣau nepathyaṁ pratikarma prasādhanam.*

śaṅkā. Fear, suspicion (X.10). *A vyabhicāribhāva;* see *NŚ,* VII.33; also *saśaṅka* (IV.12); *śaṅkita* (V.10); *pari* √*śaṅk* (VI.11); *viśaṅkamāna* (VII.12); see *bhaya.*

śubha. Bright, auspicious (n.), auspiciousness (I.15, 45; XII.14, 18); also *śobhā,* brilliance, beauty (II.4; XI.28). A *sattvabhāva* in a *nāyaka,* see *NŚ,* XXIV.32.

śṛṅgāra. Sexual love; technically, the esthetic mood of sexual love (I.3, 46; XII.21); see *NŚ,* VI.45 prose; Dimock, *PHM,* p. 138; see *adbhuta, rati, rasa, viraha.*

śrī. Radiance, beauty (VII.1; X.13); personified as Lakṣmī, the goddess of beauty and good fortune (I.2, 23); see Ingalls, "Beauty," p. 102.

sakhī. Female companion; Rādhā's friend and messenger to Krishna (I.37; II.1, 11*; IV.1, 9; V.1; VI.1, 6; VII.3*, 12, 31*; XI.8, 10, 13); Rādhā's circle of friends (IV.10; VII.40; XI.7; XII.1); Rādhā, addressed by the *sakhī* (I.27*, 46; V.2*, 11). The stock figure of the female companion in Sanskrit poetry and drama assumes special significance in the *rasa-śāstra* and theology of Bengali Vaishnavism; see De, *VFM,* pp. 208–10; *Ujjv* pp. 91 ff.; see *dūtī, sahacarī.*

samāgama. Lover's union (I.36; II.12); also *saṁgama* (VII.30); *saṁgata* (III.6; V.9); *samāgatya* (XI.10).

sarasvatī. Speech, personified as the goddess of speech (I.4); see *bhāratī.*

sahacarī. Rādhā's companion (I.26); see *dūtī, sakhī.*

sādhvasa. Fear, apprehension (XI.23); see *bhaya, śaṅkā;* see *Bh P,* I.11.18; X.29.20.

sukṛta. Favor, in reward for meritorious behavior; esp. the favor of Krishna's love (V.6, 12, 15; VII.6; XI.31).

sukha. Joy, pleasure (I.15; II.17, 18; III.14; IV.4; V.8; IX.2; X.3; XI.21); also √*sukh* (IV.18; IX.9); see *ānanda, mud, harṣa.*

sudhā. Nectar (II.2,19; III.14; IV.7; VII.40; VIII.9; XI.22; XII.4, 6); see *madhu.*

subhaga. Graceful, esp. in love (VII.19; XI.8, 30, 33); of Krishna (V.19); see Ingalls, "Beauty," p. 95.

sevā. Worship, devotion (V.15; X.13); also *sevaka* (VII.29); *upasevita* (XI.22).

smara. Love, the god of love (I.30; III.15; IV.20; VII.13; VIII.1, 4; X.8; XI.8, 10, 33; XII.1); see *anaṅga.*

smaraṇa. Remembering; esp. the act of mentally evoking Krishna (I.4; II.9; XII.19). In *kāvya,* remembering is the conventional motif that allows the juxtaposition of the modes of separation and union in love; see Ingalls, *SCP,* p. 216. *Smaraṇa* is a technical term in both orthodox and Sahajiyā Vaishnavism; it implies mental identification. Caitanya "remembers" his *līlā* as Krishna through identification; the same identification is implied in Sahajiyā *sādhana.* See De, *VFM,* pp. 370 ff.; Dimock *PHM,* pp. 235–45. Also √*smṛ* (II.2*; VII.9); *smṛti* (I.34).

svādhīnabhartṛkā. A woman whose lover is in her power (XII.11). The state of a *nāyikā* which culminates the reunion of Rādhā and Krishna; see *NŚ* XXIV. 214, 224:

> *suratātirasair baddho yasyāḥ pārśvagataḥ priyaḥ* |
> *sāmodaguṇasaṃyuktā bhavet svādhīnabhartṛkā* || 214 ||
> *vicitrojjvalaveṣā ca pramododdyotitānanā* |
> *udīrṇaśobhātiśayā kāryā svādhīnabhartṛkā* || 224 ||

harṣa. Joy (I.47; V.13; XI.24*, 32) also √*hṛṣ* (II.19); see *ānanda, mud, sukha.*

hṛd. Heart, the seat of emotion; *hṛd* and *hṛdaya,* like *cetas* and *manas,* also refer to the mind, the seat of rational thought and imagination (III.6, 11; VII.8, 10, 27, 35; XI.11, 31); *hṛdaya* (I.13, 29; II.6; III.7; IV.3; V.2, 8, 15; VII.4, 21, 38, 40; VIII.5, 10; IX.8; X.4, 6, 7; XII.19); also *hṛdya* (IV.20). Krishna is *hṛdayeśa* (V.8).